诸子百家智慧故事
Wisdom of Ancient Chinese Sages

WISDOM of SUN TZU

孙子
智慧故事

主编　陶黎铭　张　英
中文作者　张　英
英文作者　王善江
英文审订　汪榕培

Editors-in-Chief　*Tao Liming*　*Zhang Ying*
Chinese by　*Zhang Ying*
English by　*Wang Shanjiang*
Revised by　*Wang Rongpei*

上海外语教育出版社
外教社 SHANGHAI FOREIGN LANGUAGE EDUCATION PRESS

图书在版编目（CIP）数据

孙子智慧故事 / 陶黎铭，张英主编.
—上海：上海外语教育出版社，2010
（诸子百家智慧故事丛书）
ISBN 978-7-5446-1641-6

I. 孙… II. ①陶…②张… III. 孙子—生平
事迹—通俗读物—汉、英 IV. K825.2

中国版本图书馆 CIP 数据核字（2009）第 228446 号

出版发行：**上海外语教育出版社**
（上海外国语大学内）　邮编：200083
电　　话：021-65425300（总机）
电子邮箱：bookinfo@sflep.com.cn
网　　址：http://www.sflep.com.cn　http://www.sflep.com
责任编辑：唐小春

印　　刷：上海申松立信印刷有限责任公司
经　　销：新华书店上海发行所
开　　本：890×1194　1/32　印张 8.375　字数 228 千字
版　　次：2010 年 5 月第 1 版　2010 年 5 月第 1 次印刷
印　　数：5 000 册

书　　号：ISBN 978-7-5446-1641-6 / B · 0003
定　　价：26.00 元
本版图书如有印装质量问题，可向本社调换

前　言

2000多年前的春秋战国时代，是中国各种思想流派百花齐放的时期，涌现了孔子、孟子、老子、庄子、墨子、荀子、孙子、韩非子等思想家、哲学家，他们开创了儒、道、墨、法等各具特色、影响深远的思想派别，后世称为"诸子百家"。"诸子百家智慧故事"是一套介绍先秦诸子经典的汉英对照系列丛书，将先秦诸子的生平事迹、哲学思想、格言警句、哲理寓言以及与他们有关的历史故事串联成启迪智慧的短小故事，既能满足中国读者的普及型阅读需求，又照顾到国外读者的文化特点，让大家在轻松愉快的阅读氛围中走近春秋战国时代"百家争鸣"的先哲们。

为了让世界更好地了解中国的经典文化，"诸子百家智慧故事"在编写上突出了以下三个特点：

轻松阅读——本系列每本书中文不过七八万字，每个故事就是一个相对独立的阅读单位，仅几百字的内容十分钟就能读完，在当今信息爆炸的快节奏时代，这种文本便于读者随时取出翻阅。

经济阅读——中国的文字特别是古文字常常是外国人阅读中国经典的障碍，本丛书采取汉英双语对照，中文是浅显易懂的白话体，配以通顺晓畅的英语译文，读者无须钻研艰深的典籍，就能了解先哲的智慧。

趣味阅读——本丛书通过一个个短小生动的故事以及古意盎然的插图，为读者深入浅出地解读诸子经典。

先秦诸子经典是中国的宝贵精神财富，至今在中国乃至全世界都有广泛的影响。希望本丛书能够引起广大中外读者对先秦诸子百家的兴趣，并能通过书中的故事体会到博大精深的中国智慧。

编者
2009年9月

Preface

Over two millennia ago, China experienced a boom of ideas and philosophies in the form of "100 Schools of Thought". Confucius, Mencius, Laozi, Zhuangzi, Mozi, Xunzi, Han Feizi, Sun Tzu ... These are the stellar names behind the philosophical schools like Confucianism, Taoism, Mohism, Legalism, etc. in the Spring and Autumn Period and the Warring States Period (from 770 BC to 221 BC). The classics of these ancient sages contain great wisdom and have exerted profound influence on Chinese history and thought. While the classics themselves may seem difficult to understand today, you can find lucid and accessible explanations of the ancient philosophies in the books of *Wisdom of Ancient Chinese Sages*. With the help of a collection of short and interesting stories, you can get to know the lives and thoughts of the ancient sages, the axioms and allegories they employed to illustrate their ideas, and some facts about the historical era they lived in.

With the aim of presenting the ancient Chinese classics to the world audience, *Wisdom of Ancient Chinese Sages* boasts three advantages:

Easiness — Each book in the series is comprised of only a few dozen stories, each of which has no more than 2,000 words and can be glanced through in a 10-minute coffee break. Even in your busy life, you can always snatch some time to enjoy a story of wisdom and gain some spiritual nourishment.

Efficiency — The classics may seem a little obscure today since they are written in the ancient Chinese. In this Chinese-English version of *Wisdom of Ancient Chinese Sages*, however, the classics are rendered in simple, everyday English. Without having to tax your brains, you can readily comprehend the profound wisdom of the ancient sages.

Attractiveness — With all the short but lively stories accompanied by beautiful illustrations, *Wisdom of Ancient Chinese Sages* explains (to you) the ancient philosophical ideas in a friendly and agreeable way.

The ancient philosophical classics in the "100 Schools of Thought" are an important spiritual heritage of China and impose great cultural reverberations beyond the Chinese borders. We hope that the series may let the readers develop an interest in the ancient Chinese sages and their philosophies, and appreciate the quintessential Chinese wisdom that may prove useful in present day.

Editors
September 2009

目录

Contents

孙子生平

The Life of Sun Tzu

孙子，名武，字长卿，春秋末年生于齐国乐安（今山东省惠民县），生卒年月已不可考，其生活的年代大致与孔子（公元前551—前479年）同期。孙子的祖先本是陈国公子，名完，后因陈国内乱，避难逃奔齐国。古代陈、田两字音同，故公元前672年改称田完。田完的第五世孙叫田书，骁勇善战，齐景公时，他在攻打莒国的战斗中立了战功，齐景公把乐安封赐给他作为采邑（即封地），并赐姓孙氏。这样，田书又叫孙书，他就是孙子的祖父。孙子生长在这样一个军事世袭贵族家庭，从小就受到军事文化的熏陶。而他所生活的齐国，原来是古代大军事谋略家姜太公的封地，后来又有大政治家、大军事家管仲的活动遗迹，留下了极其丰富的军事文化遗产。再后来，齐桓公称霸诸侯，齐国一度成为四方豪杰荟萃之地。这样的家庭环境和社会环境，为孙子的成长提供了丰厚的养分，使他在青年时期在兵学方面就成了学识渊博的人才。

公元前532年，齐国发生了"四姓之乱"。孙子的父亲孙凭担心受田氏的牵连，带领全家离开齐国逃到了南方的吴国。这时的孙子已经是一位饱读兵书的青年。在吴国，他一面灌园种地，一面继续研究兵法。经过多年的努力，终于写成了《兵法十三篇》。

当时，吴王阖闾身边有一位他非常信赖的谋臣，姓伍，名员，字子胥。他知道了孙子在吴国潜心研究兵法的事后，就主动跟孙子结交，并且成了朋友。孙子的雄才大略令伍子胥折服，就积极鼓动他为吴国效力。伍子胥利用跟吴王阖闾一起论兵的机会，先后七次向吴王阖闾举荐孙子，吴王终于被他的热心举荐所打动，决定见见这位被伍子胥称为军事奇才的人。

在伍子胥的引领下，孙子带着他的《兵法十三篇》到吴宫晋见吴王阖闾。据《吴越春秋》记载，孙子身材高大，相貌英俊，声音洪亮，双目炯炯有神。孙子的英武气质让吴王十分喜悦，赐座以后就开始谈起兵法来。孙子先把《兵法十三篇》呈上，然后对吴王说："我对用兵的见解，都写入《兵法十三篇》里了，请您展观。"吴王阖闾也是个粗通兵法的国君，像孙子《兵法十三篇》这样，篇目那么精到、结构那么宏富的兵书还是第一次看到，他不禁惊喜万分，急于想知道每篇的详细内容，于是就请孙子先回馆舍休息，约定改日再请他入宫详谈。

吴王很快就读完了《兵法十三篇》，对孙子深富哲理的用兵之道和充满智慧的计谋非常佩服，马上请孙子进宫见面。吴王对孙子说："您的兵法我已经逐篇拜读了，真是振聋发聩，让人耳目一新。但是，您的这些办法，不知道真正实行起来怎么样，您能不能实际演练一下，让我们看看？"孙子回答说："可以。"于是，吴王就命令从宫中调来180个宫女临时充当士兵，供孙子演练阵法。这就是著名的"吴宫教战"的故事。

吴王阖闾充分了解了孙子的军事才能，于是就接受了伍子胥的举荐，任命孙子为吴国的上将军，让他跟伍子胥一起辅佐自己争强争霸。

吴国地处长江下游（今江苏、浙江、安徽一带），是周王朝众多封国之一。据史书记载，周朝初期，周天子按照公、侯、伯、子、男五等进行公封，当时大大小小的封国总共有一千七百多个。到了周平王东迁以后，由于周王朝衰落和各封国之间政治经济发展不平衡，出现了诸侯国相互兼并争霸的局面。吴国西边有强大的楚国，南部与越国为邻，北边与齐国和鲁国相望。由于地域的关系，自春秋中期以来，吴国和楚国之间的战事就连绵不断。楚国地处长江上游，又是南方的大国，春秋以来吞并了不少小国，因而在力量对比上，吴国一直处于弱势。孙子成为吴国的上将军时，这种局面还没有改变。阖闾是个有野心的国君，他急于在长江流域争霸，于是就问计于孙子。孙子说："自古用兵之道，在于先除内患，之后才可外征。大王您若想向西征讨楚国，必须先除掉两个公子。"

孙子所说的两个公子，指的是原来吴国的公子掩余和烛庸，说起来，这是一段吴国王室内部自相残杀的历史。吴王诸樊有个儿子叫光，人们都称他为公子光，是个很有野心的人。诸樊还有三个弟弟：余祭、夷昧和季札。按照周朝的继位传统，王位可以父子相继，也可以兄弟相继。诸樊死的时候，没有把王位传给公子光，而是传给了二弟余祭，后来余祭又传给了三弟夷昧，夷昧死时应该把王位传给四弟季札，但是季札不愿意继承王位，于是就逃走了。夷昧有个儿子叫僚，夷昧便传位给了僚。公子光对此极为不满，于是寻找能够刺杀吴王僚的人。伍子胥推荐了专诸。后来专诸把刀藏在鱼肚子里，利用向吴王僚献鱼的机会将他刺死。于是公子光夺取了王位，他就是后来有名的吴王阖闾。吴王僚被杀的时候，公子掩余和烛庸正奉命率军攻打楚国，听到阖闾篡位的消息，二人不敢返回吴国，于是就投降了楚国，被楚王分封在吴国和楚国之间的舒城（今安徽庐江西南）。所以，孙子建议吴王阖闾先除掉这两个内患和伐楚的障碍。吴王听从了孙子的建议，亲自和伍子胥一起率兵出征，一举攻克了舒城，扫平了进兵楚国的道路。

攻克舒城，吴王阖闾非常高兴，他想乘胜进兵楚国，直捣楚国的首府郢都。孙子听到这个消息，急忙赶到军中去劝说吴王放弃这个想法。他对阖闾说："用兵打仗，关系到国家、将士和老百姓的生死存亡，必须考虑敌我双方的情况，比较双方的力量和条件，估量胜负的可能性、量力用兵，才能够做到攻必克，战必胜。如果不考虑敌我双方的实际情况和力量对比，贸然出战，后果不堪设想。吴国这些年一连打了几次仗了，将士和老百姓都很疲劳，吴国的经济也因为打仗受到很大的影响，国家、军队和老百姓都需要休整一段时间。而现在楚国的面积比吴国大，兵力也比吴国强，在这种情况下大规模地去讨伐楚国，胜利的可能性很小。所以，伐楚的事请大王不要操之过急，还是从长计议吧。"吴王听从了孙子的劝告，放弃了马上讨伐楚国的想法。但是他让孙子和伍子胥两位将军尽快想出战胜楚国的办法来。

孙子认为，吴楚力量对比悬殊，想直接进攻楚国而取胜是非常困难的事情，必须先削弱楚国兵力，改变楚强吴弱的现状，才可能取胜。于是，孙子和伍子胥一起为吴军制订了一个"疲楚"、"误楚"的妙计，以有效地消耗楚国兵力和财力。他们把吴国的军队一分为三，每次用一支军队去袭击和骚扰楚国的边境，三支军队轮番向楚国发动进攻。楚王接到吴军大举进攻楚国的报告，马上出动全国的军队奔赴边境抵抗。楚军队一到，吴国军队立刻撤退，并不直接跟楚国军队作战。楚军长途奔来，无法长期驻扎在边境上，看到吴军已经退回去，就班师回朝了。可是，楚军刚一退兵，吴国的另一支军队又开始向楚国进攻，楚王接到报告，只得再派大军去抵抗。如此三番，吴军不仅以逸待劳，还可以轮番休整，而楚军却不断地来回奔波，弄得筋疲力尽。连续6年，孙子一直采取这种"彼出则我归，彼归则我出"的车轮战法，不仅消耗了楚国大量的人力和物力，楚国军队的战斗力也跟着削弱了。在这种以消耗楚国兵力为目标的车轮战中，吴军不仅成功地实现了既定的战略目标，而且还相继获得了掠地的战果。公元前511至公元前509年，吴军先后占领了楚国的六（今安徽六安县境）、灊（今安徽霍山县北）和居巢（今安徽六安县东北）。

吴王阖闾非常赞赏孙子的谋略和战法，他在宫中不断收到楚疲吴逸、楚败吴胜的消息，知道吴军士气必定高昂，按捺不住急于称霸的念头，于是又想马上乘胜大举进击楚国。关于此事，司马迁在《史记·吴太伯世家》中这样写道："光（吴王阖闾）欲入郢，将军孙武曰：'民营，未可，待之。'"在这里，孙子虽然仅仅说了三句话六个字，但是却表达了一个非常重要的战略思想，那就是吴国攻打楚国的条件还不成熟，需要积蓄力量，需要等待时机，不能打无把握之仗。

吴国坚持继续运用孙子的"疲楚"、"误楚"战略，6年之后，攻打楚国的机会终于来了。原来楚国昭王新继位，他既年轻没有治国经验，又昏庸不肯听取意见，把治国的大权全部交给了令尹（相当于宰相）囊瓦。囊瓦为人不仅专横跋扈，而且嫉贤妒能，把楚国内政和外交都搞得一团糟。到了公元前506年夏天，晋国指使蔡国灭掉了沈国。当时，蔡国和沈国都是楚国的附属国，囊瓦见小小的蔡国竟然也敢犯上作乱，欺凌强大的楚国，非常生气，于是派大军压境，包围了蔡国。蔡昭侯（蔡国国君）见情势危机，只好向楚国的近敌吴国求救。为了表示诚信，蔡昭侯还提出愿意把自己的独子送到吴国做人质。吴王遂问计于孙子和伍子胥。孙子说："战争是关系到国家、将士和老百姓生死存亡的大事，国君不能因恼怒就发动战争，将帅也不可因气愤就进行决战。现在楚国因怒而发兵，而楚将子常为人很贪，唐国（楚的属国之一）和蔡国早就对他有怨恨，楚军上下必不同心。我们经过6年的'疲楚'之战，已经有效地消耗了楚国的兵力和国力，现在蔡国叛楚求救，真是天赐良机！大王可以答应蔡侯。"阖闾说："破楚方可称霸东南，此次可一举成功否？"孙子回答说："王必欲大伐，必得唐、蔡乃可。"这是一个很重要的战略问题。孙子认为，楚是一个大国，也是一个强国，经过6年"疲楚"之战后，虽然国力和兵力有所削弱，但吴国要想一举吃掉楚国并不是一件容易的事情，必须在战略上进行整体谋划，先打破唐、蔡与楚国的联盟关系，剪除其羽翼，再联合唐、蔡讨伐楚国，这样方可成功。

吴王阖闾接受了孙子的建议，欣然答应了蔡侯的请求，收下蔡侯儿子做人质，允诺出兵救蔡。公元前506年冬，吴王调集全国兵力，任孙子为大将，伍子胥和伯嚭为副将，胞弟夫概为先锋，阖闾亲自率领大军出战。

按照孙子制订的战略计划，吴国先后顺利地收服了蔡国和唐国，然后组成吴、蔡、唐三国联军，直插楚国的纵深。当时，吴、蔡、唐虽是三国联军，但整体兵力并不占优势，再加上是入敌国作战，取胜的难度很大。孙子充分发挥了他的智慧和军事才能，每每出奇制胜，打得楚军措手不及。当年11月19日，吴楚两军在大别山、小别山（今安徽境内）决战，吴军一举击溃楚军主力，为最终打败楚军并占领楚国的郢都奠定了坚实的基础。这就是历史上著名的柏举之战。

柏举决战之后，楚军大举溃逃。孙子不给楚军一点喘息的机会，指挥吴军长驱追击，11天之中行军700里，五战五胜，直捣楚国的郢都。农历11月28日，吴军攻破郢都，楚昭王只好带着妹妹和几个亲信仓惶地逃到随国（今湖北省随县）去了。

吴国出征的时候，只有3万兵力，而当时的楚国却有20万。孙子不仅创造了战争史上以少胜多的奇迹，而且他的军事思想和战略战术都在伐楚之战中得到淋漓的发挥和实战的检验，为后代兵学留下了宝贵的财富。

吴军打败了西边的强敌楚国，声威大震，吴国自此进入了强国的行列。吴王阖闾遂称霸于东南，北边威凌于齐国和晋国，南边征服了越人。吴国由弱而强的变化，显然是与孙子杰出的军事才能分不开的。所以，司马迁在《史记·孙子吴起列传》中说：吴国"西破强楚，入郢，北威齐、晋，显名诸侯，孙子与有力焉"。

除了辅佐吴王图强建立卓越的战功之外，孙子最伟大的成就是给中国，也是给全人类留下一部哲理深邃、智慧绝妙、影响深远、千古不废的军事著作——《孙子兵法》。遗憾的是，关于孙子一生的详细事迹和最终结局却无从了解。我们只能从司马迁《史记》中仅有的记述得知："孙武既死，后百余岁，有孙膑。……膑亦孙武之后世子孙也。"

孙子不仅是一位伟大的军事思想家，也是一位伟大的谋略家和哲学家，《孙子兵法》中所凝聚的思想光芒、蕴含的博大智慧早已超出了军事范畴，以至于一切具有竞争、竞赛因素的领域及行业，如商业、企业、体育、外交、政治乃至人生，都从《孙子兵法》中汲取智慧和营养。现在，《孙子兵法》早已超越时空界限，成为一把开启人类智慧的金钥匙。

Sun Tzu, alias Sun Wu, styled Changqing, was born in Le'an of the State of Qi (Huimin County of Shandong Province today) in the late Spring and Autumn Period (770 BC – 476 BC). His dates of birth and death remain unknown. He was a contemporary of one of the great Chinese thinkers of ancient times — Confucius (551 BC – 479 BC). Sun Tzu's ancestor was Prince Wan of the State of Chen. Because of domestic disorder, Prince Wan fled to the State of Qi to seek refuge. In ancient China, Chen and Tian shared the same pronunciation, therefore, in 672 BC, he was renamed Tian Wan. His fifth generation grandson, Tian Shu, was brave and well-versed in battle. In the reign of Duke Jing of the State of Qi, he won honor in attacking the State of Ju. Duke Jing bestowed upon him Le'an as his feud and Sun as his surname. This was why Tian Shu was also called Sun Shu. His grandson Sun Tzu was brought up in a family of masters of war and had been nurtured by military culture since his childhood. Besides, the State of Qi, where Sun Tzu lived, was originally the feud of Jiang Taigong, a great ancient strategist, and also the home of Guan Zhong, a famous politician and military strategist. Both left behind them rich military cultural heritage. Afterwards, Duke Huan of the State of Qi became the overlord, which attracted talents who came far and near. A family with such a social background exerted a positive influence on Sun Tzu, who distinguished himself as a talent knowledgeable in military science from his youth.

In 532 BC, "the Rebellion of Four Clans" broke out in the State of Qi. To avoid being involved because of his surname, Sun Tzu's father, Sun Ping, fled to the State of Wu, a southern state, together with his family. At that time, Sun Tzu was a young man well-read in military works. In the State of Wu, he grew crops and studied the art of war. After years of efforts, he finally completed his famous *Thirteen Chapters of the Art of War*.

At that time, King Helü of the State of Wu had a trusty councilor, Wu Yuan, styled Zixu. After he learned that Sun Tzu steeped himself in the art of war in the State of Wu, Wu Zixu took the initiative and succeeded in making friends with him. Sun Tzu's great talent and bold vision won Wu Zixu's admiration. Wu Zixu did his utmost to persuade Sun Tzu to serve the State of Wu. When discussing the art of war with King Helü, Wu Zixu took every possible opportunity to recommend Sun Tzu. After Wu recommended Sun Tzu for seven successive times, King Helü was finally moved by his warm-heartedness and decided to grant an audience with Sun Tzu, who was regarded as a military wizard by Wu Zixu.

Accompanied by Wu Zixu, Sun Tzu had an audience with King Helü in the palace, taking his *Thirteen Chapters of the Art of War* with him. According to *Annals of the States of Wu and Yue*, Sun Tzu was of a large stature, handsome, with a sonorous voice and radiant eyes. Sun Tzu's soldierly bearing pleased King Helü, who first offered him a seat and then discussed the art of war with him. Sun Tzu presented to the King his *Thirteen Chapters of the Art of War*, saying, "Your Lordship, please have a look. All my views on the art of war are expounded in this book." King Helü did not know much about the art of war, nor had he come across such a masterpiece containing rich military knowledge and was only too pleased to learn about it in detail. He asked Sun Tzu to have a rest back at the lodging and set another date for a further talk with him.

The King read through the book quickly and was filled with admiration for Sun Tzu's military philosophy and brilliant stratagems. He immediately met Sun Tzu again in his palace and said to him, "I have had the honor to read through your work chapter by chapter. It can really rouse the deaf and awaken the mute. Everything is fresh and new. But how about the application of your stratagems? Do they work? Will you demonstrate them before us?" Sun Tzu answered, "Sure." King Helü ordered to call in one hundred and eighty palace maids as temporary soldiers for Sun Tzu. This is the famous story of "Sun Tzu's training of an army in the palace of the State of Wu".

King Helü was well acquainted with Sun Tzu's military capability, so he appointed Sun Tzu as Senior General of the State of Wu on the recommendation of Wu Zixu, who, together with Sun Tzu, assisted him in obtaining dominance.

The State of Wu was located in the lower reaches of the Yangtze River (around Jiangsu, Zhejiang and Anhui Province today). It was one of the numerous vassal states of the Zhou Dynasty (1046 BC–256 BC). According to historical records, in the early years of the Zhou Dynasty, the King conferred land according to the five noble titles: Duke, Marquis, Count, Viscount and Baron. There were over 1,700 vassal states at that time. After King Ping of the Zhou Dynasty moved his capital eastward, the royal family was on the wane and imbalance existed in the political and economic development of different vassal states, thus resulting in frequent military struggles for annexation and power among them. The State of Wu adjoined the powerful State of Chu in the west and the State of Yue in the south. It faced the State of Qi and the State of Lu in the north. Along the borders, the State of Wu and the State of Chu had been in constant wars since the mid Spring and Autumn Period. The State of Chu lay in the upper reaches of the Yangtze River. Being a big power in the south, it had annexed quite a few small states since the Spring and Autumn Period. As a result, it was superior to the State of Wu in military strength. The situation did not change for the better when Sun Tzu was appointed Senior General of the State of Wu. Full of ambition, Helü consulted with him about a strategy to dominate the basin of the Yangtze River. Sun Tzu said, "According to the art of war from time immemorial, one has to end the civil strife before one attacks external enemies. Your Lordship, if you are about to attack the State of Chu in the west, you'll have to get rid of the two princes first."

The two princes mentioned by Sun Tzu were Yanyu and Zhuyong, the two former princes of the State of Wu. As a matter of fact, it was the history of a fratricidal war among the royal family of the State of Wu. King Zhufan had a son named Guang, who was the ambitious Prince Guang. Zhufan also had three younger brothers, Yuji, Yimei and Jizha. According to the tradition of the Zhou Dynasty, a king could pass on his throne either to his brother or to his son. On his death, Zhufan passed on the throne to his second brother Yuji instead of his son Prince Guang. Yimei, Zhufan's third brother, succeeded the throne after the death of Yuji. Yimei had chosen his fourth brother Jizha as the successor on his death, but Jizha was reluctant to be the king and fled. Therefore, Yimei passed on the throne to his own son Liao, which irritated Prince Guang. He wanted to find someone who could assassinate King Liao. Wu Zixu recommended Zhuan Zhu as the assassin. Later, when presenting a fish to King Liao, Zhuan Zhu managed to kill him with a dagger hidden in the fish. Prince Guang succeeded in ascending the throne, who later became the famous King Helü of the State of Wu. When King Liao was assassinated, Prince Yanyu and Zhuyong were executing the order to attack the State of Chu. The news of Helü's ascending the throne compelled them to surrender themselves to the State of Chu, whose king granted them Shu City (a city between the State of Wu and the State of Chu, southwest to Lujiang of Anhui Province today). Sun Tzu recommended that King Helü should clear these two obstacles. King Helü followed his suggestion. Together with Wu Zixu, the King led his troops in person to attack Shu City. He conquered it at one stroke, thereby clearing the way for his attack on the State of Chu.

The military conquest of Shu City delighted the King so much that he was eager to follow up his victories by marching on the State of Chu and swooping down on its capital, Ying City. On hearing the news, Sun Tzu quickly dissuaded him. He said to Helü, "War is a matter of vital importance to the state, a matter of life or death, a road either to survival or to ruin. We must take into account the situation of the antagonistic sides, contrast the military strength and conditions, estimate the outcome of the battle and act according to our capability. Only by doing so can we achieve victory. Otherwise, if we went in war without careful considerations, the consequences would be disastrous. In recent years, our state has been involved in a few battles. Both our troops and our people are exhausted. The domestic economy has also been badly affected. Now we need a time of rest for our state, our troops and our people. Besides, the State of Chu has a larger territory and more powerful military strength. Under such circumstances, chances of victory are slim if we attack them on a large scale, therefore, Your Lordship, it's no good to be overhasty. Let's wait till the right time." King Helü followed his advice and gave up the idea of attacking the State of Chu immediately, but he asked Sun Tzu and Wu Zixu to come up with a stratagem to defeat the State of Chu as soon as possible.

According to Sun Tzu, there was a striking contrast between the two states. It would be hard to defeat the State of Chu by direct fighting. The State of Wu stood a chance of winning only by weakening Chu's strength and reducing its superiority. To exhaust Chu's army and treasury, Sun Tzu and Wu Zixu joined efforts in making the ingenious stratagem of "exhausting Chu" and "misleading Chu". They divided the Wu troops into three branches. Only one branch was sent to encroach on Chu's border at one time. The three branches took turns in annoying Chu. Each time the King of the State of Chu got the news of their attack, he sent his main forces to the border. When they arrived at the border, the Wu troops would hurry back without fighting with them. The Chu troops had covered a long distance and could not be stationed at the border for long. At the retreat of the Wu army, the State of Chu withdrew its troops. Once they returned home, another branch of the Wu army would attack the Chu border again. The Chu forces then had to come back once more. This went on for six successive years, during which the Chu army was exhausted by marching to and fro while the Wu troops were at ease by taking turns to rest. Sun Tzu adopted the tactic of fighting his enemies by turns to wear them down. When the Chu forces advanced, the Wu army would retreat; when the Chu forces retreated, the Wu army would advance. As a result, the stratagem effectively exhausted Chu's army and treasury, and at the same time, it guaranteed the realization of Wu's strategic intention, and enabled the State of Wu to capture three Chu cities from 511 BC to 509 BC — Lu City (Lu'an County of Anhui Province today), Qian City (north to Huoshan County of Anhui Province today) and Juchao (northeast to Lu'an County of Anhui Province today).

King Helü thought highly of Sun Tzu's stratagem. When he got frequent news of Chu's being exhausted and defeated, he was sure that the morale among his troops must be very high at the moment, so he could not hold back his eagerness to start immediate attacks on the State of Chu. In *"Wu Taibo's Noble Family"* of *Records of the Grand Historian*, Sima Qian recorded this event in the following words, "When Guang (King Helü of the State of Wu) was eager to attack Ying City, General Sun Wu said, 'People's livelihood, not ready, keep waiting.'" Sun Tzu's six words in the three clauses conveyed a very important military thought — the time was not ripe to attack Chu; Wu had to keep gathering strength, wait for the right time and fight no battles that it was not sure of winning.

The State of Wu persisted in carrying out Sun Tzu's stratagem of "exhausting Chu" and "misleading Chu". Six years later, the time was ripe for an attack on the State of Chu. King Zhao of the State of Chu had just succeeded to the throne. He was too young to manage the state affairs, and too fatuous to listen to the others as well. He handed over the power of running the state to Prime Minister Nang Wa. Nang Wa was arrogant and domineering. Besides, he was jealous of the talented and the able. Both Chu's internal affairs and the diplomatic relations were in a complete mess. In the summer of 506 BC, acting on the instigation of the State of Jin, the State of Cai captured the State of Shen. At that time, both the State of Cai and the State of Shen were Chu's dependencies. Nang Wa was so irritated by Cai's rebellious behavior that he ordered the Chu army to crush the State of Cai by force. At this critical juncture, Marquis Zhao of the State of Cai sought help from the State of Wu, Chu's close enemy. To show his sincerity, Marquis Zhao suggested that his only son be held hostage in the State of Wu. When King Helü consulted with Sun Tzu and Wu Zixu, Sun Tzu said, "War is a matter of vital importance to the state, a matter of life or death, a road either to survival or to ruin. A king should not stage a war out of rage; neither should a general fight a decisive battle out of anger. Now fury drives the State of Chu to war. Its general, Zichang, is greedy. The State of Tang (one of Chu's dependencies) and the State of Cai have long harbored a grudge against him. There must exist internal disorders amongst the Chu troops. After six years of 'exhausting Chu', we have effectively reduced its military strength and national power. Now that the State of Cai comes to us for help, it is indeed a heaven-sent opportunity. Your Lordship, please accede to its request." Helü said, "Only by conquering the State of Chu can I be the overlord in the southeast area. Can we make it this time?" Sun Tzu answered, "To stage an attack on Chu, we have to win over the State of Tang and the State of Cai." This was an important strategic issue. From Sun Tzu's viewpoint, the State of Chu was strong as well as big. Though the State of Wu had weakened Chu's power after six years of "exhausting Chu", it was no easy job to conquer Chu at one stroke. Overall estimates were a must before military action. In terms of strategy, to achieve a victory, Wu must first break Chu's alliance with Tang and Cai, get rid of its assistants, and then attack it with the help of Tang and Cai.

King Helü followed Sun Tzu's advice and readily acceded to the Marquis' request. Keeping his son as the hostage, Helü promised to send troops to Cai's rescue. In the winter of 506 BC, King Helü assembled the military force across his state, appointed Sun Tzu as the Senior Commander, Wu Zixu and Bo Pi as the Vice Commanders and his brother Fugai as the Vanguard. Commanding the troops in person, Helü led the army to go into battle.

Acting on Sun Tzu's strategic plan, the State of Wu succeeded in subduing the State of Cai and the State of Tang successively, formed an alliance with them, and then thrust deep into Chu. Though having the allied forces from three states, Wu was still inferior to Chu in military strength. Besides, fighting in the enemy's state added difficulty to its chances of victory. Sun Tzu brought his wisdom and military talent into full play. He attacked the Chu army when it was unprepared and won a victory by using the extraordinary means each time. On November 19 that year, a decisive battle broke out between the two armies in the Dabie Mountains and the Xiaobie Mountains (within Anhui Province today). The Wu army defeated Chu's major force at one fell swoop, which laid a solid foundation for the overall victory and the conquest of Ying City. This was the historic Battle of Boju.

After the Battle of Boju, the Chu troops were put to rout. Sun Tzu gave the enemy no breathing time and led his army deep into the State of Chu. The Wu troops covered 700 *li* (a Chinese unit of length, equivalent to 1/2 kilometers) in 11 days and after five successive victories, they drove straight on to Ying City. On November 28 by lunar calendar, the Wu army captured Ying City. King Zhao of the State of Chu had no alternative but to flee with his younger sister and several henchmen to the State of Sui (Sui County of Hubei Province today).

At the beginning of the battle, the Chu forces stood at 200,000 whereas the figure for Wu was 30,000. Sun Tzu had not only created the military miracle of a speedy war, where a numerically smaller army defeated a much larger force, he had also successfully applied and verified his military thoughts and stratagems. He left a rich heritage in the military science to the posterities.

Having defeated Chu, its strong opponent in the west, the State of Wu gained a great fame and prestige and entered the ranks of the powerful states. King Helü became the overlord of the southeast area, overriding the State of Qi and the State of Jin in the north, and conquered the Yue people in the south. It was self-evident that the tremendous change in the position of the State of Wu was closely related to Sun Tzu's outstanding military talent. In "*Sun Tzu and Wu Qi*" of *Records of the Grand Historian*, Sima Qian recorded, "The State of Wu defeated its powerful foe, Chu, in the west and captured its capital, Ying

City. In the north, Wu overawed the State of Qi and the State of Jin. It was due to Sun Tzu's efforts that Wu distinguished itself among the states."

In addition to assisting King Helü in building a strong state and achieving miraculous feats in battles, Sun Tzu made the greatest contribution by leaving to the world as well as to China a military work, *Sun Tzu's Art of War*, which was profound in philosophy, ingenious in wisdom, far-reaching in influence and eternal in application. It is a real pity that little is known about his achievements and the ending of his life. The only account is found in *Records of the Grand Historian* by Sima Qian, "Over a hundred years after Sun Tzu's death, Sun Bin lived … Sun Bin was a direct descendant of Sun Tzu."

Sun Tzu is not only a great military thinker but also a strategist and philosopher. The brilliant thoughts and sharp wisdom contained in *Sun Tzu's Art of War* go far beyond the scope of military science. They can be applied successfully today in such competitive areas as diverse as business, enterprise, sports, diplomacy, politics and even people's lives. Nowadays, *Sun Tzu's Art of War* has transcended the bounds of time and space, and has become a golden key to human enlightenment.

孙子智慧故事
Wisdom of Sun Tzu

出其不意——吴楚柏举之战

《孙子兵法·始计篇》：攻其无备，出其不意。此兵家之胜，不可先传也。

公元前 506 年，地处长江下游的吴国，跟地处长江上游的楚国在柏举（今湖北麻城东北一带）发生了一次大战，孙子是吴国军队的统帅，这是孙子亲自指挥的一次经典战役。

吴国和楚国同处中国的东南地区，自春秋开启诸侯争霸的历史之后，由于地缘关系，两个都想称霸长江流域的国家就战事不断。但是，楚国是东南地区的大国，春秋以来又吞并了很多小国，因此在国力和兵力方面都比吴国强大。吴国按照孙子的"疲楚"、"误楚"计谋，把吴国军队一分为三，连续六年轮番进攻楚国边境地区，并采取调动楚国军队但不与主力部队决战的策略，有力地消耗了楚国的国力和兵力。公元前 506 年，楚国的属国蔡国叛楚投靠吴国，吴王阖闾抓住机会，调集全国兵力，任孙子为大将，伍子胥和伯嚭为副将，胞弟夫概为先锋，阖闾亲自率领大军出战，决心一举打败楚国，独霸东南。

根据楚强吴弱的客观情况，孙子制订了一个先"伐交"后"伐兵"的战略计划，即先顺利地收服了楚的两个属国蔡国和唐国，组成吴、蔡、唐三国联军，做到弱楚强吴，逐渐改变敌我力量对比，然后率领联军进击楚国本土。当时，吴国的水军力量很强大，仅战船就有大翼、小翼、突冒、楼船、桥船、桥舡等许多种。据《国语·齐语》记载，大翼相当于辎重车，小翼相当于轻便战车，突冒相当于冲锋车，楼船相当于建有楼橹的巢车，桥舡相当于剽悍轻捷的骑兵。楚军见吴军主力乘战船溯淮河直奔楚国，急忙调集主力，以汉水为界，加紧设防。

孙子看到楚军把主要兵力用于对付吴国的水军，立即改变了原来沿淮水进军的路线，放弃战船，改从陆路进攻，直插楚国纵深。副将伍子胥担心地问孙子："吴军习水性，善于水战，现在弃长就短，不是太危险了吗？"孙子说："楚军已严阵以待，吴国水军的优势已经被削弱了。况且，出征千里，日费万金，我们现在是逆水行舟，速度迟缓，楚军必然借机加强防备，这样的话就很难破敌了。军队远征，无法打持久的消耗战，故兵贵神速。所以，吴军必须出奇兵，走敌人料想不到的路，以快速进攻打他个措手不及。这就叫做攻其不备，出其不意，兵贵速胜，不贵久。"在孙子的指挥下，吴军毅然放弃战船登陆，经豫章、小别山、大别山，突然出现在楚军的面前，楚军匆忙渡河作战，结果三战三败，最后被迫在柏举与吴军进行决战。

吴军先锋夫概探知楚军内部不和，军心不稳，便向吴王阖闾建议趁机先发制人，突袭楚军，然后掩杀溃逃的敌人，必定取得大胜。吴王觉得是冒险，没有同意。夫概返回驻地，想到孙子的教导：将帅应该根据战场实际情况灵活地决定进退。有取胜的把握，即使国君不同意打，也可以坚决去打；没有取胜的可能，即使国君命令进攻，也可以不打。夫概想，战机一旦失去，就很难再遇到。孙子说得对，"将在外，君命有所不受"。于是乘雾气未散之机，率领5000士卒突袭楚军主帅营帐，楚军主帅囊瓦猝不及防，士兵纷纷溃逃。孙子得知夫概发动突袭，立刻命令伍子胥、伯嚭率主力军前去会战。这一战，打得楚军溃不成阵，死的死，伤的伤，逃的逃，散的散，连主帅囊瓦也受伤了，吴军大获全胜。柏举之战，使吴楚两军的力量对比发生了根本性转变。

孙子指挥吴军继续追击，终于在清发（今湖北安陆）追上溃逃的楚军主力部队，待楚军渡河到一半的时候，孙子命令吴军发动攻击。这时，没有过河的楚军忙着争夺船只过河，过了河的楚军已经饿得要命，忙着埋锅做饭。吴军一发动进攻，楚军毫无斗志，丢下刚做熟的饭顾不得吃，仓惶逃跑，吴军却借机饱餐一顿，然后精神饱满地继续追击楚军。孙子不给楚军任何喘息的机会，一路追杀，连战连胜，直逼楚国的郢都（今湖北江陵西北纪南城），终于在公元前506年农历11月28日一举攻破城，楚昭王仓惶带着妹妹和几个亲信逃到随国（今湖北随县）去了。在吴楚柏举决战之后，孙子指挥吴军长驱直入，11天中行军700里，以弱胜强，并一举拿下楚国的郢都，不仅创造了以少胜多、速战速决的军事奇迹，而且成就了吴王阖闾的霸业，从此吴国声威大震。

吴楚柏举之战是孙子军事思想的一次伟大实践，他的先计而后战的谋略观，以正合、以奇胜的制胜论，兵贵速不贵久的指导思想，将在外，君命有所不受的独立指挥观，都得到充分的验证。其高明的战略决策、灵活的战略战术、迅雷不及掩耳的作战速度、以少胜多的智谋，都得到充分展现。吴楚柏举之战是中国战争史上的一个经典战役。

APPEAR WHERE YOU ARE NOT EXPECTED
— The Battle of Boju between the State of Wu and the State of Chu

According to *Sun Tzu's Art of War*, "Attack the enemy where he is unprepared, and appear where you are not expected. These are the keys to victory for a strategist. It is not possible to formulate them in detail beforehand."

In 506 BC, a fierce battle broke out in Boju (northeast to Ma City of Hubei Province today) between the State of Wu (in the lower reaches of the Yangtze River) and the State of Chu (in the upper reaches of the Yangtze River). It was a classic battle conducted by Sun Tzu, who was the Commander-in-chief of the Wu troops.

The two states of Chu and Wu were both located in the southeast area of China. Since the Spring and Autumn Period, dukes had contended for power, and these two states had been in constant wars along the borders. The State of Chu was a big power in the southeast area and was superior to the State of Wu in national power as well as military strength after annexing several small states. The State of Wu followed Sun Tzu's strategies of "exhausting Chu" and "misleading Chu". It divided its troops into three branches and encroached on Chu's borders alternately for six successive years. It led the Chu troops by the nose, moved them hither and thither but avoided decisive battles with their major forces. The Wu troops successfully carried out Sun Tzu's strategies, and as a result, the Chu army as well as its treasury was greatly exhausted. In 506 BC, the State of Cai, Chu's dependency, came to the State of Wu. King Helü took this opportunity and assembled his troops throughout the state. He appointed Sun Tzu as the Senior Commander, Wu Zixu and Bo Pi as the Vice Commanders and his brother Fugai as the Vanguard. Commanding the troops in person, Helü was determined to defeat the State of Chu at one stroke and to be the overlord of the southeast area.

As Wu was inferior in military strength, Sun Tzu mapped out the strategic plan of "disrupting the enemy's alliances by diplomacy" before "attacking the enemy's army". To be specific, the State of Wu first subdued the State of Cai and the State of Tang, Chu's dependencies, and then formed alliances with them, thus turning the table by gaining superiority over Chu. Then the allied forces attacked the State of Chu. At that time, the State of Wu stood out in its navy.

They had different types of warships, *dayi*, *xiaoyi*, *tumao*, *louchuan*, *qiaochuan*, etc (equivalent to battleship, sloop, fast attack craft, towered ship and cutter respectively). As recorded in *"The State of Qi"* of *Discourses on the States*, *dayi* was similar to a covered chariot, *xiaoyi* to a light chariot, *tumao* to an assaulting chariot, *louchuan* to a double-decker chariot and *qiaochuan* to an agile and brave cavalryman. On sight of Wu's major forces rowing against the Huai River, heading directly for Chu, the State of Chu quickly assembled its major force and strengthened the defense, with the Han River as the dividing line.

Seeing that the State of Chu had deployed its major force to deal with his navy, Sun Tzu immediately changed his original plan of marching by the waterway. The Wu troops abandoned their warships and thrust into Chu in depth by land. Vice Commander Wu Zixu asked Sun Tzu anxiously, "Our troops are good at battles on the water. Isn't it dangerous for us to forsake our strength for weakness?" Sun Tzu explained, "The Chu troops have stood ready, thus our strength in water battles have been weakened. Besides, we are covering thousands of *li* at huge expenses per day. Our marching is slowed down by rowing against the river. The Chu troops must have reinforced their defense, which adds to our difficulty. If an army covers a long route, it is not advisable for it to be involved in a prolonged battle. Speed is what counts in war. So, we have to launch a surprise attack out of expectation of our enemy, that is, 'Attack the enemy where he is unprepared, and appear where you are not expected.' What is valued in war is speed, not prolonged operations." At the command of Sun Tzu, the Wu army abandoned their warships and went ashore. After they passed through Yuzhang, trekked over the Xiaobie Mountains and the Dabie Mountains, they turned up before the Chu army as if from nowhere. The Chu troops were forced to fight after crossing the river, only to suffer three successive defeats. Finally, they were forced into a decisive battle with the Wu troops at Boju.

When Wu's Vanguard Fugai learned that there was internal discord in the

Chu army and its morale was shaky, he recommended to King Helü that they should forestall the enemy, stage a surprise attack and kill those fleeing in disorder. According to him, this would guarantee Wu a sweeping victory. However, the King thought that his idea was too risky and disapproved of it. After Fugai returned to his campsite, he thought of Sun Tzu's words, "A general should make decisions as to whether to attack or retreat according to the specific situations. If the situation is favorable, he should be determined to fight even if the king disagrees; if the situation is unfavorable, he should order his army to retreat even if the king orders him to attack." Fugai was sure that opportunity knocked but once. What Sun Tzu had said was right, "A general at the front was not bound by orders from his king". So under the cover of fog, he led 5,000 soldiers to stage a surprise attack on the campsite of Chu's General Nang Wa and caught him unprepared. His soldiers fled in a rout. Learning that Fugai had staged a surprise attack, Sun Tzu ordered Wu Zixu and Bo Pi to join in the battle. The Chu troops were badly defeated and suffered heavy casualties, with the survivors fleeing in a flurry. Nang Wa was also wounded. As a result, Wu won a sweeping victory. The Battle of Boju fundamentally shifted the military strength of the two states.

Sun Tzu ordered his army to pursue the fleeing enemy closely, and caught up with them at Qingfa (Anlu of Hubei Province today). When the Chu troops were halfway across the river, Sun Tzu ordered an attack. At that moment, the Chu soldiers who had not crossed the river were busy fighting for boats; those who had crossed the river were hungry to death so they were busy setting cooking ranges or cooking meals. When the Wu army staged the attack, the Chu soldiers had no appetite for fighting at all and fled, leaving the cooked meal behind. The Wu troops kept chasing them energetically after having a big meal. Sun Tzu gave the enemy no breathing spell, pursuing and fighting with them all the way. The enemy was defeated repeatedly. Sun Tzu pressed the enemy hard till they reached Chu's capital Ying City (Jinan City, northwest to Jiangling of Hubei

Province today). On November 28 of the year 506 BC, the Wu troops conquered the city. King Zhao of the State of Chu fled with his younger sister and several henchmen to the State of Sui (Sui County of Hubei Province today). After the decisive battle at Boju, Sun Tzu led his army to drive deep into the State of Chu. They covered 700 *li* in 11 days and captured Ying City at one fell swoop. Sun Tzu not only created the military miracle of a speedy war, where a numerically smaller army defeated a much larger force, he also facilitated King Helü in building up the power. Ever since, the State of Wu had gained great fame and high prestige.

The battle of Boju between Wu and Chu was a great application of Sun Tzu's military thoughts — his strategic opinion of "estimation before attack", his theory of obtaining a victory "by using the normal forces to engage and using the extraordinary means to win", his guiding ideology of "what is valued in war is speed, not prolonged operations" as well as his viewpoint on commanding the army of "a general at the front was not bound by orders from his king". All these ideas were fully verified. The Battle of Boju witnessed Sun Tzu's ability of making strategic decisions, flexible application of stratagems, fighting with lightning speed and defeating the many with the few. The Battle of Boju between the State of Wu and the State of Chu is classic in the Chinese war history.

虚虚实实——孙膑智擒庞涓

《孙子兵法·始计篇》：用兵是一种狡诈的行为。所以能打而装作不能打，要打而装作不能打……攻其无备，出其不意。

孙膑是齐国人，庞涓是魏国人，年轻的时候，他们俩曾一起跟鬼谷子学习兵法。后来，庞涓受到魏王的重用，当了魏国的将军，他把孙膑也邀请到魏国。庞涓的才能不如孙膑，眼见着魏王越来越欣赏孙膑，心里又妒又恨，于是设计陷害，当孙膑被判死罪后又假装救他，由死刑改为"膑刑"和"黥面"，剔掉了他的膝盖骨，又用刀在他面额上刻字，再涂上墨。孙膑以前的名字不详，自从他受了"膑刑"之后，人们都称他孙膑，后来就成了他正式的名字。孙膑感念庞涓的救命之恩，答应把研习《孙子兵法》的心得和自己的用兵经验写下来送给庞涓。一个偶然的机会，孙膑知道了事情的真相，原来这一切都是庞涓的计谋，既把他变成一个废人，又谋取他的兵法。为了逃出庞涓的魔掌，孙膑只好装疯。后来，他借齐国使臣出使魏国的机会得以逃脱。

　　孙膑回到齐国后，得到齐威王和将军田忌的赏识和重用。公元前353年，齐威王派兵救赵时就要任孙膑为主将，但孙膑推说自己是身残之人，不宜做主帅。按照中国古代军制，出兵打仗，帅旗上要写上主将的姓，孙膑不想让自己的名字暴露出来，以免引起庞涓的注意。齐威王只好任他为军师，任田忌为大将。那一次，孙膑和田忌在桂陵把庞涓打得落荒而逃。没想到10年之后，两人在战场再次相遇，这就是著名的马陵道之战。

　　公元前342年，庞涓率魏军攻打西邻韩国，韩国急忙向齐国求救。齐威王采取当年救赵的策略，先答应救援，待魏、韩两军都筋疲力尽时再派田忌和孙膑率齐军出击。这一次，孙膑仍用"围魏救赵"的老办法，直接向魏都大梁进军。庞涓有了桂陵之战的教训，立刻从韩国撤军追击齐军。孙膑对主将田忌说："魏国的军队素来骄悍贪利，看不起齐国的军队。《孙子兵法》说，对不同的敌人要有不同的对策，我们可以用逐日减灶的办法，装出齐国士兵胆怯逃亡得很多的样子，诱使魏军轻敌速进，这样我们就可以寻找机会伏击他们了。"田忌依计行事，第一天在宿营地做了十万灶，第二天减为五万个，第三天只做了三万个灶。古时兵制，十人为一火，十万个灶就是一百万军队，三万个灶就是三十万军队。果如孙膑所料，魏国在后面追击，每到齐军住过的地方，庞涓必派人查齐军的灶数，到第三天，他推定齐军逃亡士兵已超过半数，不禁暗暗高兴，当即决定甩下大部队，只率精锐部队日夜兼程追击齐军。孙膑估计了庞涓的行军速度，料定晚上必然到达马陵（今河北大名县东南），便让齐军埋伏在马陵道两旁，等待一举歼灭魏军。

　　马陵道处于两山之间，道路狭窄险阻，两旁杂草丛生，是个设伏兵的好地方。孙膑让士兵们把道路两旁的树木都砍倒，堆放在道路上以阻塞通行，只留下一棵最大的树矗立着，把那棵树朝东的皮剥下一大块，然后在白花花的树干上写下"庞涓死于此树下"几个醒目的大字。孙膑又在军中调集了一万名射箭高手，分为两队，埋伏在道路两旁的险要之处，命令他们只要看到这棵大树下火光一亮，就立即朝树下射箭。之后，孙膑又派一支部队隐蔽在离马陵道不远的地方，以截断魏军的退路。一切都布置妥当，就等魏军往"口袋"里钻了。

庞涓求胜心切，催促精锐部队日夜兼程，终于在天黑的时候到达马陵道。那棵兀然矗立的大树引起了他的注意，他隐隐约约看到树的白木处写着字，但看不清楚，于是命士卒点起火把照亮，只见那几个字是"庞涓死于此树下"。庞涓惊出一身冷汗，知道中计。就在这时，齐军的箭像雨点般射来。庞涓知道难脱虎口，遂拔剑自刎。魏军失去主帅后大乱，齐军趁机掩杀，魏军遭遇了前所未有的惨败。从此，齐魏两国形势大转，最终齐国取代了魏国的地位，成为中原地区实力最雄厚的国家。

兵者，诡道者也。孙膑智擒庞涓，用的是减灶诱敌之计，这一妙计，综合运用了"兵不厌诈"、"能而示之不能"、"利而诱之"、"卑而骄之"、"攻其不备，出其不意"等多项战略战术原则，是对孙子兵法思想的绝妙发挥。马陵道之战，也是孙膑军事生涯中的经典战役之一。

VOID AND ACTUALITY
— Sun Bin Annihilated Pang Juan

According to *Sun Tzu's Art of War*, "All warfare is based on deception. Therefore, when capable of attacking, feign incapacity; when intending to fight, feign inactivity… Attack the enemy where he is unprepared, and appear where you are not expected."

Sun Bin was born in the State of Qi, while Pang Juan was born in the State of Wei. When they were young, they studied the art of war under Guiguzi. Later, Pang Juan was appointed the important position of general by the King of the State of Wei. At Pang Juan's invitation, Sun Bin came to the State of Wei. Since

Pang Juan was not as talented as Sun Bin, and the King valued Sun Bin more and more; Pang Juan became so jealous that he conspired against him. When Sun Bin was sentenced to an extreme penalty, Pang Juan pretended to save him. The punishment was changed from death to two other forms of torture, chopping off his kneecaps and branding his face. There was no historical record of Sun Bin's original name, but since the torture of chopping off one's kneecaps was called the *bin* punishment, he was called Sun Bin afterwards. Feeling grateful to Pang Juan for saving his life, Sun Bin agreed to write for Pang Juan his understanding of *Sun Tzu's Art of War* and his own military experience. In doing this work, Sun Bin learned the truth that it was Pang Juan who had ambushed him, who had caused him to be disabled and who had angled for his art of war. To escape the clutches of Pang Juan, Sun Bin had no alternative but to pretend to be insane. Later on, when the Qi envoy was accredited to the State of Wei, Sun Bin took the opportunity and fled.

After his return to the State of Qi, Sun Bin was greatly valued by the King and General Tian Ji. In 353 BC, when King Wei of the State of Qi was about to send troops to save the State of Zhao, he wanted to appoint Sun Bin the Leading General. His offer was declined, for Sun Bin pleaded that his disability disqualified him for the post. According to ancient Chinese rules in war, the surname of the Leading General should be put on his flag. Sun Bin did not want to capture Pang Juan's attention by revealing his surname. King Wei could do nothing but appoint him Military Consultant, and Tian Ji was appointed Leading General of the Qi troops. It was through the joint efforts of Sun Bin and Tian Ji that Pang Juan was defeated at Guiling and fled the battlefield. It was also out of expectation that Pang Juan and Sun Bin could meet again on the battlefield ten years later. This was the famous Battle of Maling.

In 342 BC, Pang Juan led the Wei troops to attack the State of Han, which was in west of the State of Wei. The State of Han rushed to seek help from the State of Qi. King Wei of the State of Qi took the same strategy that the state had adopted in the rescue of the State of Zhao. He agreed to offer help, but did not send troops until the troops of the State of Wei and the State of Han were exhausted. In this battle, Sun Bin adopted the strategy of "besieging Wei to rescue Zhao", and directly marched towards Daliang, the capital city of the State of Wei. Having learned from the lesson of the Battle of Guiling, Pang Juan immediately withdrew his forces from the State of Han to pursue the Qi troops. Sun Bin said to Leading General Tian Ji, "The Wei troops have always been overbearing and rapacious, looking down upon our army. According to *Sun Tzu's Art of War*, we should adopt different strategies to deal with different enemies. We may reduce the cooking ranges day by day to mislead our enemy into believing that the reduction is due to the drop in the number of our soldiers, who are so cowardly that they flee. When the enemy starts to chase us at full speed, we might easily ambush them." Tian Ji followed his suggestion. On the first day, there were 100,000 cooking ranges at their campsite. The number was reduced to 50,000 on the second day, then 30,000 on the third. According to ancient military rules, ten soldiers shared one cooking range in general. 100,000 ranges suggested the number of 1,000,000 soldiers and 30,000 ranges meant 300,000 soldiers. Just as Sun Bin expected, Pang Juan asked his men to count the number of the cooking ranges whenever he found traces of camping by the Qi troops. On the third day, he could not help laughing when he calculated that less than half of the soldiers remained. He decided to leave the majority of the troops behind and pursue the Qi troops round-the-clock with only a contingent of crack forces. Sun Bin estimated that Pang Juan would be arriving at Maling (in the southeast of County Daming of Hebei Province today) at the marching speed of his army. He ordered the Qi troops to lie in ambush beside the road, waiting to annihilate the enemy.

The road being a dangerous and difficult mountain path, Maling was a perfect spot for an ambush. Sun Bin asked his soldiers to cut the trees beside the path, stacked them up to block it, and left the tallest tree standing. The bark of the trunk that faced the east was stripped off. Several Chinese characters stood out against the background of the bare trunk, which said, "Pang Juan is doomed to die beneath this tree." Sun Bin then assembled 10,000 master archers and divided them in two columns. The archers were hidden beside the path. They were ordered to shoot toward the tree root when torches were lit under the tree. To cut off the enemy's retreat, a contingent of troops was sent to hide at a place not far from Maling. When all was ready, the only thing to do was wait for the Wei troops to fall into the ambush.

Pang Juan was so eager to win that he urged his force to march day and night. At dusk they finally reached Maling. A towering tree caught his attention. The words on the bare trunk loomed through the darkness. When torches were lit, the words became clear, which said, "Pang Juan is doomed to die beneath this tree." Pang Juan broke into a cold sweat with fear as he realized that he had fallen into the trap. At this very moment, arrows rained down on them. Seeing no chance of escape, Pang Juan drew his sword and committed suicide. The death of its Leading General threw the Wei army into chaos and confusion. The Qi troops took the chance and made a surprise attack. The Wei troops suffered the most severe defeat that they ever encountered. Ever since, the situation of the two states had been reversed. The State of Qi finally replaced the State of Wei in becoming the strongest state on the Central Plains.

All warfare is based on deception. In capturing Pang Juan, Sun Bin adopted the strategy of reducing cooking ranges, which was a combination of several military laws: feigning is the soul of fighting a war; when capable of attacking, feign incapacity; hold out baits to lure the enemy; if the enemy is arrogant, try to encourage his egotism; attack the enemy where he is unprepared, and appear where you are not expected. Sun Bin showed these laws of Sun Tzu in the Battle of Maling, one of the classic battles in Sun Bin's military career.

利而诱之——齐、郑大败北戎

《孙子兵法·始计篇》：利而诱之，乱而取之。

公元前 706 年夏，位于中国北部的游牧民族北戎大举侵袭齐国，除了掠夺边境之外，还举兵向齐国的纵深入侵，威逼历城。齐军奋力抵抗，但是面对北戎如此强势的进攻，有点招架不住，于是齐僖公急忙向友邦郑国、鲁国和卫国借兵抗击北戎。

郑庄公接到求救信后，立即派世子忽率军前往救援，郑军第一个到达齐国的历城之下。齐僖公与世子忽商量共同破敌的对策。世子忽说："北戎性轻而不整，贪而无亲，胜不相让，败不相救，可以诱而取之。"齐僖公很赞赏世子忽的分析和破敌之策，便一起商定了用兵计划，然后分头去部署和准备。

一切准备就绪之后，齐、郑联军开始行动。齐将公孙戴仲奉命打开历城北门，率领齐军出城向围城的戎兵挑战，北戎将领小良见状即刻率军迎战，双方交锋，你来我往地打了约二十个回合，公孙戴仲找准机会诈败，掉转战车绕城向东门逃去，小良不知是计，紧追不舍，北戎另一位将帅大良则率大部队紧随其后。眼看快要追到东门之际，预先埋伏在那里的齐军突然杀出，给敌人一个措手不及。小良见状，方知中计，急忙勒马回撤，恰与紧随其后的大部队相撞，把大良的军队冲乱。这时，公孙戴仲立刻回军与伏兵一起掩杀乱了阵的敌人，北戎被迫狼狈逃窜，当溃逃到鹊山时，突然遭到埋伏在那里的郑军的截击。大良和小良接连遭伏击，失魂落魄，部队已经失去了士气，被郑军打得落花流水。在激战中，小良被射死于马下，大良则被世子忽斩首，齐、郑联合打了一个漂亮的歼灭战，保卫了齐国的北部边境。

这一战取胜的关键，是因为世子忽非常了解敌人，做到知彼知己，能根据敌人贪利、轻敌、败不相救等弱点，制订出有针对性的作战计划，即"利而诱之，乱而取之"。孙子认为，两军交锋，皆为争利，问题在于如何使对方"贪"起来，而自己避免因贪利而陷于灭顶之灾。所以，聪明的将帅总是在具体的战斗中要考虑得失两个方面，即"必杂于利害"，不能只见"利"不看"害"。在敌情不明、危险很大、对全局不利的情况下，就要权衡利害，有的路就不能走，有的敌人就不能打，有的城就不能攻，有的地盘就不能争。孙子在《九变篇》中总结说："是故智者之虑，必杂于利害。杂于利，而务可信也；杂于害，而患可解也。"显然，孙子把以前战争的宝贵经验，从正反两个方面加以总结和提升，成为《孙子兵法》的精彩内容。所以后人说，《孙子兵法》是先秦兵法思想的一大结集。

HOLD OUT BAITS TO LURE THE ENEMY
— The Qi and Zheng Troops Defeated the Beirong People

According to *Sun Tzu's Art of War*, "Hold out baits to lure the enemy. Strike the enemy when he is in disorder."

In the summer of 706 BC, the Beirong people, a nomadic ethnic group living in the north of China, attacked the State of Qi. They seized Qi's borderland by force, and invaded the state in depth, even approaching Li City. The Qi troops resisted strenuously, but were unable to withstand. Duke Xi of the State of Qi then sought help from its three friendly states: the State of Zheng, the State of Lu and the State of Wei.

When Duke Zhuang of the State of Zheng got the message, he immediately gave the order that Shi Zihu was to lead troops to Qi's rescue. They were the first troops who got to Li City in the State of Qi. When Duke Xi and Shi Zihu discussed a plan to assault the invaders together, Shi Zihu said, "The Beirong people always underestimate their opponents. They are greedy for honor, immodest in victory, and reluctant to offer help in an emergency. So we can hold out baits to lure them." Duke Xi heaped praise on him. After the battle strategy was set, they went to deploy troops respectively.

When all were prepared, the allied forces took action. General Gongsun Daizhong of the State of Qi opened the north gate of Li City and led the army to challenge the Beirong troops that were besieging the city. General Xiaoliang led the Beirong troops to meet them head-on. After fighting for about twenty rounds, Gongsun Daizhong feigned defeat and escaped in the chariot toward the east gate of the city. Not seeing through the stratagem, Xiaoliang closely pursued them, followed by the majority of the Beirong troops who were led by General Daliang. Close to the east gate, they were ambushed and beaten by the Qi troops. It was not until then that Xiaoliang realized the stratagem. He retreated hastily, only to run head-on into Daliang's troops. At the very moment, Gongsun Daizhong gave the Beirong troops a back thrust. They fled in panic and were again ambushed by the Zheng troops at Mount Que. Having encountered one ambush after another, the Beirong troops were demoralized. In fierce fighting, Xiaoliang was shot to death under his horse, while Daliang was beheaded by Shi Zihu. The allied forces of Qi and Zheng fought a brilliant battle of annihilation and protected the northern border of the State of Qi.

The key to winning the battle lies in Shi Zihu's knowledge of the enemy. He knew the enemy and his own troops well. The enemy was greedy for honor, always underestimated its opponents and never saved its companion in defeat. Based on the analysis of these weaknesses, Shi Zihu made the battle plan, "Hold out baits to lure the enemy." According to Sun Tzu, people fight for advantages. The key to success lies in how to make one's opponent become greedy and to free oneself from greed which always results in complete annihilation. Therefore, in war, a wise general would take both gains and losses into consideration. He must consider favorable and unfavorable factors. He should not overlook the losses for the gains. When he is not clear of the state of the enemy, or when the situation is unfavorable with high risks, the general should weigh the pros and cons and then decide what ways to follow, what enemies to fight, what cities to attack and what territory to vie for as well as to choose what ways to drop and what enemies and cities to avoid. As Sun Tzu summed up in *Sun Tzu's Art of War*, "Therefore, a wise general takes into account both favorable and unfavorable factors. By considering the favorable factors, he makes his plan feasible; by considering the unfavorable factors, he may avoid potential disasters." It is self-evident that Sun Tzu summarized and developed the valuable experience of previous battles from both the positive and negative perspectives. These are the important teachings in *Sun Tzu's Art of War*, which was valued by the later generations as a collection of military thoughts prior to the Qin Dynasty (221 BC–206 BC).

攻其不备——齐讨蔡伐楚

《孙子兵法·始计篇》：攻其不备，出其不意。

公元前 656 年，齐桓公已经取得了霸主地位，但是，处于南方的楚国在兼并了许多小国之后，国力日渐强大，也怀有称霸野心，屡次进攻齐的盟国郑国。这一年的春天，齐桓公决定号令诸侯对楚国实行打击，一来彰显一下齐国的霸主地位，二来借机打破楚国妄想争霸的野心。

楚国毕竟也是一个实力很强的大国，齐桓公想以偷袭的方式给楚国一个出其不意的打击。但是，齐楚相距很远，中间隔着大大小小的国家，由几个国家组成的军队长距离地奔袭，要想隐蔽偷袭的战略意图，给楚国一个出其不意的打击，在当时军队机动能力十分低下的情况下，非常不容易。为此，齐国君臣费尽了脑筋。

管仲是春秋时代最伟大的谋略家，也是辅佐齐桓公登上霸主地位的功臣。他对齐桓公说："数国军队，千里奔袭，如此大的军事行动要做到让别人不知道，几乎没有可能。不如以讨蔡之名，行伐楚之实。这样方可掩人耳目，实现出其不意，攻其不备的战略意图。"齐桓公一听，连连称奇，因为蔡国也是他想惩罚的诸侯国之一。

蔡国位于楚国的北边，原来跟齐国关系很好。蔡穆侯为了加强与齐国的关系，把自己的妹妹嫁给了齐桓公。有一次，齐桓公带蔡姬一起去水上游玩，来自南方的蔡姬在船上玩得很高兴，见齐桓公怕水，故意把小船摇得来回晃荡，惹恼了齐桓公，结果被送回了蔡国。按照周代的礼法，女人结婚以后被送回娘家，就是被丈夫休了，这是很耻辱的事情。蔡穆侯认为，齐桓公这么点小事就休妻，是故意给蔡国难堪，恼怒之下又将妹妹嫁给了楚成王。从此，蔡国结好楚国，疏远齐国。为此，齐桓公对蔡侯十分恼恨。以讨蔡之名兴兵，既掩盖了伐楚的战略意图，又教训了蔡国，一举两得，真是太妙了！

齐桓公率领诸侯军队顺利地拿下蔡国，正要实施突袭楚国的行动时，却意外地在边境见到了楚国的使者。原来，在齐桓公伐蔡时，齐军先锋坚貂率领一支军队先到达蔡国攻城。蔡姬在齐国时，坚貂曾服侍蔡姬并得到过恩惠，蔡姬退回娘家时，他又是送使。蔡穆侯认出坚貂，知道他是个贪利之人，于是，便在深夜派人偷偷送他金帛一车，求其缓兵。坚貂接受了贿赂，便把齐桓公以讨蔡之名行伐楚之实的战略计划都告诉了蔡侯，劝蔡侯赶快到别国避难。蔡侯立刻把消息传递给楚国。楚王得到蔡侯的报告，一面严加戒备，一面派使者去质问齐桓公为什么伐楚。管仲看到楚国已经有了充分准备，原来的计划不可行了，马上调整战略，一方面打着维护周天子的旗号，指责楚国对王朝无礼，保持在政治上压制住楚国；另一方面，把军队调集到汉水边，与楚军隔水相望，军事上保持对楚国的压力，迫使楚国就范。果然，楚国一方面为没有按周礼朝贡周天子辩护，一面积极谋求与齐桓公和解。这次战争，最终以齐、楚两国在召陵缔结盟约而告终。

虽然这次战争最终没有完全实现预定的"突袭楚国"的战略意图，但是，它留下的军事遗产却十分丰富。首先，齐桓公当时号令了八个诸侯国一同伐楚，这样庞大的军事行动却巧妙地以讨蔡掩盖了其伐楚的战略意图，这在战争史上是一个伟大的创举；其次，当"讨蔡伐楚"之谋功溃于消息泄漏之时，管仲及时调整了战略，变被动为主动，避免了功亏一篑；第三，作为军事谋略家和指挥家，管仲的因利而制权能力给后人很多启示，他巧妙地把原本只是刀光剑影的军事斗争，变成谈与打相互结合的综合斗争。这些闪耀着管仲谋略智慧和指挥艺术光芒的经典战役，都成为孙子军事思想的不朽源泉。《孙子兵法》中说："善攻者，敌不知其所守；善守者，敌不知其所攻。""合于利而动，不合于利而止。""能因敌变化而取胜者，谓之神。"

ATTACK THE ENEMY WHERE HE IS UN-PREPARED
— The State of Qi Attacked the State of Cai to Invade the State of Chu

According to *Sun Tzu's Art of War*, "Attack the enemy where he is unprepared, and appear where you are not expected."

By 656 BC, Duke Huan of the State of Qi had long obtained power. The State of Chu, located in the south, had also become a power after annexing several small states and harbored the ambition of taking Qi's overlord position. It attacked the State of Zheng, the ally of the State of Qi, several times. In the spring of that year, Duke Huan of the State of Qi was determined to order the other dukes to attack the State of Chu together, to demonstrate his supreme power and to destroy Chu's ambition.

Since the State of Chu was also powerful, Duke Huan planned a surprise attack. But the plan was infeasible because it was hard to disguise their strategic intention, for the combined troops of several states had to travel a long distance to reach the destination by way of several big and small states. Besides, the low mobility of troops at that time also added to the difficulty. Therefore, Duke Huan and his officials racked their brains to figure out a solution.

Guan Zhong was a great strategist in the Spring and Autumn Period. He was also the one who helped Duke Huan to become the overlord. He told Duke Huan, "There is no way to disguise our military action with the combined troops of several states covering a thousand *li* for a surprise attack. Why not cover our real intention of attacking the State of Chu by feigning to attack the State of Cai? In this way, we may deceive the others and realize our strategic intention." Duke Huan profusely praised him because the State of Cai was also one of the vassal states he wanted to punish.

The State of Cai lay to the north of the State of Chu. It used to be in good relations with the State of Qi. To enhance the friendship between the two states, Marquis Mu of the State of Cai married his younger sister to Duke Huan of the State of Qi. Once, Duke Huan went boating with Concubine Cai, who was brought up in the southern area. When she noticed that Duke Huan was afraid of water, she shook the boat deliberately, which annoyed the duke. As a result, she was sent back to the State of Cai. According to the etiquette of the Zhou Dynasty, if a married woman was sent back to her parents' home, she was discarded by her husband, which would bring a great shame to her family. Marquis Mu of the State of Cai was offended. He thought that Duke Huan was intentionally embarrassing the State of Cai by discarding his wife over such a trifling matter. Out of rage, he married his younger sister to Duke Cheng of the State of Chu. Since then, the State of Cai had been on good terms with the State of Chu, but chilled its relationship with the State of Qi. Duke Huan was irritated by this action. Guan Zhong's plan could help him "kill two birds with one stone". On the one hand, Duke Huan could cover his real intention of attacking the State of Chu under the cover of attacking the State of Cai; on the other, he was able to teach the State of Cai a good lesson. How wonderful the idea was!

Duke Huan succeeded in conquering the State of Cai with the combined troops. When he was just about to stage a surprise attack on the State of Chu, he accidentally met Chu's messenger near the border. As it was, Marquis Mu of the State of Cai recognized Jian Diao, Qi's Spearhead who led the vanguard at their arrival in the State of Cai. Jian Diao was the attendant of Concubine Cai when she was in the State of Qi and had obtained her favor. He was also the envoy who took her back to her home state. As Jian Diao was greedy for money, Marquis Mu sent someone under cover of darkness to bribe him with a chariot of gold and silk. In return, the Marquis asked for a delay in attack. Jian Diao took the bribe and revealed Duke Huan's real intention of attacking the State of Chu. He suggested that Marquis Mu should take refuge in other states. Marquis Mu immediately delivered the message to the State of Chu. After he was informed, the King of the State of Chu called for a full alert, and at the same time sent an envoy to question Duke Huan about the reasons of attacking his state. Seeing that the State of Chu had been well prepared, Guan Zhong realized that his original plan could not be carried out, and immediately adjusted his strategy. On the one hand, under the banner of defending the honor of the King of the Zhou Dynasty, he condemned the State of Chu for being rude to the royal family, thus obtaining an overwhelming position in politics; on the other hand, he assembled his troops on the bank of the Han River, facing the Chu troops on the opposite bank, thus exerting pressure on the State of Chu in military forces and compelling it to submit. Just as expected, the State of Chu defended itself for violating the etiquette of the Zhou Dynasty and paying no tribute to the King of the Zhou Dynasty, and at the same time it took active measures to seek compromise with Duke Huan. The battle ended in a treaty of alliance between the two states.

Although the strategic intention of "staging a surprise attack on the State of Chu" was not entirely fulfilled, the battle did leave behind it a rich military heritage. Duke Huan assembled troops from eight vassal states to attack the State of Chu. It was remarkable in the war history that their strategic intention was so well disguised despite their huge military operation. Besides, after the disclosure of the secret, Guan Zhong adjusted the strategy promptly and avoided failure by regaining the initiative. Furthermore, as a commander and military strategist, Guan Zhong was able to act in accordance with what was advantageous. He left his descendants abundant revelations. He ingeniously changed the bloody military fighting into a combination of fighting and negotiation. These classical battles shining with Guan Zhong's wisdom and tactics are the endless sources of Sun Tzu's military thoughts. As is stated in *Sun Tzu's Art of War*, "Against those skilled in attack, the enemy does not know where to defend, and against the experts in defense, the enemy does not know where to attack. Fight when the situation is advantageous, and stop fighting otherwise. One able to win the victory by modifying his tactics in accordance with the enemy situation may be said to be divine."

亲而离之——晋献公假道伐虢

《孙子兵法·始计篇》：利而诱之，乱而取之，实而备之，强而避之，……亲而离之。

公元前 658 年，晋献公打算出兵讨伐虢国。虢位于晋国南部，国君名字叫丑，为人骄悍好斗，多次用兵进犯晋国边界。晋献公无法容忍一个弹丸小国对晋国的冒犯，于是决定出兵讨伐。

与晋、虢相邻的还有虞国，也是一个小国。虞与虢不仅毗邻，而且是同姓，因此两国关系一直很好。攻打虢国，晋献公很担心虞国会出来帮助虢国。晋大夫荀息对献公说："何不用借道的办法来伐虢？"晋献公问："怎么借呢？"荀息说："虞、虢关系虽好，但两国国君的性情完全不同，虢公性骄，虞公性贪，如果我们用重宝收买虞公，借虞国之道去伐虢，只要虞公收了贿赂肯借道，就一定不会出兵援救虢国。"晋献公采纳了这一计谋，于是派荀息为使，带着两件至宝去见虞公。

荀息拜见虞公，给他戴了许多高帽子，把虞公夸得心花怒放以后，荀息趁机呈上礼物，一个是出产于垂棘的美玉，叫做"垂棘之璧"，一个是晋献公最钟爱的名马，叫做"屈产之乘"，因出产于屈地而得名。荀息说："这些都是天下罕见的至宝，晋君特以此结欢于您。"虞公被一席美言和眼前的至宝感动得不知如何是好，便巴结地对荀息说："晋国若有用得着我的地方，不要客气。"荀息趁势讲了借道伐虢的事，并许诺："一旦伐虢得胜有所收获的话，全部奉送给虞公作为回报，晋国愿与虞国永世结好。"虞公经不住这样的诱惑，满口答应了晋国借道伐虢的要求。

虢国西邻有少数民族犬戎，常常骚扰和掠夺虢国边境。晋军趁虢国与犬戎在桑田（今河南灵宝县）交战之机，途经虞国向虢国发动了进攻。为了讨好晋国，虞公还派兵充当晋军的先头部队。虢军见到虞军，还以为是来帮助自己抗击犬戎的，便打开了下阳的城门。下阳位于今山西平陆县大阳之南，是虞国北部的门户，结果一下子就落入了晋军之手。

事隔3年，即到了公元前655年，晋献公再次向虞公借道伐虢。虞国大夫宫之奇对虞公说："虞、虢两国，就像辅与车的关系，辅（车轮外的两条直木，用以增强车辐的承载力）在则车在，辅去则车亡，虞虢相依犹如辅车相依。虞国不能再借道给晋军了。"虞公听了，默然不应。宫之奇担心虞公没有明白，于是又打了个比方说："虞、虢两国就像嘴唇和牙齿的关系，如果嘴唇失去了，牙齿就没有了遮挡，直接暴露在外面了，所以唇亡而齿寒。虢国若亡，虞国就难以生存了，这就是唇亡齿寒的道理。因此，虞不但不能借道给晋军，还应联合虢国防备晋国。"但是，虞公贪眼前之利，不听劝告，还是答应了晋军再次借道伐虢的要求。宫之奇说："借道与晋，虞、虢必同归于尽。"遂带家眷逃往其他国家。

公元前655年秋冬，晋国再次举兵伐虢。虢国的都城上阳在南部，其北部的门户下阳早已被晋军夺取，这样就失去了依托和保护，很快上阳就被晋军攻破了，虢君丑逃亡。晋军灭了虢国之后，凯旋回师，经过虞国的时候，乘其不备，发动突然袭击，一举把虞国拿下。虞公只好将受贿所得的"至宝"又全部交出来。《韩非子·十过》篇中记载了这件事，说：当荀息牵着名马"屈产之乘"、拿着至宝"垂棘之璧"奉还给晋献公的时候，晋献公幽默地说："璧玉倒还是原来的，只是良马的牙齿比原先长长了！"

晋国假道伐虢，从战争谋略的角度值得总结的东西很多。从晋国的角度说，首先以至宝"利诱"，成功地离间了虢、虞两国的关系，实现了"伐交"和"分敌"；其次，又利用虞国的麻痹发动突然袭击，实现了"攻其不备"的军事效果。可以说是一举两得，大获全胜。从虢、虞两国的角度来看，既不知"诸侯之谋"，又不进行"庙算"，一味贪利，以至于亡国。

孙子兵法说，"利而诱之，乱而取之，……亲而离之。"善于用兵的人是使敌军屈服而不靠直接交战，夺取敌人的城堡而不靠硬攻，毁灭敌人的国家不须旷日久战，晋献公假道伐虢是对孙子兵法的成功运用。

IF THE ENEMIES ARE UNITED, TRY TO SOW DISSENSION AMONG THEM
— Duke Xian of the State of Jin Borrowed a Road to Invade the State of Guo

According to *Sun Tzu's Art of War*, "Hold out baits to lure the enemy. Strike the enemy when he is in disorder. Prepare against the enemy when he is secure at all points. Avoid the enemy for the time being when he is strong… If the enemies are united, try to sow dissension among them."

In 658 BC, Duke Xian of the State of Jin planned to attack the State of Guo, which lay to its south. Duke Chou of the State of Guo was aggressive and overbearing; he often encroached on the borders of the State of Jin. The offence by this tiny state was past endurance to Duke Xian, who decided to send a punitive expedition against it.

Adjacent to these two states lay another tiny state, the State of Yu, which not only adjoined the State of Guo but was also on good terms with the state because of their shared surname. Duke Xian feared that the State of Yu might offer military aid to the State of Guo. Minister Xun Xi said, "Why not attack the State of Guo by way of the State of Yu?" Duke Xian asked, "How?" Xun Xi answered, "Though these two states are on good terms with each other, their dukes differ in characters. Duke Chou of the State of Guo is overbearing, while the Duke of the State of Yu is greedy. We may easily buy him with treasures and ask for his permission to pass through his state. If he takes the bribe and consents to our proposal, he won't offer military aid to the State of Guo." Duke Xian adopted his strategy and appointed him the envoy to bribe the Duke of the State of Yu with two treasures.

At the audience with the Duke of the State of Yu, Xun Xi made lots of flattering remarks. When the Duke was elated, he took the chance to present him with two treasures: a piece of precious jade from Chuiji and a fine horse from Qu. Xun Xi said, "These two treasures are priceless, and they symbolize our Duke's friendship with you." The Duke was so flattered by his words and treasures that he fawned over Xun Xi, "Please don't hesitate to tell me whenever your state needs my help." Xun Xi took advantage of this occasion and asked to borrow a road. He also promised, "As long as we win the battle, we will present you with whatever loot we get in return for your help. We wish that our friendship will last forever." The Duke could not resist the temptation and readily promised to let the Jin army pass through his state.

The Quanrong people, an ethnic group living to the west of the State of Guo, frequently encroached on its border. When the Guo army and the Quanrong army were fighting a war at Sangtian (Lingbao County in Henan Province today), the Jin army took the chance and attacked the State of Guo by way of the State of Yu. To curry favor with the State of Jin, the Duke of the State of Yu sent his troops as Jin's vanguard. At the sight of the Yu army, the Guo troops opened the gate of Xiayang City, for they mistook them for their allies. The Jin troops captured Xiayang without any trouble. Xiayang lay to the south of Pinglu County of Shanxi Province today. It was the northern gateway to the State of Yu.

Three years later, in 655 BC, Duke Xian asked to borrow a road to invade the State of Guo again. Gong Zhiqi, an official of the State of Yu, hastened to admonish his Duke, saying, "The State of Guo and our state are neighbors as close as spokes and carts. We are interdependent. If one is gone, it will be difficult for the other to continue to exist. It won't do at all to allow the Jin army to pass through our state." The Duke was silent and made no response. To make it clear, Gong Zhiqi made another comparison, "We two states are like lips and teeth. If the lips are gone, the teeth will be exposed without any protection. This is also the case with our two states. If the State of Guo is destroyed, it will be hard for us to survive. So don't let them pass through our state. Instead, we should be on guard against the State of Jin in alliance with Guo." But the Duke was too greedy to listen to his words, and agreed to allow the Jin army to pass through his state again. Gong Zhiqi sighed repeatedly, "The State of Yu and the State of Guo will be doomed to the same fate." He then left for another state together with his family.

Later that year, the State of Jin invaded the State of Guo again. Since they had already captured its northern city Xiayang, Shangyang, Guo's capital, located in the south, lost the backing and protection and was soon seized. Duke Chou of the State of Guo fled. On their return trip, the Jin troops staged a surprise attack and destroyed the State of Yu. The Duke of the State of Yu had to return all the priceless treasures he had received. "*Ten Sins*" in *The Philosophy of Hanfeizi* recorded, "When Xun Xi returned Duke Xian the fine horse from Quchan and the priceless jade from Chuiji, Duke Xian said humorously, 'The jade is the same, while the teeth of the horse are longer.' "

A lot can be learned from Jin's borrowing the road. From Jin's perspective, it successfully drove a wedge between the State of Guo and the State of Yu by the temptation of treasures. Thus, it realized the goals of "disrupting the enemy's alliances by diplomacy" and "dividing the enemy". Later, it staged a surprise attack on the State of Yu when Yu was off guard, and won a sweeping victory by "killing two birds with one stone". In terms of the State of Yu and the State of Guo, they were ignorant of the plans of its neighboring state; neither did they make any estimate before the battle. Their only concern was greed for the treasures. No wonder they were eventually destroyed.

Sun Tzu's Art of War says, "Hold out baits to lure the enemy. Strike the enemy when he is in disorder... If the enemies are united, try to sow dissension among them." Those skilled in war could defeat the enemy without fighting, capture its cities without storming, and destroy its country without prolonged warfare. Duke Xian's borrowing the road to invade Guo is a case in point of the application of Sun Tzu's stratagem.

逸而劳之——楚庄王疲敌平内乱

《孙子兵法·始计篇》：辞卑慎行的敌军要骄纵他，休整好的敌军要劳累他，团结的敌军要离间它。

公元前 606 年，楚国发生了一起内乱，令尹斗越椒借楚庄王率兵出征之机，发动一场兵变。楚庄王在班师回国的途中受到叛军的阻拦，双方展开了斗智斗勇的角力。

楚庄王是在公元前 613 年继承王位的。此前的楚穆王一心要报其父楚成王在城濮被晋国打败之仇，积极操练兵马，不断吞并周围的小国，雄心勃勃，发誓要雪城濮惨败之耻。正当楚穆王要大展身手的时候，突然暴病而亡，其子旅继位，他就是后来赫赫有名的楚庄王。但楚庄王在继位之初的表现并不让臣民们满意。一连三年，他整天不是邀人在宫中喝酒就是带人出去打猎，既不关心国内的政事，也不关心强敌晋国的发展。为了阻止大臣来进谏，他特地让人在宫门口挂了一个牌子，上面写着："进谏者，杀毋赦!"大臣们都很着急，不知道该怎么办。

有一天，右司马(官职，主管军事)对楚庄王说："南山有一只大鸟，停在那儿三年了，从未展开过翅膀，不飞也不叫，默然无声，你知道这是什么鸟吗？"楚庄王明白了右司马的意思，于是他回答说："那可不是一只平凡的鸟，不展开翅膀，是为了长羽翼，不飞不鸣，是为了观民情，虽然现在它不飞不鸣，一旦奋飞必定冲天，一旦鸣叫必定惊人。"右司马明白了楚庄王的心思，暗暗高兴。

过了一段时间，楚庄王还是没有什么动静，大夫苏从也忍不住了，他也不顾禁令跑去劝谏庄王。楚庄王说："你明知故犯，真是太傻了。"苏从说："您比我更傻。我进谏被杀，死后可得一个忠臣的名声，您这样荒废下去，必将亡国，那时您就成了亡国之君，什么都没有了。"庄王知道时机已经成熟，于是一改往日颓废的生活，开始理政。楚国当时的令尹叫斗越椒，是个野心勃勃的家伙。楚庄王首先任命了三个大臣去分担令尹的工作以达到分权的目的，防止斗越椒篡位。然后整顿朝政，亲自管理国家大事。斗越椒手中的权力被大大地削弱了，引起他的不满和仇恨。于是他借楚庄王率兵北伐戎兵的机会，举兵先占领了郢都，然后率军在途中拦截楚庄王，企图把楚庄王消灭在郢城之外。斗越椒是以逸待劳，楚庄王的军队是刚刚打仗归来，所以双方一交战，庄王的军队就损失不小。楚庄王知道硬拼不行，便假装败退，悄悄地把主力军埋伏在漳水东岸，留一支小部队引诱敌人。

斗越椒求胜心切，不仅要击垮庄王的军队，还想一举活捉楚庄王。他见庄王的兵败退，便督军奋力追击。庄王则利用斗越椒的这一心理，引诱他率兵不停地追击，派人假扮百姓向斗越椒报信说："楚王就在前边"，把敌人紧紧地吸引住。斗越椒顾不得让士兵吃饭休息，一路狂追，疲惫不堪，当发现中计打算回军时，河中的桥已经被庄王的军队拆了。斗越椒失去了回路，顿时惊慌起来，只好命令隔河射箭与庄王的军队对峙。

庄王军中有一神箭手，叫养由基。他对斗越椒说："河面很宽，彼此的箭很难射到对面。早就听说您善于射箭，不如我们两个站在桥堵之上，各射三支箭，决个高低。" 斗越椒问过对方姓名，见是个无名小辈，自恃善射，便答应了。比赛开始了，斗越椒先射。第一箭射来，养由基用弓轻轻一拨，箭便掉到河里去了。第二箭射来，养由基稍微一蹲，箭就从头顶飞过去了。斗越椒见状，便大叫道："不许躲！" 第三箭射来，养由基手一伸，把箭接在手中。轮到养由基射箭了，他连续两次只拉弓未放箭，斗越椒发左躲右闪都落了空，就在他心神未定之时，第三箭已经射出，恰中他的脑门，一命呜呼。士卒见状，逃跑的逃跑，投降的投降。一场内乱就这样被平息了。

乱起之时，楚庄王处于劣势，但他巧妙地施行计谋，成功地把敌人拖疲拖垮，置敌于险境，进而掌握了战场的主动权。孙子说的"调动敌人而不被敌人所调动"，"休整好的敌军要劳累他，团结的敌军要离间它"，这些都是"立于不败之地"的精妙战略。

WEAR THE ENEMY TROOPS DOWN IF THEY ARE WELL PREPARED AFTER A GOOD REST

— King Zhuang of the State of Chu Suppressed the Internal Rebellion by Wearing Down the Rebels

According to *Sun Tzu's Art of War*, "If the enemy is humble and cautious, try to make him arrogant. Wear the enemy troops down if they are well prepared after a good rest. If the opponents are united, try to sow dissension among them."

In 606 BC, an internal rebellion broke out in the State of Chu. Prime Minister Dou Yuejiao launched a mutiny when King Zhuang was on an expedition. On his return trip, King Zhuang was intercepted by the rebel forces. A battle of wits and valor ensued.

King Zhuang came to the throne in 613 BC. King Mu, his predecessor, constantly held military maneuvers and kept annexing small neighboring states. Being ambitious, he swore to wipe out the humiliation of his father, King Cheng's fiasco in Chengpu by the State of Jin. When he was just about to take actions, he unfortunately died of a sudden illness. His son Lü succeeded to the throne to become the famous King Zhuang later. However, in the first three years of his reign, King Zhuang neglected state affairs, which disappointed his officials and people. He wasted his time hunting excessively or partying lavishly, showing no concern for the development of his rival, the State of Jin. To prevent his officials from admonishing, he asked to put up a sign at the gate of his palace, which said, "Let whoever admonishes die without mercy!" The officials were all anxious but could do nothing.

One day, Right Minister who was in charge of military affairs said to King Zhuang, "A big bird has perched on the southern hill for three years. It did not flap its wings, nor did it fly or sing. It remains still and silent. What should it be called?" The King made sense of his words, and replied, "It is anything but ordinary. It did not flap but grew the feathers on its wings. It neither flew nor sang but observed the condition of its people. Once the bird starts to fly, it will soar to the sky in one flight. Once it starts to sing, it will amaze the world with one cry." Having read the King's mind, the Right Minister was delighted secretly.

After a period of time, King Zhuang still took no action. Minister Su Cong could not wait any longer and risked admonishing him. King Zhuang said to him, "How silly you are to deliberately break my rule!" Su Cong answered, "You are sillier. If I am killed, my death will win me immortal fame. If you keep in a state of inertia, our state is doomed to its fate, which will leave you nothing but a title of the King of a Conquered State." Knowing the time was ripe, King Zhuang thereupon turned over a new leaf and devoted himself to his duties. Dou Yuejiao, his prime minister, was full of ambition. The first step King Zhuang took was to cripple Dou Yuejiao's power by appointing three ministers lest he should usurp the throne. Then he reorganized the court and handled state affairs in person. The weakening in power stoked up Dou Yuejiao's resentment and hatred. When King Zhuang attacked the Rong troops in the north, he took the chance and occupied the city of Yingdu. Then he led the army to block the King's way, attempting to kill him outside the city. Dou's army was at ease, while the King's army had been exhausted back from the battlefield, and suffered great losses when they started fighting. Knowing that direct confrontation would do no good, King Zhuang pretended to flee. He ordered a contingent to lure the enemy, while the major forces lay in ambush at the bank of the Zhang River.

Dou Yuejiao was so eager to win that he intended to defeat King Zhuang's army and capture him alive, so he asked his soldiers to spare no effort in pursuing the King's army. The King played upon his eagerness and lured him into hot pursuit. He asked his soldiers to disguise themselves as civilians to pass the message to Dou Yuejiao, "The King is just ahead of you." Dou ordered his army to follow closely, neglecting meals and rest. Only when they were extremely exhausted did he find out the truth. But it was already too late. Their way back was cut off because the bridge over the river had been torn down. Dou Yuejiao was at a loss, and had to ask his troops to confront the King's army and shoot arrows across the river.

There was an unerring shooter called Yang Youji in the King's army. He shouted to Dou Yuejiao, "The river is wide, and it is hard to shoot arrows to the opposite bank. I am told that you are good at shooting. Let's stand on the bridge abutment and fight it out by shooting three arrows respectively." Dou Yuejiao first asked his name, and then agreed promptly as Yang Youji was just a small potato compared with his own fame. The competition began. Dou Yuejiao shot first. Yang Youji used his bow to flick his first arrow aside, which fell into the river. When the second arrow came, Yang Youji ducked to let it fly past. Dou

Yuejiao shouted, "No dodging." His third arrow was grabbed by Yang Youji. It was Yang Youji's turn. He shot twice without arrow. Dou Yueji hastened to dodge, only to be cheated. When he was unsettled, Yang Youji shot the last fatal arrow, which hit into his forehead. At the sight of his death, his soldiers either fled or surrendered. An internal rebellion was thus appeased.

When the rebellion cropped up, King Zhuang was in an unfavorable situation. However he adopted an ingenious strategy and successfully exhausted his enemy. He regained the initiative when his enemy was in danger. Sun Tzu once said, "Those skilled in war bring the enemy to the field of battle and are not brought there by him." "Wear the enemy troops down if they are well prepared after a good rest. If the opponents are united, try to sow dissension among them." All these are the keys to remaining invincible in warfare.

以仁激勇——楚庄王巧设"绝缨会"

《孙子兵法·始计篇》：将者，智、信、仁、勇、严也。

　　公元前 606 年，楚庄王平定了斗越椒之乱后，在宫中大宴群臣，一来庆祝平叛胜利，二来招待一下平叛有功的百官们，所以号称"太平宴"。消灭了斗越椒，除掉了庄公的心腹之患，君臣都特别高兴，酒也喝得格外有兴致，直到夜幕降临，大家都还在兴头上。庄王命令点烛继续欢饮，同时还把他最宠幸的许姬叫出来为大家敬酒助兴。正喝得热闹，突然一阵风吹来，把烛都刮灭了。席中有一人，见许姬美艳惊人，趁烛灭之际，借着酒劲，偷偷扯许姬的裙子，拉她的手。许姬很厉害，趁势把那人的帽缨揪了下来，握着帽缨走到楚庄王旁边，附耳禀报了此事。她向庄王建议道："我已把那人的帽缨揪了来作为证据，大王您快命人点烛，察看一下是谁干的。"庄王听罢，并不回话。他对那些正忙着找火点烛的人说："不要点烛！就这样很好。"然后庄王又转向各位大臣说："我今天要跟你们一起喝个痛快，各位都把帽缨摘掉，把帽子拿下来，大家开怀畅饮！"虽然各位官员觉得莫明其妙，但还是按照庄王的话做了。当所有的人都绝缨摘帽之后，庄王才命令点烛。就这样，那个调戏许姬的人被遮掩过去了。

许姬不明白庄王的用意，散席之后问庄王为何不追究那个人的罪责，反而替他掩护。庄王说："今日是我请文武官员来赴宴，大家都很高兴，从白天喝到晚上，都有几分醉意了，在这种情况下，出现失态失礼的行为不足为奇。如果我按照你说的做，把那个人查出来并惩罚了他，别的官员也都会尴尬，宴会就会不欢而散，这可不是我请群臣来参加宴会的目的。"许姬说："还是大王您想得远，有肚量。"此后，人们把这个宴会叫做"绝缨会"。几年以后，楚庄王发兵讨伐郑国，有一位副将名叫唐狡，自告奋勇要当先锋，率百名勇士在前边为大军开路。唐狡勇猛善战，攻无不克，战无不胜，使楚军伐郑进展顺利。伐郑结束后，楚庄王论功行赏，要厚赏那位开路先锋唐狡。唐狡不好意思地对庄王说："我怎么还敢讨赏呢！当年绝缨会上失态冒犯许姬，蒙大王昔日不杀之恩，今番讨郑才有机会舍命相报，怎敢再领赏呢！"楚庄王回宫对许姬感叹道："当初若明烛治他的罪，今天怎么会有这样肯为我效死杀敌之人啊！"

按照中国古代的礼法，调戏君王的宠姬就是大逆不道，按罪当死。楚庄王并没有单纯从礼法的角度处理问题，而是从维护大局的角度，把原本会导致不欢而散的局面巧妙地转化为一场别开生面的酒会，既维护了自己的面子，保证"太平宴"的目标顺利实现，又给那位有不轨行为的官员以悔过的机会，让他清楚地知道楚王的恩德和宽宏大量，激发他自新和感恩。《孙子兵法》在《始计篇》中说，战争是关系到百姓生死和国家存亡的大事，军事要从道、天、地、将、法五个方面来经营。孙子在具体论述将帅的素质要求时说："将者，智、信、仁、勇、严也。"它包括了"德"、"才"、"能"几个方面，古人统称之为"武德"。在孙子看来，一个好的将帅应该是"智、信、仁、勇、严"具备，而不只是有"勇"，君王用将、将帅用兵过程中所体现出来的"智、信、仁"，则常常备受推崇，这成为中国古代评价将帅、选拔将帅的一个传统。

STIMULATE BRAVERY BY BENEVO-LENCE
— "The Feast of Taking off the Tassels" by King Zhuang of the State of Chu

According to *Sun Tzu's Art of War*, "The commander stands for the general's qualities of wisdom, sincerity, benevolence, courage, and strictness."

In 606 BC, after King Zhuang of the State of Chu had suppressed the rebellion of Dou Yuejiao, he held a feast in his palace in celebration of the victory and for the entertainment of the heroes, which was called "the peace feast". The killing of Dou Yuejiao was like getting rid of the thorn in King Zhuang's flesh, so both the King and his officials were extremely happy. They were all so much in high spirits that they were still reveling in drinking at dusk. The King asked people to light candles and continue drinking, at the same time, he let Concubine Xu, his favorite, to propose toasts to add to the fun. When everyone was having a jolly time, the candles were suddenly blown out by a gust of wind. Enchanted by Concubine Xu's beauty, an official availed himself of the moment and secretly pulled her skirt and touched her hand out of drunkenness. However, Concubine Xu was tough to handle. She pulled out his hat tassel in passing. Then she went to King Zhuang and whispered in his ear. She told the King, "I have pulled out his tassel as an evidence. Your Lordship, please ask them to light candles to see who did it." The King was silent and made no response. Then he told those who were busy looking for flames to light candles, "Don't light candles! It's quite OK." He turned to his officials and said, "Let's drink our fill. Take off your hat and pull your tassels. Drink to your hearts' content." All present were puzzled, but still followed his words. It was not until all the hats were taken off and tassels pulled out that King Zhuang told his attendants to light the candles. In this way, the man who had harassed Concubine Xu was not exposed.

Concubine Xu could not figure out the King's real intention, so when the feast was over, she asked him why he did not hold the man accountable but protected him instead. King Zhuang answered, "I invited all my officials here for entertainment. Everyone was delighted and became tipsy after drinking for the whole day. It's nothing strange for a person to forget himself in his cups. If I had done what you told me, found out who he was and punished him, the other officials would be so embarrassed that the feast would end in discomfort. This is anything but my real intention of inviting them here." On hearing his words, Concubine Xu answered, "Your Lordship, you are really far-sighted and broad-minded." Ever since, the feast had been known as "the feast of taking off tassels". Several years later, when King Zhuang attacked the State of Zheng, a vice-commander, Tang Jiao, volunteered to be Vanguard with a hundred warriors. His bravery and resourcefulness ensured the victory of the battle. After the triumph, King Zhuang rewarded his officials according to their contributions. When he was about to give bounteous reward to Tang Jiao, the Vanguard said in embarrassment, "How dare I expect rewards? But for Your Lordship's forgiveness, I would have been killed for my offence to Royal Concubine Xu at the feast without my tassel. You spared my life, so I could have the chance to repay your kindness today on the battlefield. How could I accept the rewards?" After he returned to his palace, King Zhuang said to Concubine Xu, "If I had asked to light candles and punish him at the feast, who would be willing to give his life on the battlefield for me today?"

According to the ancient Chinese etiquettes, it was the worst offence to harass the king's favorite concubine and could result in the death penalty. King Zhuang did not handle the situation merely in terms of etiquettes; instead he protected the general interests and ingeniously kept the feast in a unique way which would have otherwise ended in discomfort. In this way, he defended his own honor, realized his original intention of "the peace feast", and offered the offender an opportunity to repent for his error. In return, the King's forgiveness and benevolence would stimulate the offender to be grateful and make a fresh start. As is said in *Sun Tzu's Art of War*, "War is a matter of vital importance to the state and a matter of life or death to the people. Therefore, it should be appraised in terms of the five fundamental factors of politics, weather, terrain, commander and doctrine." Sun Tzu dealt with the qualities of the commander in detail, "The commander stands for the general's qualities of wisdom, sincerity, benevolence, courage and strictness." They included the aspects of "integrity", "talent" and "competence", which were generally called "martial ethics" in ancient China. According to Sun Tzu, a capable commander should not only be valiant, but should also possess the qualities of wisdom, sincerity, benevolence, courage and strictness. It was highly praised for a king to appoint generals, for generals to use soldiers in terms of wisdom, sincerity and benevolence, which was tradition in the evaluation and selection of generals in ancient China.

上兵伐谋——郑庄公智解五国之围

《孙子兵法·谋攻篇》：用兵打仗，上策是在未战之前就挫败敌人的计谋；其次是从外交上挫败它，使它孤立无援；再次就是在战阵间打败它，最下策就是攻打敌人的城池了。

公元前 719 年春，由卫国牵头，联合了宋、鲁、陈、蔡四国，组成五国联军，出动甲车一千三百乘，把郑国都城东门围了个水泄不通。原来，卫国新君州吁刺死了哥哥卫桓公夺得君位，他担心国内外不服，急于立威以服众。郑国位于卫国的南边，曾与卫国发生过矛盾，于是州吁决定拿郑国开刀立威。但是，郑国跟位于东部的齐国结有盟约，卫国攻郑，齐国必然来救，齐是大国，这样卫国就很难取胜立威。州吁遂利用矛盾，重贿拉拢，组成了五国联军，威逼郑国都城，郑国顿时陷于险境之中。

面对五国联军声势浩大的包围，郑庄公急忙召集群臣商议对策。

大臣们有的主张讲和，有的主张死拼。郑庄公听完大臣们的意见之后，觉得都不是好办法。他说："围郑虽是五国，但他们出兵的动机和目的却不一样，州吁刚刚篡了他哥哥的君位，还没有赢得本国的民心和诸侯的信任，所以借口跟我们有旧怨，牵头前来攻打我们，其目的不过是想以此立威压众。鲁国与郑相隔很远，又无矛盾，鲁国出兵围郑，是因为掌管鲁国兵权的公子翚贪图卫国的贿赂。陈、蔡两国虽然是我们的近邻，但一直没有大的矛盾。所以，这三国之兵，都没有一定要跟郑国拼死打仗的意思。只有宋国跟我们有些小矛盾，因宋国的公子冯在郑国，宋殇公一直担心我们支持公子冯回国夺取君位，所以这次借机出兵围郑，如果把公子冯移出都城送到长葛去，那么宋军必然也会移向那里。这样的话，真正想打仗的就只剩卫国了。我们只要做做样子，派少量军队出东门专门跟卫军打一打，假装兵败退回城内，让州吁既没有太大的损失又得个战胜之名，满足了他立威的目的，他必然会撤军回去。"群臣们都觉得郑庄公说得很有道理，于是就依计行事。

郑国先把公子冯送到长葛，然后派使臣对宋殇公说："当初公子冯逃命来到郑国，我们不忍心将他杀死。现在我们已经让他在长葛等待您的处罚，希望您到那里去解决你们的矛盾吧!"听到这个消息后，宋殇公果然命令宋军移兵去围长葛了。

蔡、陈、鲁三国军队看见宋军离去，军心也发生了动摇。这时，郑国派出一支500人的军队，出东门单找卫军交战，蔡、陈、鲁三国军队都乐得袖手旁观，纷纷登上壁垒观战。按照预订的计划，郑军只打了几个回合便佯败逃入东门，卫军追至东门，见城门紧闭，无法再战，便命令把东门外已经成熟了的庄稼全部割去以慰劳士兵。见此情景，鲁、陈、蔡三国将士都来祝贺卫军的胜利。

郑国示弱不战，各国军队便纷纷班师回国。卫君州吁觉得"立威"的目的已达到，同时又担心国内不稳，于是顺水推舟，命令卫军高唱凯歌，风光地撤军回国去了。

卫、鲁、陈、蔡、宋五国围郑，历史上称为"东门之役"，郑庄公智解五国之围的故事，详见于历史演义小说《东周列国志》第五回。郑国从被合围到解围，前后只有五天的时间，一场联军压城的惊险战争被郑庄公巧妙地解围了。孙子后来提出的"用兵打仗，其策之上者，是在未战之前就挫败敌人的计谋；其次是从外交上挫败它，使它孤立无援；再次就是在战阵间打败它，最下策就是攻打敌人的城池了。攻城的办法，是不得已而为之。"的思想，可以看做是对其理论升华。

ATTACK THE ENEMY'S STRATEGY AS THE PRIME CHOICE
— Duke Zhuang of the State of Zheng Ingeniously Stopped the Siege by Armies from Five States

According to *Sun Tzu's Art of War*, "What is of supreme importance is to attack the enemy's strategy before the war. Next best is to disrupt his alliances by diplomacy. The next best is to attack his army. And the worst policy is to attack cities."

In the spring of 719 BC, the State of Wei assembled allied forces from the states of Song, Lu, Chen and Cai. With 1,300 chariots, the allied forces besieged Zheng's capital outside its east gate. As a matter of fact, the new Duke of the State of Wei, Zhou Xu, seized the throne after he murdered his elder brother Duke Huan. In fear of disobedience at home and abroad, he was eager to flaunt his power and win the popular support. The State of Zheng was located to its south, and used to have conflict with it. Therefore, Zhou Xu decided to make Zheng the first target of attack. The State of Qi, located to Zheng's east, was its ally, who would definitely come to Zheng's rescue if Zhou Xu attacked it. Since the State of Qi was powerful, it would be hard for the State of Wei to achieve victory. Zhou Xu took advantage of the conflicts between different states and won over the other four states by offering high bribes. With the allied forces from five states, he besieged the capital city of the State of Zheng. A horrible pang of danger immediately struck the state.

In face of the siege by large troops of the five states, Duke Zhuang quickly called a meeting of his officials for counter-measures. Some advocated reconciliation while others maintained last-ditch defense, neither of which sounded good to Duke Zhuang. He said, "Though there are troops from five states besieging our capital, they differ from each other in their motivations and purposes. Zhou Xu has just seized the throne at the cost of his brother's life, yet he has not won the support of his people and the trust of other dukes. It is his eagerness to win the popular support that has driven him to war on the pretext of our past conflict. The State of Lu is far away from our state and has no conflicts with us. Prince Hui's greediness for Wei's bribes lies at the bottom of his sending troops, because he holds the military power of his state. The states of Chen and Cai are our close neighbors, but have never been in conflict with us, therefore the troops of these three states will not fight desperately against us. the State of Song is the only one we have ever had minor conflicts with. Its Prince Feng is taking shelter in our state, while Duke Shang is in constant fear of his returning to seize the throne. That's why he sends troops here. If we transfer Feng to Changge, the Song troops will certainly follow. In such a case, Wei will be the only state intending to fight. Let's play a game. We may send only hundreds of soldiers to fight with the Wei troops, and then pretend to flee back to the city. Therefore, Zhou Xu will suffer no loss at all and win the fame of victory. His needs to earn the popular support will be well satisfied. He is bound to withdraw his troops." All the officials thought that his idea did make sense, so they acted according to the plan.

First of all, the State of Zheng transferred Prince Feng to Changge, and then Duke Zhuang sent an envoy to pay an audience with Duke Shang of the State of

Song, "When Prince Feng fled to our state, we could not bear to kill him. Now we have sent him to Changge awaiting your punishment. We sincerely hope that you will settle your problem there." On hearing this, Duke Shang ordered his troops to transfer and besiege Changge.

When the Cai, Chen and Lu troops saw the transfer of the Song troops, the morale was shaken. Just at that time, the State of Zheng sent a contingent of merely 500 soldiers to fight only with the Wei troops outside the east gate. The Cai, Chen and Lu troops were only too happy to stand by and watch the fight on the ramparts. As planned, the Zheng troops pretended to flee into the east gate after several rounds. The Wei troops pursued to the east gate, only to see the gate tightly closed. As a result, they could not fight any longer, so they harvested the ripe crops that were outside the east gate as rewards to the soldiers. At this scene, troops of Lu, Chen and Cai all came to their celebration.

On seeing Zheng's showing weakness, troops from the other three states returned in triumph. Zhou Xu thought that his aim was well realized. At the same time, he was in fear of internal instability, so he took the favorable opportunity and returned amidst songs of triumph.

The battle was historically known as "the Battle of the East Gate". The story of Duke Zhuang's stopping the siege by wisdom was recorded in Chapter Five of *Annals of the States in the East Zhou Dynasty*, a novel of history. The siege lasted for only five days, and the dangerous battle with the allied forces was avoided by Duke Zhuang ingeniously. As is stated in *Sun Tzu's Art of War*, "What is of supreme importance in war is to attack the enemy's strategy before the war. Next best is to disrupt his alliances by diplomacy. The next best is to attack his army. And the worst policy is to attack cities. Attack cities only when there is no alternative." Sun Tzu's words may be seen as a theoretical distillation of Duke Zhuang's stratagem.

以全争天下——郑庄公 "远交近攻"

《孙子兵法·谋攻篇》：善于用兵的人，使敌人屈服不一定非得靠交战，占领敌人的城池不一定非得靠强攻，毁灭敌人的国家不一定非得靠久战。一定要用全胜的战略争胜于天下。

公元前 714 年，郑庄公假借周天子之命，要求诸侯一起去讨伐宋国，理由是宋殇公失礼于王室，没有去朝见周天子。其实，自周平王东迁以后，周王室衰落，诸侯们常常不按周礼去朝拜周天子，郑庄公不过是找个借口攻打宋国罢了。

宋国位于郑国的东边，当年宋国新君继位的时候，宋国的公子冯争君位失败后逃到郑国，郑庄公收留了他，引起宋殇公的不满，由此郑、宋两国结下恩怨。公元前 719 年，位于郑国北部的卫国发生了弑君篡位的事件，州吁杀死了同父异母的兄弟而自立为君，为了求得诸侯的承认和稳定国内的民心，他向宋殇公提出联合攻打郑国以除掉他的政敌公子冯，宋殇公当然很高兴。当时，卫国与陈、蔡两国关系很好，于是卫、宋、陈、蔡等国便在这年的夏天联合伐郑，包围了郑国都城的东门，即历史上所说的"东门之役"。那一次，郑庄公用"伐谋"的战略，巧妙地解了东门之围，但是，郑国被宋、卫两国夹击的危险并没有解除。除了地理上宋、卫对郑国处于包围之势外，在国家关系上，郑国也处于两国包围之中，因为郑国与卫国也有很深的矛盾。当年，郑庄公的弟弟段在母亲的纵容和支持下密谋夺取君位，郑庄公发现并击败了这一阴谋，杀死了弟弟段，幽禁了母亲，但是段的儿子公孙滑却逃到了卫国。卫桓公不但收留了他，而且帮助滑夺取了郑国的廪延，之后两国的矛盾日趋恶化。所以，郑庄公视宋、卫两国为大患，必欲除之而后快。

公元前717年，宋国夺取了郕国的土地，郕国向郑国求助雪耻，这给郑国提供了机会。于是，郑庄公便用兵伐宋。宋国急忙向鲁国求救，因使者愚蠢，不但没有搬来救兵，还把鲁隐公惹生气了。郑庄公得到消息，急忙派使者去结好鲁国，答应把以前侵占的鲁国土地归还给鲁国，化敌友为己友。宋国求鲁失败后，又转求齐国，齐国答应出面调停郑、宋两国的冲突。本来，郑、宋两国的矛盾是不可调和的，但是，齐是大国，郑庄公不能不给面子，于是答应齐国接受调停，以赢得齐国的好感。其实，郑庄公与鲁国、齐国的周旋，都是从战略上切断了宋国的外交关系，即孙子所说的"伐交"，是实现远交近攻目标的第一步。到了公元前714年，郑庄公见时机成熟，便以宋公没有朝见周天子为由邀鲁、齐一同讨伐宋国。这是郑庄公远交近攻战略的第二步"伐兵"。

郑、鲁、齐三国伐宋之役开始，宋国则联合友邦卫国抵抗，但力量对比上无法与郑、鲁、齐三个大国抗衡。宋军很快就在菅（今山东单县北）地被鲁军打败，宋国的郜（今山东成武县东南）、防（今山东金乡县西南）两邑相继被郑军和齐军占领。宋、卫两军见正面较量不过郑、鲁、齐三军，便乘郑国国内空虚之机，转而进攻郑国，得手后又接着攻打戴国。郑庄公把占领的郜、防二邑送给齐国和鲁国，自己率兵返回，在戴国全歼了戴、宋、卫三国军队。接着又顺道灭了郕、许，并再次伐宋，宋军大败，宋、卫被迫向郑求和，郑国声威大增。从此，郑庄公便以霸主自居。

郑国之所以能够步步取胜，根本的原因在于郑庄公有一套完善的战略，即"远交近攻"，先"伐交"，化敌友为己友，再"伐兵"，以替周天子讨伐宋公无礼的名义联合鲁、齐用兵，做到万无一失。郑庄公败宋降卫的用兵智谋，必然给其后的孙子以启发。《孙子兵法·谋攻篇》说：善于用兵的人，使敌人屈服不一定非得靠交战，占领敌人的城池不一定非得靠强攻，毁灭敌人的国家不一定非得靠久战。一定要用全胜的战略争胜于天下。这样既不使自己的军队疲惫受挫，又能取得圆满的胜利。这就是以谋略胜敌的法则。

TAKE ALL UNDER HEAVEN INTACT BY STRATEGIC CONSIDERATIONS
— Duke Zhuang of the State of Zheng Attacked His Neighbors and Made Friends with States Afar

According to *Sun Tzu's Art of War*, "Those skilled in war subdue the enemy's army without fighting battles. They capture the enemy's cities without assaulting them and overthrow enemy's state without protracted operations. Their aim is to take all under heaven intact by strategic considerations."

In 714 BC, Duke Zhuang of the State of Zheng asked the other dukes to join him in attacking the State of Song under the pretext of the King of Zhou. His reason for the attack was that Duke Shang of the State of Song had breached the etiquette and did not have audience with the King. As it was, the royal family of Zhou had been on the wane after King Ping moved the capital eastward, and the dukes frequently breached the etiquette by having no audience with the King. Duke Zhuang was just inventing an excuse for his attack.

The State of Song lay to the east of the State of Zheng. When Duke Shang of the State of Song came to power, Prince Feng intended to seize the throne from him but failed, so he fled to the State of Zheng to seek shelter. Duke Zhuang of the State of Zheng took him in, which irritated Duke Shang and the seed of hatred was thus sown between the two states. In 719 BC, in the State of Wei, which lay to Zheng's north, Zhou Xu killed his half-brother and seized the throne. To win the support of his people and to be recognized by the other dukes, Zhou Xu made the proposal to Duke Shang that they should join efforts to attack the State of Zheng. Duke Shang was only too eager to agree as this would help him to get rid of his political foe, Prince Feng. At that time, the State of Wei was on good terms with the State of Chen and the State of Cai. So, these states formed allied forces and attacked the State of Zheng in the summer of that year. They besieged the east gate of Zheng's capital, which was historically known as "the Battle of the East Gate". Duke Zhuang stopped the siege ingeniously by attacking their strategy. But the danger still existed as the State of Zheng was located between the two states geographically. Besides, the two states were against Zheng in terms of relationship because of the serious conflicts between the State of Zheng and the State of Wei. Years ago, Duke Zhuang's younger brother Duan schemed for power with the connivance and help of his mother. Duke Zhuang discovered it and defeated their plot by killing Duan and house arresting his mother. But Duan's son, Gongsun Hua, succeeded in fleeing to the State of Wei. Duke Huan of the State of Wei not only provided him with shelter but also helped him capture Linyan, a city of the State of Zheng. As a result, the relationship between the two states took a drastic turn for the worse. Both the State of Song and the State of Wei were just like thorns in Duke Zhuang's flesh, so he would be only too happy to destroy them.

In 717 BC, the State of Song captured some land of the State of Zhu, who turned to the State of Zheng for help. This was a golden opportunity for Duke Zhuang, so he attacked the State of Song without any hesitation. Song intended to seek aid from the State of Lu, but was refused because its silly envoy irritated Duke Yin of the State of Lu. On hearing this, Duke Zhuang quickly sent an envoy to seek alliance with Lu by promising to return the land Zheng had occupied. In this way, he converted the enemy's friend to his own friend. Refused by the State of Lu, the State of Song turned to the State of Qi for help, who promised to mediate in their dispute. Though their conflict was irreconcilable, Duke Zhuang gave face to the State of Qi for fear of its power. He accepted the mediation to win Qi's favor. As a matter of fact, all his efforts were to realize what Sun Tzu called the "strategy of disrupting the enemy's alliances by diplomacy". This was the first step of Duke Zhuang's strategy to attack his neighbors and make friends with states afar. In 714 BC, when the time was ripe, Duke Zhuang asked the State of Lu and the State of Qi to join him in attacking the State of Song under the pretext of Song's not having audience with the King. This was the second step of his strategy of "attacking the enemy's army".

When the battle broke out, the State of Song, together with its ally, the State of Wei, put up a stubborn resistance, but they were no match for the combined forces of the three powerful states of Zheng, Lu and Qi. The Song troops were soon defeated at Jian (north to Dan County of Shandong Province today) by the Lu troops. Gao City (southeast to Chengwu County of Shandong Province today) and Fang City (southwest to Jinxiang County of Shandong Province today) were occupied one after the other by the State of Zheng and the State of Qi. Seeing that they had no way to win in the head-on confrontation, the Song and Wei troops changed their strategy and attacked the State of Zheng because it was weakly defended. After their success, they went on to attack the State of Dai. Duke Zhuang of the State of Zheng transferred Gao City and Fang City to the State of Qi and the State of Lu, and then he returned to his state with his troops. When they were in the State of Dai, the Zheng troops annihilated the troops of Dai, Song and Wei. On the way, they destroyed the State of Cheng and the State of Xu as well. After that, they attacked the State of Song again, whose troops were utterly defeated. The State of Song and the State of Wei were reduced to reconciliation with the State of Zheng, which earned it an awe-inspiring reputation. Ever since, Duke Zhuang had posed as the overlord.

The reason why the State of Zheng could succeed step by step lies in the perfect set of stratagems Duke Zhuang adopted, that is, attacking his neighbors and making friends with the states afar. By "disrupting the enemy's alliances by diplomacy", he succeeded in converting the enemy's friends to his own friends; by "attacking the enemy's army", he took no risk by allying with the State of Lu and the State of Qi and by flaunting the banner of Song's offending the King. The wisdom of Duke Zhuang in defeating the State of Song and conquering the State of Wei must have enlightened Sun Tzu, who wrote in *Sun Tzu's Art of War* that those skilled in war subdue the enemy's army without battle. They capture the enemy's cities without assaulting them and overthrow enemy's state without protracted operations. Their aim is to take all under heaven intact by strategic considerations. This could help one's own troops free from fatigue and frustration and at the same time achieve a complete success, which is the principle of the offensive strategy.

不战而屈人之兵——齐桓公收郭国

《孙子兵法·谋攻篇》：百战百胜，还算不上高明的，不经交战就能使敌人屈服，才是高明中最高明的。

公元前 666 年，齐桓公想用兵郭国，于是问计于管仲。管仲给他出了一个"示以欲伐"的主意，用现代的军事术语说，就是实行"战略威慑"。

郭国，位于今江苏省的赣榆县一带，是春秋时期的一个小国，原来是纪国的附属。公元前 693 年，齐国把纪国吞并了，但作为纪国附庸的郭国却一直没有归附齐国，一心谋求称霸的齐桓公对此不能容忍，所以想用兵征讨。管仲是齐桓公最重要的谋臣，他说："您刚刚赢得诸侯们认可，登上霸主地位，要是想巩固霸主地位，赢得人心很重要。如果以战争手段吞并郭国，必然引起诸侯恐惧。再说，郭国虽然很小，但他们的先人是姜太公孙子中的一支，跟齐国是同姓。灭同姓的话，不合乎道义。为了取信诸侯，巩固霸主地位，您眼下要做的应该是使那些快要灭亡的小国能够生存下去，让那些已经灭亡的国家复兴起来，建立'存亡兴灭之德'，这样您就可以长久地在诸侯中称霸了。至于欲得郕国，您可以采取'示以欲伐'的策略。""什么叫'示以欲伐'？"齐桓公问。管仲说："做出要讨伐郕国的样子，但并不真的去打它。比如，您可以命王子成父率领大军去巡视纪城，做出要讨伐郕国的架势，郕国必然害怕，会主动来投降齐国。"齐桓公问："这样做有什么好处呢？"管仲说："您可以一举两得，有得郕国土地之实，而无灭亲之名。"齐桓公听了非常高兴，于是就按管仲的策略行事。果然，郕国看到齐国大军压向自己的近邻纪城，大有一口吞掉郕国之势。郕国乃弹丸之地，根本不是齐军的对手，只好乖乖地向齐国投降。齐国未动一刀一枪，尽得郕国。齐桓公高兴地称赞管仲说："仲父（即管仲）之谋，万不失一！"

　　管仲的"示以欲伐"之计的核心，就是用军事力量威慑敌人，给对方造成巨大的心理压力，迫使其就范，以达到不用兵即可实现战略目标。这与《孙子兵法》中"不战而屈人之兵"制胜论是相通的，照孙子的说法就是"百战百胜，还算不上高明的，不经交战就能使敌人屈服，才是高明中最高明的"。管仲是齐桓公称霸时代的重臣，也是春秋时代最重要的思想家、军事家、谋略家之一。他给齐国留下的文化遗产，必然哺育了生长在齐国的孙子。所以《孙子兵法》既是孙子兵法思想的结晶，也是先秦兵法思想的结集。

SUBDUE THE ENEMY WITHOUT FIGHT-ING

— Duke Huan of the State of Qi Subdued the State of Zhang

According to *Sun Tzu's Art of War*, "To win one hundred victories in one hundred battles is not the acme of skill. To subdue the enemy without fighting is the supreme excellence."

In 666 BC, Duke Huan intended to attack the State of Zhang. When he consulted with Guan Zhong, Guan Zhong proposed the strategy of "showing the enemy their intention to attack", that is, "strategic threat" in the modern military term.

The State of Zhang (near Ganyu County in Jiangsu Province today) was a small state in the Spring and Autumn Period. It had attached itself to the State of Ji before Ji was annexed by the State of Qi in 693 BC. However, as a dependent state of Ji, the State of Zhang did not submit to Qi's power, which was intolerable to Duke Huan. At that time, Duke Huan was eager to dominate the Central Plains, so he decided to attack the State of Zhang. His major counselor, Guan Zhong, said to him, "Your Lordship, you have just achieved dominance and succeeded in gaining the other dukes' recognition. To strengthen your position, winning the popular support should be your top priority. Your annexation of Zhang by force will strike terror into the hearts of the other dukes. Besides, in spite of its small territory, the State of Zhang shares the same surname with us, because the people there are the offspring of Jiang Taigong's grandson. It is not ethical to destroy people of the same surname. To establish credibility among the other dukes and to strengthen your position as the overlord, your chief concern, for the time being, should be to help those small states on the verge of perishing to survive and to resurrect those perished states. If you succeed in helping them, you will dominate the Central Plains for a long time. As to the State of Zhang, we may adopt the strategy of 'showing them our intention to attack'." "But how?" Duke Huan asked. Guan Zhong answered, "We may feign to attack the State of Zhang, but do not take any concrete action. Let Wangzi Chengfu lead the troops to inspect Ji City, pretending to attack the State of Zhang. Out of fear, it must submit to us of its own accord." Duke Huan asked, "What benefits can I get by doing so?" Guan Zhong replied, "You can 'kill two birds with one stone' — occupy Zhang's territory and save yourself from the ill fame of killing your blood relations." Hearing his analyses, Duke Huan was quite happy. Then he carried out his strategy. Just as expected, at the sight of Qi's overwhelming army in its neighbor Ji City, the State of Zhang, a tiny state who was no match for Qi at all, surrendered without resistence. The State of Qi subdued the State of Zhang without the slightest effort. Duke Huan sang highly of Guan Zhong, "How miraculous Sir Guan's strategies are!"

The strategic threat by the overwhelming army was at the core of Guan Zhong's strategy of "showing the enemy our intention to attack". It was the great psychological pressure that forced the enemy to submit. In this way, he realized his strategic intention to subdue the enemy without fighting, which accorded closely with Sun Tzu's theory of achieving a victory. Sun Tzu once said, "To win one hundred victories in one hundred battles is not the acme of skill. To subdue the enemy without fighting is the supreme excellence." Guan Zhong was the most important court official in the reign of Duke Huan. Besides, he was also one of the most important thinkers, military scientists and strate-gists in the Spring and Autumn Period. The cultural heritage he left to the State of Qi nurtured Sun Tzu who was brought up there. Sun Tzu's *Art of War* is a collection of military thoughts prior to the Qin Dynasty and the distillation of Sun Tzu's military thoughts as well.

不战而胜——弦高犒师退秦

《孙子兵法·谋攻篇》：军队不疲惫受挫却可以圆满取得胜利，这就是以计谋攻取敌人的法则。

  秦穆公被烛之武说服从郑国撤军以后，听说郑国又与晋国结了盟，非常生气，于是想找机会再讨伐郑国。公元前 627 年春，留守在郑国的杞子派人向秦穆公密报，说郑国让他掌管着都城北门的钥匙，如果秦军来偷袭，他里应外合，可以得手。秦穆公召集群臣商议此事，老臣蹇叔和百里奚都不赞同。蹇叔说："调动大军想偷袭这么远的国家，我们赶得精疲力乏，而对方可能早就有了准备，怎么能够取胜？况且行军路线这样长，还能瞒得了谁？"秦穆公只想听赞同的话，见蹇叔反对，就不客气地说："你真是老糊涂了，要是你不活这么老，你坟上的树都该有碗口粗了。"秦穆公执意要偷袭，于是就派百里奚的儿子孟明视为大将，蹇叔的两个儿子西乞术、白乙丙为副将，率领三百辆兵车，偷偷地向郑国进发。

郑国有一位商人，名字叫弦高，赶着牛群去洛阳贩卖，恰巧在离郑国不很远的滑地（今河南偃师）与秦军的偷袭部队相遇。当他弄清了秦军的意图，便急中生智，一边派人火速去报告郑君，一边假扮郑国使者去犒劳秦军。他从自己的牛群中选了十二头肥牛，另外又带了四张熟牛皮，送到秦军驻地，谎称是郑国的使者，奉国君之命来犒劳远道而来的秦军。秦军听说郑国已经知道他们的行动，非常吃惊。弦高故意不慌不忙地对秦将说："郑国处于强国之间，军队不得不厉兵秣马，边境戒备森严，您见了这种情况请不要介意"。

再说郑穆公接到弦高的报告，急忙派人到客馆察看杞子等人的动静，发现秦军将士果然已把行装捆好放在车上，兵器都已磨好，战马也已喂饱，只等秦国的偷袭部队到来后从内接应了。于是郑穆公便召见杞子等人，对他们说："郑国又小又穷，没有办法长期供养你们，听说你们要回秦国了，那么就请便吧。"郑穆公正式向留守郑国的秦军下了逐客令。杞子等人见郑穆公已经看破他们的计谋，只得灰溜溜地离开郑国。秦国的偷袭部队先被弦高的犒劳所迷惑，以为郑国真的早有戒备，接着又失去了内应，觉得偷袭已无胜利的可能，只好放弃原来的计划。但是，秦军远道而来，又不愿空手而归，于是顺手牵羊，灭了滑国，然后班师回国。结果在途中被晋军伏击，这就是著名的秦晋崤之战。这段战史详见下文。

弦高犒师退秦军，可以称是"伐谋"的典范。郑国一场生死存亡的危急，被弦高以十二头牛的犒劳化解了。弦高"犒师"，彻底打破了敌人的计谋和战略。可见，智谋对战争的胜负有着巨大的作用。所以，孙子在《谋攻篇》中说："是故百战百胜，非善之善者也；不战而屈人之兵，善之善者也。"军队不疲惫受挫却可以圆满取得胜利，这就是以计谋攻取敌人的法则。

的确，弦高与秦军打了一场没有硝烟的战争，并且赢得很漂亮！

WIN A VICTORY WITHOUT FIGHTING
— Xian Gao Averted the Qin Troops by Rewarding Them

According to *Sun Tzu's Art of War*, "To triumph without wearing out the troops is the principle of winning victories by way of stratagems."

Persuaded by Zhu Zhiwu, Duke Mu of the State of Qin withdrew troops from the State of Zheng. The Duke flew into a rage at the news of the alliance between the State of Zheng and the State of Jin, and decided to seek another chance to invade it. In the spring of 627 BC, Qizi, an official of the State of Qin, whose troops were stationed in the State of Zheng, sent someone to make a secret report to Duke Mu that he was in charge of the key to the north gate of the capital. If the Qin troops made a sneak raid, he would act from inside in coordination with them to take the city. When the officials convened for a discussion, both Jian Shu, an old minister, and Baili Xi strongly disagreed about the plan. Jian Shu said, "To cover such a long distance will only exhaust our troops. The enemy may be well prepared, but how can we win the battle? Besides, how can we conceal ourselves on such a long overland march route?" Duke Mu did not want to hear any contrary views and said bluntly, "You are too old to think clearly. Otherwise, the trees on your grave would be as thick as a bowl." Determined to make a sneak attack, Duke Mu appointed Mengming Shi, the son of Baili Xi, as the General; Xiqi Zhu and Baiyi Bing, the sons of Jian Shu, as the Assistant Generals. With three hundred chariots, the troops secretly marched to the State of Zheng.

A merchant of the State of Zheng, Xian Gao, who was on his way to Luoyang to sell his cattle, encountered the Qin troops in Huadi (Yanshi in Henan Province today) which was close to the State of Zheng. When he figured out the intentions of the Qin troops, he hit upon a plan in an emergency. He sent someone to report to the Duke of the State of Zheng, and at the same time, he pretended to be the messenger from the State of Zheng, who was sent to reward the Qin troops. He picked twelve fat cattle and four pieces of cooked cattle hide and then took them to the campsite of the Qin troops. There he lied that he was the messenger of the State of Zheng, and was sent at the command of the Duke to reward the Qin troops coming from afar. The Qin troops were astonished to learn that their plan was already known by the State of Zheng. Xian Gao told the generals of Qin in a firm manner, "Surrounded by several powerful neighboring states, the State of Zheng has to get ready for war. Our horses are fed, weapons are sharpened, and the borders are heavily guarded. Please don't be shocked by such a sight."

When Duke Mu of the State of Zheng received the report from Xian Gao, he quickly sent someone to Qizi's residence. The man found that Qizi's subordinates had prepared troops, with horses fed and weapons sharpened, fully prepared to coordinate an attack from the inside on the arrival of the Qin troops. Under such circumstances, Duke Mu of the State of Zheng summoned Qizi with his subordinates and said to them, "Our state is too small and poor to support you any further. I was told that you are about to leave for your own state, please feel free to go." In this way, Duke Mu formally ordered the Qin troops that were stationed in the State of Zheng to leave. Realizing that their conspiracy had been revealed, Qizi and his subordinates were forced to retreat in submission with their tails between their legs. First, confused by the reward of Xian Gao, the Qin troops thought that the State of Zheng was indeed well prepared for the war. The subsequent loss of their contact inside made their chance of winning slim, so the Qin troops gave up their initial plan. But they did not want to go back empty-handed after such a long march, so they conquered the State of Hua en route. However, on their way home, the Qin troops were ambushed by the Jin troops. This was the famous Battle of Mount Xiao between Qin and Jin in history. The details of this battle will be covered in the following chapter.

The fact that Xian Gao opposed the Qin troops by rewarding them is a case in point for an offensive strategy. The danger of being conquered was eliminated by merely twelve cattle. Xian Gao's rewarding the Qin troops ruined the enemy's plan. This is evidence that strategies play a decisive role in the outcome of a battle. In *Sun Tzu's Art of War*, Sun Tzu said, "Therefore, winning one hundred victories in one hundred battles is not real excellence, winning a victory and subduing the enemy without fighting is the supreme excellence." To triumph without wearing out the troops is the principle of winning victories by way of stratagems.

As it was, Xian Gao waged a war without gun smoke with the Qin troops, and swept to victory.

因利制权——楚军"筑室耕田"降宋军

《孙子兵法·谋攻篇》：善于用兵的人，是使敌军屈服而不靠直接作战；夺取敌人的城堡而不靠硬攻；毁敌国而不靠旷日持久的战斗。

公元前594年秋，楚庄王发兵攻打离楚千里之遥的宋国，理由是楚国出使齐国的使者途径宋国时被害，而真正的原因则是为了解晋军攻郑之围。

三年前，即公元前597年，在争夺郑国的战争中晋军被楚军打败，郑国投靠了楚国并与之结盟，引起晋国的强烈不满。晋国围郑，其实就是对那一次兵败和郑国叛晋就楚的报复，楚国当然不愿意郑国再落入晋国之手，遂找借口去围攻晋国的友邦宋国，以期解郑国之围。

宋国位于晋国的东部，隔卫国与晋为邻。自晋文公称霸以后，卫、宋两国一直是晋的盟国。楚国大军压境，把宋国都城睢阳围得水泄不通。宋急忙向晋国求救。晋景公召集群臣商量派兵救宋的良策。大夫伯宗力主虚应而实不救之策。他说："上次荀林父率六百乘去救郑国，结果被楚军打得一败涂地。这次即便再派六百乘，也不一定有获胜的把握，何况现在正用兵郑国，若再分兵救宋，势必冒双重风险。楚、宋两国相距千里，楚军的粮草补给一定很困难，不可能支持太长时间。我们不如答复宋君，假说援军很快就到，让他们坚守城池就是。只要他们能坚守几个月，楚军不攻自退。"晋景公听了伯宗的分析，觉得这是两全其美的好计策。遂依计行事。果然，宋军坚守待援，一点也没有要投降楚军的意思。

楚军自公元前594年9月开始围困睢阳，宋军一直坚守到次年5月，楚、宋两军足足对峙了9个月。楚军所剩粮草仅仅够维持几天了，睢阳城内也是粮草俱尽。楚、宋两军都接近了崩溃点。楚庄王眼见着军中粮草殆尽，是进是退，必须马上做出选择。他登高向睢阳城内眺望，发现宋军的守卫依然固若金汤。遂打算放弃围城，撤军回国。其手下一员副将对庄王说："宋军之所以坚持不降，大概是估计到我们离楚国遥远，粮草补给困难，在这里待不长。我们不如来个将计就计，抽出部分士卒，让他们去种庄稼和盖营房，假装要在这里长期驻守下去。这样的话，宋军必然害怕，或许会动摇他们守城的决心。"庄王正在进退为难之际，听到这个妙策，大加称赞，立刻命令部队分头行动，围城的围城，种庄稼的种庄稼，建营房的建营房。守城的宋军马上把消息报给宋文公。文公见晋国援军毫无音讯，城中早就粮草告罄，现在楚军又筑室耕田，打算长期围城，无可奈何，君臣上下的守城意志都被动摇了，只好派大将华元出城与楚军签订降约。一场持续9个月的攻守消耗战，就这样被楚将的一个计策给打破了。此后，宋国脱离晋国而成为楚国的盟友。

《孙子兵法》说："兵贵速，不贵久"，因为久战于国无利。楚国千里出师，且采取孙子称之为最下的"攻城之策"，犯的都是用兵大忌。但是，在最后的关头，楚庄王能听取将士的建议，及时调整战略，动摇宋军守城信念，不费一刀一箭，拿下宋国。这个建议的实质就是《孙子兵法》说的"根据有利的原则而采取应变措施以保持战略主动，从而实现'不战而屈人之兵'"。

FORMULATE TACTICS ACCORDING TO WHAT IS EXPEDIENT
—The Chu Troops Subdued the Song Troops by "Building Camps and Growing Crops"

According to *Sun Tzu's Art of War*, "Those skilled in war subdue the enemy without fighting; they capture the enemy's cities without assaulting them; they overthrow the enemy's state without protracted operations."

In the autumn of 594 BC, King Zhuang of the State of Chu sent troops to assault the State of Song which was thousands of *li* away, under the pretext of revenging on the State of Song, because King Zhuang's ambassador to the State of Qi was murdered when he passed through the State of Song. However, the real reason was to rescue the State of Zheng from the siege by the State of Jin.

Three years earlier (597 BC), in the battle for the State of Zheng, the Jin troops were defeated by the Chu troops. When the State of Zheng crossed over to the State of Chu and made an alliance, the State of Jin was irritated. By laying a siege, the State of Jin actually took revenge on the State of Zheng's disloyalty and its alliance with the State of Chu; whereas, the State of Chu did not want the State of Zheng to fall under the rule of the State of Jin again. Therefore, it invented an excuse and besieged the State of Song, the friendly state of Jin, with an expectation to rescue the State of Zheng from Jin's siege.

The State of Song lay to the east of the State of Jin, with the State of Wei in between. Since Duke Wen of the State of Jin dominated over the Central Plains, the State of Wei and the State of Song had been his allies. When the Chu troops heavily surrounded Suiyang, the capital of the State of Song, Song immediately sought help from the State of Jin. Duke Jing of the State of Jin summoned his officials for a plan to rescue the State of Song. Minister Bo Zong strongly recommended that the Duke should appear to promise to render help but not take any concrete actions. He said, "Last time, when Xun Linfu intended to rescue the State of Zheng with six hundred chariots, they were hammered by the Chu troops. Even if we send troops with six hundred chariots now, we still do not stand a chance of winning. What's more, our military forces are besieging the State of Zheng. If we send troops to rescue the State of Song, our risk is surely doubled. The State of Chu is thousands of *li* away from the State of Song, so it will be difficult for the Chu troops to get food supply in time. As a result, they cannot hold on for too long. We may as well tell the Duke of the State of Song that our relief troops are right on the way, meanwhile they should stay where they are. As long as they can hold on for several months, the Chu troops will be forced to retreat without fighting." Duke Jing thought that this was a perfect plan, so he adopted it. As expected, the Song troops held on, waiting for the arrival of the relief troops and they did not intend to surrender at all.

The confrontation between the two armies lasted for about nine months from September 594 BC to May 593 BC. The food supply could only sustain the Chu troops for another several days, and the food in Suiyang was also running low. Both sides were in total breakdown. In such a case, King Zhuang of the State of Chu had to solve the dilemma: to quit besieging or to continue fighting. He climbed to the top of a hill to have a bird's eye view of Suiyang, only to find that it was still strongly fortified by the guards. So he decided to give up the siege and return to his own state. At that time, an assistant general said to him, "The reason why the Song troops do not surrender is probably because they think we are far away from our state. It is difficult for us to get food supply in time, so we may not hold on for long. We may as well turn their trick against them. Why not let some soldiers grow crops and build camps, as if we were going to stay here for long? This would frighten the Song troops and shake their morale." King Zhuang was upon a gum tree, so when he heard this good idea, he thought highly of it and immediately gave orders to the troops. Some soldiers were to keep surrounding the city, some were sent to grow crops, while others were asked to build camps. The news was soon reported to Duke Wen of the State of Song. As the relief troops were still nowhere to be seen, the food was running out, and the Chu troops seemed to be determined to besiege the city for good by building camps and growing crops; the morale of the State of Song was shaken. Duke Wen had no alternative but to send General Hua Yuan to sign a treaty of surrender with the Chu troops. Thus, the nine-month confrontation was brought to an end by the strategy of the assistant general. Since then, the State of Song broke off relations with the State of Jin and formed alliance with the State of Chu.

Sun Tzu's Art of War says, "What is valued in war is victory, not protracted operations." Because protracted operations are no good for the state. The Chu troops covered thousands of *li* and adopted the strategy of "besieging cities", which were regarded as the last resort by Sun Tzu. However, at the crucial moment, King Zhuang followed the advice of the assistant general, adjusted his strategy in time to depress the morale of the Song troops and finally took the State of Song without any cost. The essence of the advice can be seen in *Sun Tzu's Art of War*: "Contingency measures should be taken to maintain the strategic initiative and finally to subdue the enemy without battle".

将能不御——魏文侯用人不疑

《孙子兵法·谋攻篇》：预知胜有五个方面：知可以战与不可以战者胜；知道兵多兵少的不同战法者胜；全军上下意愿一致者胜；以准备对无准备者胜；将帅有指挥能力而君王不牵制者胜。

公元前445年至前369年，魏文侯在位。他是战国初期比较有作为的国君之一。他曾任用李悝进行变法，尽地力之教；重用吴起、西门豹等人，建立武卒，治理地方，发展经济。在他的统治下，魏国成为战国初期第一个强国。战国时期的兼并战争较之春秋时代有过之而无不及。据统计，从公元前475年至公元前221年的255年中，大小战争达230次之多。战争的目的，主要是掠夺更多的土地、财富和人口，以扩大自己的国力。魏文侯派大将乐羊讨伐中山国，就发生在战国初期。

魏国的首都在大梁，其疆域主要在今山西省西南部的河东地区和河南省北部的河内地区。中山国的前身为鲜虞国，公元前774年以前，鲜虞国是周王室的姬姓封国。春秋战国时期，周王朝衰落，周王室的姬姓公国虢国、虞国等遭到晋国等诸侯国灭国。鲜虞国虽然也备受歧视，但得以幸存，公元前506年前改名中山国。战国初，晋国曾灭中山国，但中山国灭而不亡，于公元前414年又复兴起来。公元前406年，魏国再次把战火引向中山国。

魏文侯任命乐羊为大将。乐羊本是中山国人，后来投奔了魏国。乐羊奉命征伐中山国时，他的儿子还留在中山国为官，所以很多官员觉得派乐羊率兵攻打中山国不妥，但魏文侯不改初衷，依然派乐羊率兵出征。

乐羊是个很会用兵的将军，魏军在他的指挥下，进军势如破竹，一直逼到中山国城下。中山国在兵力上无法与魏军匹敌，眼见着国破城危，他们想利用乐羊的儿子去游说他退兵。于是乐羊将计就计，要求中山国王投降魏国，并把攻城的日期一改再改，连续三次延缓攻城日期。消息传到魏国，那些本来就不相信或者嫉妒乐羊的人纷纷上书魏文侯，有的说乐羊假公济私，为了保全儿子不肯奋力攻城；有的说中山国王私下与乐羊定约，要是乐羊不攻城，将分一半土地给乐羊，乐羊就要自立为王了；还有的说乐羊要与中山国联合起来进攻魏国，等等。总之，随着乐羊延缓攻城的日期加长，向魏文侯告他状的人越来越多。接到这些告状信，魏文侯既不撤换乐羊，也不催乐羊攻城，而是亲自派人到前线去慰劳将士，并在都城内为乐羊修建了新的住宅。

乐羊宽限中山国王在三个月内投降，所以一连三个月对中山城围而不攻。中山城的守备力量逐渐薄弱。乐羊见攻城时机已经成熟，于是一举破城，灭了中山国。魏军班师回朝，魏文侯亲自出城迎接凯旋的魏军，然后在宫中大摆筵席庆贺胜利，乐羊自然是酒宴中最受恭维的人，他确实有点飘飘然了。庆功宴会结束之后，魏文侯送给乐羊一个密封的大箱子。乐羊想，一定是魏文侯赏给他的财宝。回到家打开箱子一看，满满一箱子都是官员们揭发他围城不攻、对魏国怀有二心的奏章。乐羊惊出一身冷汗，才知道魏文侯对他是如此的信任和器重，自己是多么幸运！

　　第二天一早，乐羊去拜见魏文侯，他说："没想到朝中有那么多人如此造谣诽谤我。要不是魏王您心胸宽广，明察秋毫，用而不疑，我恐怕早就变成刀下鬼了。"从此以后，乐羊更加死心塌地为魏文侯效力了。后来，魏文侯把灵寿封给了乐羊。乐羊死后，就葬在灵寿，他的后代子孙们就在那里安了家。

　　孙子在《谋攻篇》中曾透彻地分析国君干预将帅指挥权对战争胜负的影响，他说：国君危害军事行动的情况有三种：不了解军队不能前进而命令军队前进，不了解军队不能后退而命令后退，这叫做束缚军队；不了解军队的内部事务而去干预军队的行政，就会使将士迷惑；不懂得军事上的权宜之变而去干涉军队的指挥，就会使将士产生疑虑。军队既迷惑又心存疑虑，那么灾难就要降临了。这叫做自乱其军，自取灭亡。所以孙子说："故知胜有五：知可以战与不可以战者胜；识众寡之用者胜；上下同欲者胜；以虞待不虞者胜；将能而君不御者胜。"正因为魏文侯懂得这一点，他始终信任乐羊，赋予他独立军事指挥权，不干预前线的军事，所以才能够取得这样的胜利。魏文侯可谓是懂得兵法的国君。

ABLE GENERALS SHOULD NOT BE INTERFERED WITH
— Marquis Wen of the State of Wei Did Not Suspect the Person He Employed

According to *Sun Tzu's Art of War*, "There are five points from which victory may be predicted. He who knows when he should fight and when he should not will win; he who knows how to adopt the appropriate military art according to the number of his own troops and his enemy's will win; he whose general and soldiers can fight with one heart and mind will win; he who is well prepared while his enemy is underprepared will win; and he who is a wise and able general and whom the sovereign does not interfere with will win."

From 445 BC to 396 BC, Marquis Wen of the State of Wei was in power and he was one of the most successful dukes in the early Warring States Period (475 BC–221 BC). He once appointed Li Kui to carry out agricultural reform to make full use of the soil resources and improve the soil fertility. Marquis Wen also placed Wu Qi and Ximen Bao in important positions to train infantry armies, rule the local governments and develop the economy. It was under his reign that the State of Wei became the first power in the early Warring States Period. Annexations between the states were even more frequent in the Warring States Period than in the Spring and Autumn Period. According to the statistics, there were more than 230 battles, either big or small, during the 255 years from 475 BC to 221 BC. Most wars were waged for land, property, population to develop the national strength. It was at the early time of this period that Marquis Wen of the State of Wei sent General Yue Yang to invade the State of Zhongshan.

Daliang was the capital of the State of Wei, whose territory was mainly the Hedong area in the southwest of what is now known as Shanxi Province and the Henei area in the north of Henan Province. The State of Zhongshan had been formerly known as the State of Xianyu, a vassal state because its Duke shared the same surname "Ji" with the royal family of the Zhou Dynasty. During the Spring and Autumn Period and the Warring States Period, the Zhou Dynasty was on the decline and its vassal states, such as the State of Guo and the State of Yu, were destroyed by the State of Jin and other states. Although the State of Xianyu suffered extreme discrimination, it survived and changed its name to the State of Zhongshan before 506 BC. At the beginning of the Warring States Period, the State of Jin once destroyed the State of Zhongshan, but it did not perish and resurrected itself in 414 BC. In 406 BC, the State of Wei engaged the State of Zhongshan in war again.

Marquis Wen of the State of Wei appointed Yue Yang, who was born in the State of Zhongshan and later sought refuge in the State of Wei, as General. When Yue Yang got the order, his son was still living in the State of Zhongshan as an official, so lots of officials considered the order inappropriate. But Marquis Wen stuck to his plan and sent Yue Yang there.

Yue Yang was very adept at military operations. Under his command, the Wei troops won one victory after another with irresistible force and they approached the City of Zhongshan. The military forces of the State of Zhongshan were no match for those of the Wei's. Seeing that the city was in danger, the State of Zhongshan made Yue Yang's son the lobbyist to ask his father to retreat. Yue Yang made a counterplot, demanding that the State of Zhongshan surrender itself to the State of Wei and Yue Yang delayed the storming of the city for three successive times. When the news was spread to the State of Wei, those who had always been suspicious or jealous of Yue Yang submitted written statements to Marquis Wen. Some said that Yue Yang feathered his own nest. According to them, Yue Yang was reluctant to assault the city merely for the purpose of protecting his son. Some said that the King of the State of Zhongshan had signed an agreement in privacy with Yue Yang, promising to allot half of the land to him as long as he did not take any military actions, so that Yue Yang would come to the throne himself. Others asserted that Yue Yang would team up with the State of Zhongshan to fight against the State of Wei. There were a growing number of complaints about him as Yue Yang delayed the storming of the city. On hearing these complaints, Marquis Wen neither recalled or replaced Yue Yang, nor did he urge Yue Yang to storm the city. Instead, he sent someone to the frontline to reward officers and soldiers and even built a new residence for Yue Yang in the capital city.

Yue Yang had already extended the deadline three months for the King of the State of Zhongshan to surrender, so he just besieged the city without storming it during this time. The defense of the city was gradually weakened. Seeing that the time was ripe for attack, Yue Yang led his soldiers to capture the city in one quick stroke and destroyed the State of Zhongshan. When the Wei troops returned home triumphantly, Duke Wen left the capital to welcome them in person and held a celebration feast in the Imperial Palace. Of course, Yue Yang was the most celebrated person at the banquet and he was somewhat complacent. After the banquet, Marquis Wen gave him a big sealed box. Yue Yang thought it must be full of treasure. But when he opened it after he got home, he found there was nothing inside except the complaints about him by other officials. He broke into a cold sweat with fear. It was then that he realized how deeply Marquis Wen trusted him and how lucky he was to have such a trust.

Early the next morning, when Yue Yang had an audience with Marquis Wen, he said, "I never realized that there were so many people in the court slandering me. I could have been executed if Your Lordship were not broad-minded, sharp-eyed and determined." Ever since, he was even more determined to serve Duke Wen. Later, Marquis Wen conferred Lingshou to Yue Yang. After Yue Yang's death, he was buried in Lingshou, where his descendants settled.

In *Sun Tzu's Art of War*, Sun Tzu thoroughly analyzed the impact of the interference of the king with his generals on the outcome of a battle. He said that a ruler might bring great misfortune upon his army in three ways. Firstly, if he ordered an advance while not knowing that his army could not go forward, or ordered a retreat while being ignorant that his army could not fall back, his orders would, of course, tie down the army. Secondly, if he interfered with the administration of the army without understanding its internal affairs, his action would, of course, baffle his officers and soldiers. Thirdly, when he interfered with the direction of the army without knowing the principles of the military stratagem, it would raise doubts and misgivings in the minds of the officers and soldiers. This would necessarily lead to their confusion and suspicion, and disasters would happen. This was what was meant by the saying, "throwing his own army into confusion and paving the way for the enemy's victory". Therefore,

Sun Tzu said, "There are five points from which victory may be predicted. He who knows when he should fight and when he should not will win; he who knows how to adopt the appropriate military art according to the number of his own troops and his enemy's will win; he whose general and soldiers can fight with one heart and mind will win; he who is well prepared while his enemy is underprepared will win; he who is a wise and able general and whom the sovereign does not interfere with will win." Knowing this, Marquis Wen trusted Yue Yang all along, entitled him to command the army and did not interfere with the military operations at the frontline, so he finally won such a victory. In this sense, Marquis Wen of the State of Wei demonstrated that he knew the art of war.

先战而后求胜——晋齐鞍之战

《孙子兵法·军形篇》：胜利的军队总是首先创造必胜的条件而后才去寻求与敌交战；失败的军队则往往是先贸然与敌交战，然后再在交战过程中去争取侥幸的胜利。

　　公元前 589 年春，齐军伐鲁，卫穆公趁机兴兵入侵齐国。卫军与齐军在新筑（今河北魏县南）相遇，结果卫军不敌齐军，主将孙良夫只好到晋国去求援。此时，恰好鲁国大夫臧孙许也来向晋国求助。鲁、卫是晋的盟国，晋景公位居霸主，自然答应两国的请求，遂派执政大臣郤克率七百乘驰援鲁、卫。郤克对晋景公说："当年晋楚城濮之战时，晋军也是七百乘，但那时有先王的机智和先大夫的机敏，所以能够取胜。我与先大夫的聪明机敏相比，还不足以做他们的随从。所以，请大王再多派些兵车方可。"于是晋景公又加一百，合为八百乘。郤克率中军，士燮领上军，栾书领下军，韩厥为司马，浩浩荡荡向齐国进发。这一年的六月十六日，晋军在今济南千佛山附近追上了齐军。

齐军既讨伐了鲁国，又打败了进犯的卫军，正高高兴兴地班师回国，没想到晋军追踪而至。齐顷公大怒，派使者向晋军主帅郤克挑战说："您率军光临敝邑，敝国士卒虽少，但是愿意明天早上与你们相见。" 郤克回复说："鲁、卫都是晋国的友邦，他们对晋君说，贵国不分早晚都在他们的土地上发泄气愤，晋君不忍，特派下臣来向贵国请求。况且，晋君有命，不允许我们在您这儿长期停留，所以，您的命令我们会照办的。" 齐顷公听了使者的回话，傲慢地说："无论晋军同意不同意，都必有一战。"大将高固对齐顷公说："齐晋未曾交过兵，不知道晋军勇怯如何，不如我去打探一下。"于是驾一辆单车，径直闯入晋军营门，此时，正好有一晋军末将乘车从营门出来，高固灵机一动，弯腰捡起一块石头砸向那位末将的头部，那人中石倒下， 高固趁势跳到对方的车上，驾车在晋军营中巡走一圈，然后回到齐营。他对齐顷公说："晋军虽然势众，但真正能打仗的人少，不值得担心。" 齐顷公备受鼓舞。

　　第二天早上，晋、齐两军依照约定摆开战阵。齐顷公对将士们说："我们打败晋军再吃早饭！"战斗开始了。齐顷公登上战车，邴夏为其驾车，逢丑父为车右。晋军主帅郤克也登上了战车，张侯为其驾车，郑丘缓为车左。齐顷公的战车不披甲就驶向了晋军，齐军随之掩杀过来。混战之中，晋军主帅郤克和驭者张侯都受了重伤，鲜血一直流到鞋子上，但郤克坚持指挥，进击的鼓声一直没有中断。郤克的伤势十分沉重，渐渐支持不住了，张侯在手掌和手肘被射穿的情况下，一手抓住四根缰绳驾车，一手接过鼓槌擂鼓指挥进攻。在郤克的激励和指挥下，晋军奋勇拼杀，打得齐军溃败而逃。晋军司马韩厥驾战车紧紧追击齐顷公，为齐顷公驾车的邴夏想射杀韩厥，齐顷公不许，因为韩厥是王子。于是邴夏只射杀了韩厥的车左和车右。为了防箭，韩厥只好躬身躲避，齐顷公趁机逃脱。为了防止万一，车右逢丑父与齐顷公交换了位置以冒充齐顷公。后来，他又让齐顷公换乘郑国父驾驭的副车才得以冲出重围。

　　韩厥发现齐顷公逃跑，驾战车猛追，误把逢丑父当成了齐顷公，将其活捉。按照周礼，刑不上大夫，齐顷公贵为国君，就更不能冒犯了。虽然他已经成了晋军的俘虏，但韩厥依然毕恭毕敬地对待他。韩厥拿着绊马索站在顷公车前，执礼如仪，先向他行了再拜稽首礼，然后取过酒杯，配上玉璧，献给"齐顷公"。之后，才开始说话。他说："晋、鲁、卫是盟国，鲁、卫被你们打败，求救于晋国，所以晋侯派我们来求您放过他们。晋侯告诫我们，不要深入齐国国土。不幸的是我们在这里碰见齐侯的军队，如果躲避齐侯的车驾会成为晋侯的耻辱，于齐侯您也不大光彩。我作为一个不称职的士卒，现在不得不履行自己的职责了。"言外之意是：现在我要俘虏你齐侯了。韩厥的这番话，鲜明地体现了春秋时代的行事规则和交际特点，形式上要彬彬有礼，语言上要委婉含蓄，即要合乎"礼"，但从骨子里流露出的却是逞强逞霸的强硬和狠毒。虽然逢丑父随机应变使齐顷公免遭被俘之灾，但这一仗，齐国是彻底地失败了。

晋军继续追击溃逃的齐军，一直追到丘舆附近（今山东省益都县西南），齐顷公只好派执政大臣国佐把国宝玉器和以前霸占鲁、卫两国的土地奉送给晋国，以求晋国罢兵。晋军主帅郤克不依不饶，提出要让齐国国母萧太后到晋国做人质，要求齐国把境内的田垄都改为东西向。齐臣国佐说："您的要求太过分了。要是您有意刁难不答应的话，那么齐国将收集残余力量，同你们决一死战。"鲁、卫两国赶紧从中斡旋，最终晋国接受了齐国的讲和条件。公元前589年7月，晋、齐在爰娄（今山东省临淄西）结盟。作为条件，齐国把汶阳（今山东省宁阳县北）以南地区归还给鲁国。次年十二月，齐顷公到晋国行朝聘礼。由此，齐国成为晋的附属国。

齐、晋交兵之初，晋军并没有明显的优势。但是，齐顷公骄兵轻敌，盲目乐观，导致惨败。孙子说，善于用兵打仗的人，总是使自己立于不败之地，而不放过敌人可能被击败的机会。所以，"胜兵先胜而后求战，败兵先战而后求胜"。意思是说，胜利的军队总是首先创造必胜的条件而后才去寻求与敌交战；失败的军队则往往是先贸然与敌交战，然后再在交战过程中去争取侥幸的胜利。齐顷公所指挥的鞍之战，可谓是"先战而后求胜"的典型，所以，齐军才有这样的惨败。

START THE FIGHT FIRST AND EXPECT TO HAVE VICTORY LATER

— The Battle of An between the State of Jin and the State of Qi

According to *Sun Tzu's Art of War*, "A victorious army is one that will not fight with the enemy until it is assured of the conditions for winning, while a defeated army is one that starts the fight first and expects to have victory later."

In the spring of 589 BC, when the Qi troops attacked the State of Lu, Duke Mu of the State of Wei took the chance to invade the State of Qi. The two armies encountered each other in Xinzhu (in the south of Wei County of Hebei Province today), where the Wei army was defeated by the Qi troops. Sun Liangfu, Commander-in-chief of the Wei troops had to go to the State of Jin for military aid. Minister Zang Sunxu of the State of Lu happened to be there for help, too. Because the State of Lu and the State of Wei were allies of the State of Jin, and Duke Jing of the State of Jin had power over them at the time, he promised to offer help and decided to send Xi Ke, the Major Minister, to lead seven hundred chariots to rescue them. Xi Ke said to Duke Jing, "In the battle of Chengpu between our state and the State of Chu, we sent seven hundred chariots, but thanks to the wisdom of our late duke and the quick-wittedness of the former minister, we finally won the battle. Compared with the former resourceful minister, I am not even qualified to be his attendant. Please dispatch more chariots." Thus, Duke Jing sent one hundred more chariots. Xi Ke led the middle army, Shi Xie led the upper army, Luan Shu led the lower army and Han Jue acted as Commander. The troops marched to the State of Qi with great strength and vigor. On June 16th that year, they overtook the Qi troops near what is known as Mount Qianfo of Jinan Province today.

After the attack on the State of Lu and the triumph over the invasive Wei troops, the Qi troops proceeded home cheerfully. They did not anticipate the pursuit of the Jin troops at all. Duke Qing of the State of Qi flew into a rage, so he sent a messenger to issue a letter of challenge to Xi Ke, the Commander-in-chief of the Jin troops. The letter said, "Welcome to my humble country. Though we do not have enough soldiers, we are ready to challenge you tomorrow morning." While Xi Ke replied, "Both the State of Lu and the State of Wei are the allies of our state, and they told our Duke that your honored state had been finding fault with them day and night. Our Duke could not bear to stand by, so he sent me to make a request. Besides, he ordered us not to remain here for too long. Therefore, we will follow your order." Hearing the replies, Duke Qing said arrogantly, "We are bound to launch a battle against them, whether they approve it or not." General Gao Gu said to him, "Since we have never fought with the Jin troops, we don't know whether they are courageous or not. I may as well exploit it." He drove one chariot to run into the Jin campsite, when one junior officer of the Jin troops happened to go out of the gate in a chariot. On a sudden inspiration, Gao Gu bent down, got a piece of stone and threw it at his head. The officer was knocked down and Gao Gu took the chance to jump into the chariot. He went around the Jin barracks and then went back to the Qi campsite. He told Duke Qing, "Although the Jin troops are overwhelming with number, there are few people who can really fight. So please do not worry." Duke Qing was greatly inspired.

The next morning, both sides deployed their troops in battle formation, according to prior agreements. Duke Qing of the State of Qi said to his officers and soldiers, "Let's wipe them out before breakfast!" The battle started. Duke Qing got on the chariot, with Bing Xia as the charioteer and Pang Choufu standing on the right side of him. Xi Ke also got on the chariot, with Zhang Hou as the charioteer and Zheng Qiuhuan standing on the left side of him. The chariot of Duke Qing was not even armored. It sped to the Jin troops, followed by the Qi troops. A tangled warfare ensued with both Xi Ke and Zhang Hou badly wounded, their blood running down to their boots, but Xi Ke kept directing the operations and beating the battle drum. When he was too badly wounded to hold out any longer and Zhang Hou, with his palm and elbow penetrated by arrows, held the four reins of the chariot in one hand and got the drumsticks in another to beat the drum to direct the operations. Inspired and directed by Xi Ke, the Jin troops fought vigorously and the Qi troops were utterly defeated. Han Jue, Commander of the State of Jin, drove his chariot to follow the chariot of Duke Qing. Bing Xia, Duke Qing's charioteer, wanted to shoot Han Jue but was stopped by Duke Qing because Han Jue was the prince of the State of Jin. So Bing Xia only shot the men who stood at Han Jue's sides. To avoid being shot by the arrows, Han Jue had to bend from the waist and Duke Qing took the chance to escape. In case of being captured, Pang Choufu, standing on the right side impersonated Duke Qing by changing positions with him (At that time, monarchs and ministers wore the same military uniforms on the battlefield, and they were recognized by their positions and banners.) Later, Duke Qing transferred to another chariot driven by Zheng Guofu and finally broke through the tight encirclement of the warring soldiers.

When Han Jue found that Duke Qing had escaped, he drove his chariot in hot pursuit. He mistook Pang Choufu for Duke Qing and captured him alive. According to the rites of the Zhou Dynasty, a minister who had committed an offense could not be punished like commoners, so Duke Qing, noble as the monarch of a state, could not be offended. Although Duke Qing had become the captive of the Jin troops, Han Jue still treated him reverentially. Courteously standing in front of Duke Qing's chariot, with a stumbling rope in hand, he kowtowed twice. He took a cup, matched it with a piece of jade and then presented them to "Duke Qing". After that, he started to talk. He said, "The State of Lu and the State of Wei are our allies. When they were defeated, they turned to us for military aid, so our Duke sent us to beg you to spare them. Duke Jing warned us not to drive deep into your territory. Unfortunately, we encountered your troops here, and if we bypassed your chariot, it would bring shame on both you and our Duke. As an unqualified soldier, I have to fulfill my responsibility now." Implied in his words was his intention to capture Duke Qing. What Han Jue said reflected vividly the code of conduct and the characteristics of communication in the Spring and Autumn Period. In communication, people were polite in form with tactful and implicit remarks which must conform to the "rites", but actually in their heart of hearts they expressed toughness and viciousness to parade their superiority. Though Pang Choufu rose to the occasion and saved Duke Qing of the State of Qi from being arrested, the State of Qi was totally defeated in this battle.

The Jin troops kept running after the Qi troops who fled in rout until near Qiuyu (in the southwest of Yidu County of Shandong Province today). Duke Qing had to send Guo Zuo, the Major Minister, to present to the State of Jin lots of treasure, jade and the formerly annexed territories of the states of Lu and Wei. By doing so, Duke Qing anticipated that the State of Jin would withdraw their troops. But Xi Ke was hard to satisfy. He demanded Duke Qing's mother, Queen Mother Xiao, as the hostage, and wanted to change the trends of ridges between fields in the State of Qi into eastwest. Guo Zuo said, "You are too demanding. If you are deliberately making things difficult for us, we have to collect the remnants of our army and wage a life-or-death battle." The State of Lu and the State of Wei quickly mediated, and finally the State of Jin accepted Qi's conditions to make peace. In July of 589 BC, the State of Jin and the State of Qi formed alliance in Yuanlou (in the west of Linzi County of Shandong Province today). As a condition, the State of Qi returned the region to the south of Wenyang (in the north of Ningyang County of Shandong Province today) to the State of Lu. In December of 588 BC, Duke Qing of the State of Qi went to the State of Jin to pay homage to its Duke. From then on, the State of Qi became a dependency of the State of Jin.

At the beginning of the battle, the Jin troops did not have an obvious advantage over the Qi troops. However, Duke Qing of the State of Qi was puffed up with pride and his unfounded optimism resulted in a complete fiasco. Sun Tzu said, "The skillful warriors always free themselves from defeat by the enemy and grasp every opportunity to destroy the enemy." So "A victorious army is one that will not fight with the enemy until it is assured of the conditions for winning, while a defeated army is one that starts the fight first and expects to have victory later." The Battle of An, directed by Duke Qing of the State of Qi, is a case in point of "starting the fight first and expecting to have victory later". It was no wonder that the Qi troops suffered such a fiasco.

攻守相依——田单"火牛阵"复齐

《孙子兵法·军形篇》：创造不可被战胜的条件，是我方在防御过程中所要解决的问题；一旦敌方出现可以被战胜的条件，那么我方就需采取攻势了。

公元前284年，燕昭王以乐毅为上将军，率领燕、赵、秦、韩、魏五国之兵讨伐齐国。初战告捷后，赵、秦、韩、魏四国之兵撤回本国，乐毅独率燕军连续攻下齐国七十余座城池，连都城临淄也被燕军拿下，齐国只剩下莒、即墨两城还顽强地坚守着。乐毅想收服齐国的民心，所以除了围城攻城以外，对当地的老百姓还实施了一些怀柔政策。

乐毅派兵进攻即墨，守城将领出城抵抗，结果战死了，城里的人顿时恐慌起来。田单是齐王的远房亲戚，曾经带过兵，于是大家就公推他为将军，带领大家守城。田单临危受命，组织和调配城中的力量，还把本族人和自己的家属都编在队伍里。田单不仅身先士卒，而且跟兵士们同甘共苦，守城的士气一下旺盛起来。乐毅把莒城和即墨围困了三年也没有攻下来。有人在燕昭王面前诋毁乐毅，说他想当齐王，故意不攻下莒城和即墨。燕昭王坚定不移地信任乐毅，不但没有干涉乐毅的军事指挥权，还派使者到临淄去慰劳乐毅，真的要封他为齐王，乐毅坚决不受。他非常感激燕昭王的信任和厚爱，更加努力地为燕国尽力。不久，燕昭王死了，燕惠王继位，他本来就与乐毅不和，田单便乘机暗中派人到燕国散布谣言说："要是燕国派别的将领，齐国莒城和即墨早就攻下来了。"燕惠王听信了谣言，就派大将骑劫去齐国取代了乐毅。田单一看燕惠王中计，加紧实施破围复国的计划。

骑劫一到齐国，就下令围攻即墨，围了好几层也没有能破城。过了几天，围城燕军听到附近的老百姓在议论，有的说："以前乐将军太好了，抓了俘虏还好好对待，守城的人当然不怕。要是燕国人把俘虏的鼻子都削去，齐国人还敢打仗吗？"还有的说："我的祖宗的坟都在城外，要是燕国军队真的刨起坟来，可怎么办呢？"这些话都传到了骑劫的耳朵里，他就真的把齐国俘虏的鼻子都削去，又叫兵士把齐国城外的坟都刨了。其实，那些话都是田单故意派人散布的。

守城的齐军听说燕军这样残酷地对待俘虏，又在城头上看见燕军在即墨城外挖他们的祖坟，都气愤极了。于是恨得咬牙切齿，纷纷向田单请战，要跟燕国人拼个死活。田单见守城将士和百姓同仇敌忾，心中暗暗高兴。他又派几个人装作即墨的富翁，偷偷地给骑劫送去金银财宝，并"告密"说："城里的粮食已经用完了，不出几天就得投降。将军进城的时候，请一定保全我们的家小。"骑劫听到这个消息，高兴地收下财物，满口答应他们的请求。燕军渐渐懈怠下来。

田单挑选了一千多头牛，在牛角上捆各绑一把尖刀，牛尾巴上系一捆浸透了油的苇束，然后再把花花绿绿的被子披在牛身上，乔装成一个个庞然怪物。一切都准备好之后，命令士兵在深夜时分凿开十几处城墙，把牛队赶到城外，把牛尾巴上的苇束点上火，赶向燕军兵营。牛尾巴的火一烧着，牛性子发作起来，一千多头牛朝着燕军方向猛冲过去。齐军的五千名"敢死队"拿着大刀长矛，紧跟着牛队冲杀过去。城里的老百姓则站在城头敲击铜壶、铜盆，顿时火光夹杂着呐喊声敲击声把燕军从睡梦中惊醒，看着成群的庞然怪物冲来，吓得胡乱逃窜，根本顾不上反击。火牛的突踏，敢死队的冲杀，再加上燕军自己乱窜狂奔中的自伤，燕军死伤无数。混战中，燕将骑劫乘战车想杀出一条活路，结果未能如愿，被齐兵团团围住，丢了性命。

田单的火牛阵不仅打败了燕军，保住了即墨城，而且成为齐军反败为胜的转折点。田单率齐军乘胜反攻，整个齐国都轰动起来了，失地的将士和百姓纷纷揭竿而起，杀了燕国的守将，迎接田单。田单的军队打到哪儿，哪儿的百姓就群起响应。不到几个月的时间，就收复了被燕国和秦、赵、韩、魏四国占领的七十多座城池，并把齐襄王从莒城迎回都城临淄，齐国终于从亡国的险境中恢复过来。田单因功被封为安平君。他的"火牛阵"成为中国古代战争史上的佳话，一直流传下来。

田单与孙子同姓，是齐国临淄人。虽然他与孙子生活的时代相距将近两百年，但他用兵的思想和谋略，仿佛都可以从《孙子兵法》中找到影子。比如用计、用间、出奇制胜，等等。特别是田单的攻守战略和转换，正像孙子在《军形篇》中说的那样："创造不可被战胜的条件，是我方在防御过程中所要解决的问题；一旦敌方出现可以被战胜的条件，那么我方就需采取攻势了。"田单善守，藏锐于九地之下，田单善攻，雷动于九天之上。孙子之言，田单之行，谁能说他们之间仅仅是巧合呢！

DEFENSE AND OFFENSE ARE INTERDEPENDENT
— Tian Dan Restored the State of Qi by "Fire Bull Attack"

According to *Sun Tzu's Art of War*, "Skillful warriors first make themselves invincible and then await the enemy's moment of vulnerability."

In 284 BC, King Zhao of the State of Yan appointed Yue Yi as the General of the armies to lead the troops from the five states (the states of Yan, Zhao, Qin, Han and Wei) to invade the State of Qi. Having won the first battle, the troops from the other four states returned home while Yue Yi led the Yan troops and captured more than seventy cities of the State of Qi. Even Linzi, its capital, was taken and the State of Qi had only two cities left — the City of Ju and the City of Jimo. But the Qi troops tenaciously held their ground. As Yue Yi wanted to gain support from the civilians of the State of Qi, in addition to besieging and storming the cities, he also implemented policies of conciliation for the local people.

When Yue Yi sent the troops to storm Jimo, the senior officers who were defending the city went out to fight, but were all killed, which led to a state of panic within the city. As Tian Dan, a distant relative of the King of the State of Qi, used to be in command of the troops, he was elected the general commander, and charged with the task of taking responsibility for the defense of the city. Entrusted with a mission at such a critical moment, Tian Dan organized and deployed forces in the city. His clansmen and relatives were also recruited to the army. Tian Dan not only charged at the head of his men, but also went through thick and thin together with them, so the morale of the troops was increased. As a result, Yue Yi did not succeed in capturing the two cities even after three years of siege. In this case, some people slandered Yue Yi in front of King Zhao. They thought that Yue Yi wanted to be the King of the State of Qi, so he intentionally did not capture the two cities. However, King Zhao had deep faith in Yue Yi and instead of interfering with his direction of the army, he sent a messenger to Linzi to reward him. King Zhao was indeed planning to appoint Yue Yi King of the State of Qi, but Yue Yi declined. Yue Yi felt extremely grateful to King Zhao for his trust and great kindness, so he made more efforts to serve the State of Yan. Before long, King Zhao died and King Hui succeeded to the throne. He had a poor relationship with Yue Yi. Tian Dan took advantage of the opportunity and secretly sent some people to the State of Yan to spread slanderous rumors, which said that Ju and Jimo would have already been captured if other generals had taken Yue Yi's place. King Hui believed the rumors and substituted General Qi Jie for Yue Yi. Seeing that King Hui had fallen into the trap, Tian Dan lost no time in implementing the plan of breaking through the encirclement and restoring the State of Qi.

Upon arriving at the State of Qi, Qi Jie ordered the troops to lay siege to Jimo, but they could not capture it though they densely surrounded the city. Several days later, the Yan troops heard the common people nearby whispering, "The former General, Yue Yi, was so nice to the captives that the defenders of the city were not frightened at all. If the noses of the captives had been cut off, who dared to fight any more?" Others said, "The graves of my ancestors are outside the city. What if the Yan troops dig them up?" When these words reached Qi Jie's ears, he ordered to have the captives' noses cut off and the graves dug up. In fact, it was Tian Dan who deliberately sent people to spread these words.

The Qi troops became extremely angry at the news of the cruel treatment to the captives and at the sight of those dug graves on the top of the city wall. So one after another, they gnashed their teeth and asked for permission to fight with the Yan troops to the bitter end. Seeing that the army as well as the common people bore a common hatred for the enemy, Tian Dan was so delighted inwardly. He sent several men disguised as rich men in Jimo to bribe Qi Jie with gold and treasure. They pretended that the food in the city was running out and that the Qi troops would surrender in several days. And they begged Qi Jie for the promise of the safety of their family members. On hearing that, Qi Jie accepted the bribes delightedly and acquiesced to their requests. Gradually, the Yan troops slacked off.

Tian Dan selected more than one thousand bulls, ordered his men to tie a sharp knife to each horn and a cluster of reeds soaked with oil to each tail. Then they disguised the bulls as huge monsters by covering them with colored quilts. When this was done, he ordered the soldiers to make a dozen exits through the city walls in the dead of night. They drove the herd out of the city and made them run toward the barracks of the Yan troops. As soon as the reeds were lit, the bulls were enraged and ran wildly in the direction of the Yan troops, followed by 5,000 soldiers of the dare-to-die corps with broadswords and lances. The common people inside the city stood on the top of the city walls, beating bronze pots and basins. The Yan troops were awakened by the flames, the shouting and the beating. When they saw flocks of huge monsters dashing to them, they dispersed and were too scared to fight back. The tramples of the fire bulls and the charges of the Qi soldiers all contributed to the numerous injuries and casualties of the Yan troops, in addition to the injuries sustained when they were randomly running away from the "monsters". Riding a chariot, Qi Jie tried to fight his way out of the heavy encirclement, but he was heavily surrounded by the Qi troops and finally died.

Tian Dan's "Fire Bull Attack" not only defeated the Yan troops and retained Jimo, but also became a turning point for the Qi troops to turn defeat into victory. Tian Dan led the Qi troops to follow up the victory in hot pursuit, which created a great stir throughout the State of Qi. The officers and soldiers, as well as the common people in the lost territories rose in rebellion one after another, killed the Yan defenders and welcomed Tian Dan. Wherever Tian Dan's troops went, the common people all rose to respond. In several months, they recovered more than seventy cities taken by the states of Yan, Qin , Zhao, Han and Wei and welcomed King Xiang of the State of Qi from Ju City back to Linzi, the capital. The State of Qi finally recovered from the brink of destruction. Because of his creditable deeds, Tian Dan was appointed as Lord Anping. His "Fire Bull Attack" became an oft-told tale in the ancient Chinese war history, which has been handed down ever since.

Born in Linzi of the State of Qi, Tian Dan had the same surname with Sun Tzu. Although he lived at a time two hundred years later than Sun Tzu, his ideas and strategies of war, such as estimates, use of spies and defeating the enemy by a surprise action, were reflected in *Sun Tzu's Art of War*. In particular, strategies and changes in defense and offense strategies were what Sun Tzu described in *Sun Tzu's Art of War*, "Skillful warriors first make themselves invincible and then await the enemy's moment of vulnerability." In defense, Tian Dan could hide his superior military forces as under the nine-fold earth (in ancient China, the number nine was used to signify the highest number); in attack, he could flash forth as from above the nine-fold heavens. How can the word *coincidence* fully express the similarities between Sun Tzu's words and Tian Dan's behaviors?

奇正之变——田忌赛马

《孙子兵法·兵势篇》：用兵作战，总是以正兵当敌，以奇兵取胜。

　　田忌是中国战国时代齐国的一位将军，说起来，他还是孙子的同乡呢，只不过他比孙子晚出生一百多年。但是他赛马取胜的策略，却是运用了孙子的兵法。

　　据司马迁《史记·孙子吴起列传》记载，战国时代，齐国贵族喜欢赛马赌胜，大将军田忌也是赛马的爱好者，他经常跟齐国的诸公子一起赛马，赌注下得都很大，但是胜败、输赢却没有十分的把握。田忌有个好朋友叫孙膑，是孙子的后世子孙，他从小特别佩服孙子的军事才能，不断研习，后来也成为一个著名的将军和兵学家，他的《孙膑兵法》就继承和发扬了孙子的思想和学说。孙膑观看了比赛，发现田忌的马跟诸公子的马在实力上相当，马中各有上、中、下三等，并没有多大差别，要想稳操胜券，必须像《孙子兵法》中说的那样，"以正合，以奇胜"。"正"是正面对阵的常规战术，"奇"是旁出奇袭的灵活战术，必须打破常规的思维定式，运用智慧来谋胜，而不是单纯地硬拼实力。他想出了一个妙策，于是就对田忌说："明天赛马赌胜，你放心地下大赌注，我能让你取胜！"田忌了解孙膑的才能，知道他一定有什么妙计，就很痛快地答应了。

第二天，按规矩，赛马前先下赌注。这一次，田忌下注特别痛快，与诸公子竞相押注，以至于达到千金。下完注之后，该安排马的比赛顺序时，孙膑悄悄地对田忌说：现在，用你的最差的马跟他最好的马比赛，用你最好的马跟他中等的马比赛，用你的中等马跟他最差的马比赛。三组马比赛完毕，田忌的马以两胜一负的比赛结果最终赢得了胜利，获得了千金。孙膑的妙计，就是"一输两赢"之策。这一妙策，一方面，可以看出是孙膑对孙子"以正合，以奇胜"的制胜理论的灵活运用，另一方面，也可以看出，《孙子兵法》所总结的规律和原则，具有普遍的指导意义。

THE VARIATIONS AND COMBINATIONS OF THE NORMAL AND EXTRAORDINARY FORCES
— Tian Ji's Horse Racing

According to *Sun Tzu's Art of War*, "Generally, in battle, use the normal forces to engage and use the extraordinary forces to win."

Tian Ji, a general of the State of Qi in the Warring States Period, was a fellow townsman of Sun Tzu, but he lived one hundred years later than Sun Tzu. However, he applied Sun Tzu's art of war to horse racing and won.

As recorded in "*Biography of Sun Tzu and Wu Qi*" of *Records of the Grand Historian* in the Warring States Period, horse betting was a popular activity among the aristocrats in the State of Qi, with Tian Ji being one of them. He often gambled with them at high stakes but was not quite sure of the outcome. Tian Ji had a good friend, Sun Bin, who was a descendant of Sun Tzu. When he was a child, Sun Bin admired Sun Tzu for his military talents and kept studying *Sun Tzu's Art of War*. Later on, he became a renowned general and military strategist. His *Sun Bin's Art of War* inherited and developed Sun Tzu's thoughts and theory. When Sun Bin watched the races, he found that Tian Ji's horses were no better than other people's horses. In horse racing, horses were divided into three classes, namely, super, plus and regular. Little difference existed between horses of the same class. To win the game, Tian Ji must act on the rules of *Sun Tzu's Art of War*, "Use the normal forces to engage and use the extraordinary forces to win." "Normal" referred to the normal tactics in confronting the enemy. "Extraordinary" referred to the flexible tactics in attacking by surprise which required a break with the conventions of thinking and the application of wisdom rather than strength to win. Sun Bin developed a good idea and said to Tian Ji, "Feel at ease to play for high stakes tomorrow and I can ensure you a victory." Knowing Sun Bin's talents well, Tian Ji was sure that he must have an ingenious idea, so he quickly agreed.

The next day, according to the rules, stakes were laid down before the horse racing. This time, Tian Ji did not hesitate to lay down high stakes. He made bets with others competitively. His bets were as much as one thousand taels of gold. When it was time to arrange the horses in order, Sun Bin secretly told Tian Ji that he should use his regular horse to race against the super horses from the others, his super against others' plus horses and his plus against others' regular ones. After three rounds of racing, Tian Ji had two wins and one defeat and thus got one thousand taels of gold. Sun Bin's ingenious idea was the strategy of "one defeat and two wins". It can be seen from this strategy that, on the one hand, Sun Bin flexibly applied the theory of "using the normal forces to engage and use the extraordinary forces to win", while on the other, the laws and principles summed up in *Sun Tzu's Art of War* were of universal guiding significance.

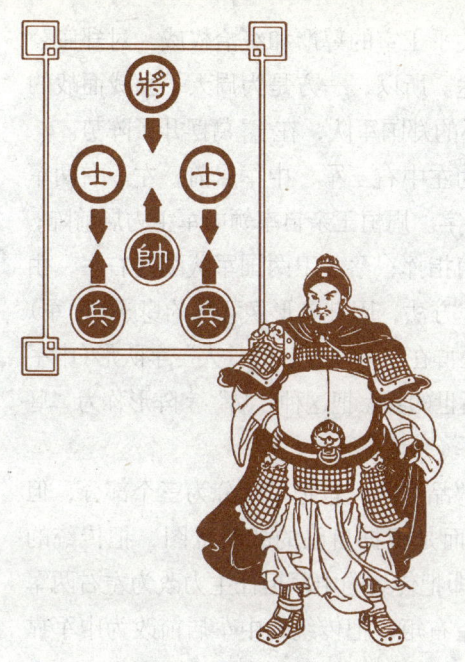

奇正相生——"鱼丽之阵"大败"鸟阵雁行"

《孙子兵法·兵势篇》 战势不过奇正，奇正之变，不可胜穷也。

公元前 707 年秋，郑庄公与周天子（即周桓王）发生了一场战争，因战地在繻葛（今河南长葛县东北），所以史称周、郑繻葛之战。

郑国是诸侯中的大国，本来跟周王室的关系不错。自周平王东迁以后，郑国国君一直是王朝卿士，但到了周桓王执政时期，中断了这一传统，引起了郑庄公的不满。郑国不再去朝拜周桓王，并借机抢收周王室的麦子和稻子，侵犯周天子的利益。让周桓王最不能容忍的是，郑国竟敢假托周天子之命，要挟诸侯攻打其世仇宋国。周桓王认为，郑国对自己威严的冒犯已经达到不能容忍的地步，于是诏命蔡、卫、陈三国一同讨伐郑国。这是一场周天子与诸侯之间的战争，胜负对双方都非常重要。对周天子来说，关乎王室的尊严和统治权威。对郑庄公来说，关乎郑国称霸诸侯的前途。所以，一方是为周天子立威而战的王师军队，一方是带着称霸野心的郑国军队，在 繻葛摆开了阵势。

周桓王把所统领的军队分为左中右三军，中军居前，左、右两军居中军两边稍后，阵形如"品"字。周桓王亲自率领中军主力居前阵；陈国军队配属左军，由周公黑肩指挥；蔡、卫两国军队配属右军，由虢公林父统率。这是传统的布阵方法，因其阵形像飞鸟的身子（中军）和双翅（左、右军）一样，也和雁群在空中飞行时的"人"字队形（中军靠前，左右军靠后）相似，所以后世的兵家把这种"品"字阵形称为"鸟阵雁行"。

郑军见王师一分为三摆开"品"阵，也把军队分为三个部分，但郑军没有按传统的阵法布阵，而是根据自己的战略意图，把传统的"品"字阵形作了相应的改变，即把传统的中军担任主力改为左右两军担任主力，并摆成方阵，名为左右矩；把传统的中军居前改为中军靠后，即放在左右两军略为靠后的地方，把三军阵形摆成倒"品"字。由于这种阵形像张开的渔网一样，便于两翼军队先把周军左右两军冲垮，然后三军合围周军中军主力，即让敌人陷入"网"中。为了万无一失，左右方阵都把战车排在前面，步卒配置在战车之后，车上有人负伤，步卒中马上抽人补上，使战阵严密如渔网，所以称之为"鱼丽之阵"。

郑军不仅根据王师"鸟阵雁行"暴露出来的弱点有针对性地创造出了"鱼丽之阵"，而且分析了王师三军的实力和士气，认为处于左翼的陈国军队力量和士气最弱，因为陈侯佗是刚刚杀了太子免自立为君的，内外都不服众，陈军奉命来参战，军心不稳，战斗力也不强，遂决定以先击陈军作为突破口。

战斗开始了，郑军左右两矩奋勇冲杀，王师左军的陈国军队本来就没有斗志，见郑军如此凶猛，不战而溃。掉头逃跑的陈军将整个左军冲乱，郑军顺势掩杀，王师左军即刻溃散。王师右军的蔡、卫两国军队，抵挡不住郑军的猛烈进攻，见左军溃逃，也纷纷寻路奔逃。左右军一溃，只剩下周桓王率领的中军孤立无援地处于郑军的包围之中，恰似鱼儿入网，顿时军心大乱。郑军左、中、右三军乘势合力攻杀，王师即刻"车倾马毙"，"将陨兵亡"，连周桓王的左肩也被郑将祝聃射中一箭，郑军大胜。

繻葛之战，郑国彻底摧毁了周天子的威严和"受命于天"的神话，揭开了春秋列国争雄的序幕。这一仗，不仅开启了一段新的历史，而且郑军创造的"鱼丽之阵"也开启了用兵战略的新思维，即不固守传统，要因势而变化。郑军的创新和经验必定给予孙子以启发，他在《兵势篇》中说，大凡用兵作战，总是以正兵当敌，以奇兵取胜。"战势不过奇正，奇正之变，不可胜穷也。"善于出奇制胜的人，其战术变化，就像天地万物那样无穷无尽，像江河之水那样通流不竭。孙子对先秦战争经验的总结及所包含的丰富哲理，成为后世用兵的重要指导思想，其影响一直延续到现在。

BOTH THE NORMAL AND EXTRAORDINARY FORCES ARE MUTUALLY REPRODUCTIVE

— "The Formation of a Fishing Net" Trounced "The Formation of Flying Wild Geese"

According to *Sun Tzu's Art of War*, "In battle, there are only the normal and extraordinary forces, but their combinations are limitless; no person can imagine or envision all of them."

In the autumn of 707 BC, a battle broke out between Duke Zhuang of the State of Zheng and King Huan of the Eastern Zhou Dynasty. Since it took place at Xuge (in the northeast of Changge County of Henan Province today), it was historically called the Battle of Xuge.

The State of Zheng was a big vassal state and had been on good terms with the royal family of the Eastern Zhou Dynasty. Since King Ping of the Eastern Zhou Dynasty moved his capital eastward, the ruler of the State of Zheng had been the major minister of the royal family of the Eastern Zhou Dynasty. But when King Huan came into power, this tradition was broken, thus irritating Duke Zhuang. The State of Zheng did not pay obedience to King Huan any longer and even took the opportunity to get the harvest of wheat and rice from the royal family, which encroached on the interests of King Huan. What was the most intolerable to King Huan was that on the pretext of his order, the State of Zheng coerced other dukes into launching an attack on the State of Song, its long-standing foe. King Huan thought that the affront to his dignity was past endurance, so he summoned the dukes of the states of Cai, Wei and Chen to subdue the State of Zheng. This was a battle between the King and a duke, so the outcome was very important for both sides. For King Huan, the outcome was related to the dignity and authority of the royal family. For Duke Zhuang, the outcome bore on the future of his dominance over other dukes. Therefore, the royal forces and the Zheng troops deployed the ranks in battle array at Xuge with different intentions, with the former for the dignity of King Huan, while the latter for the ambition of dominance over other states.

King Huan divided the forces into the left, middle and right armies. The middle army was deployed first in the lead while the other two armies were arranged on both sides and a little backward. The formation looked like an inverted "V". King Huan personally led the major forces in the front array, with the Chen troops as the left army led by Zhougong Heijian and the Cai and Wei troops as the right army led by Guogong Linfu. This was a traditional way of forming the troops, and because the formation not only looked like the body of a flying bird (the middle army) and its two wings (the left and right armies), but also was similar to an inverted "V" formation created by flying wild geese in the sky, from then on military strategists called the inverted "V" formation "the formation of flying wild geese".

The State of Zheng also divided their troops into three parts, but instead of deploying the forces in the traditional way, they made some corresponding adjustments to the traditional inverted "V" formation. According to their strategic intentions, the left and right armies, instead of the middle army, acted as the main force. A square formation was deployed, called the left and right squares; the middle army was not deployed ahead, but backward, behind the left and right army, thus the three armies were deployed in a "V" formation. This kind of formation looked like an open fishing net, which made it easy for the two wings to destroy the enemy's left and right armies first, then to encircle the Zhou's middle army, in other words, "to trap them in the net". In order to be perfectly safe, the Zheng troops arranged the chariots to take the lead in the square formation of each side, followed by foot soldiers. If soldiers in the chariots got hurt, the foot soldiers would immediately replenish them, making the formation as tight as a fishing net.

The Zheng troops not only created "the formation of a fishing net" based on the weaknesses revealed by "the formation of flying wild geese" of the royal forces, but also analyzed the strength and morale of their three armies. They concluded that the Chen troops in the left army were the weakest with the lowest morale because Marquis Tuo of the State of Chen had just proclaimed himself duke after he killed the crown Prince Mian, and nobody submitted to him. Under such circumstances, the Chen army received orders to fight. So they were in low morale with weak battle effectiveness. The Zheng troops decided to beat the Chen army first.

The battle started. The left and right armies of the Zheng troops courageously charged at the enemy. Confronted by the fierce Zheng troops, the Chen troops, with depressed morale, dispersed without fight. The left army was in chaos, so the Zheng troops took this opportunity to make a surprise attack. As a result, the left army was totally defeated. Unable to resist the fierce attack, the

Cai and Wei troops in the right army also dispersed at the sight of such an appalling scene. Cut off from help and trapped into the encirclement of the Zheng troops, the isolated middle army led by King Huan was like "a fish in the net" and the morale was immediately shaken. The charge of the three armies of the Zheng troops overturned the enemy's chariots, killed its horses, soldiers and generals. Even King Huan was shot with an arrow in the left shoulder by General Zhu Dan. The Zheng troops won a sweeping victory.

The dignity of King of the Eastern Zhou Dynasty was completely lost and the myth of "his becoming King by the grace of Heaven" was totally eradicated by the Battle of Xuge, the prelude to the struggle for power between the states in the Spring and Autumn Period. This battle initiated a new period in history. As well, the formation created by the Zheng troops initiated a new way of thinking in military strategies, namely, traditions should be challenged and changes should be made according to what was most expedient. Sun Tzu must have been inspired by the originality and experience of the Zheng troops, for he said in *Sun Tzu's Art of War* that generally, in battle, a general used the normal forces to engage and used the extraordinary forces to win. "In battle, there are only the normal and extraordinary forces, but their combinations are limitless." So those skilled in the use of extraordinary forces are capable of employing strategies as innumerable as the millions of living things on earth and as endless as the flow of water droplets in great rivers. Sun Tzu's summary of the military experience prior to the Qin Dynasty and the profound philosophies became an important guiding ideology regarding operations of war in later generations, the effects of which have continued to be felt to the present day.

取与待机——赵、魏、韩三家分晋

《孙子兵法·兵势篇》：用小利去诱动敌人，再用强兵劲卒去对付它。

公元前453年，原本是卿大夫的赵、魏、韩三家瓜分了晋国，号称"三晋"。

晋国是周成王的弟弟唐叔虞的封国。到晋文公时期，他中兴晋国，曾多次平定中原，召集诸侯会盟，被周天子封为"诸侯之长"，是春秋时期毫无争议的至尊霸主。晋文公之后的晋襄公，拒强秦于中原之外，为中原文化持续发展赢得宝贵发展时间，为诸子百家自由争鸣赢得宝贵发展空间。其后的晋景公、晋悼公等延续拒秦东进策略，均是事实上的霸主。所以在春秋五霸中，晋国是维持霸主地位时间最长的国家。

但是，到了春秋后期，晋国公室衰弱，当权的卿大夫逐渐强盛起来，如智伯瑶、赵襄子毋恤、韩康子虎、魏桓子驹等，都是权倾公室。

本来晋国六卿还有范氏和中行氏两家，但被势力强大的智、韩、赵、魏四家兼并，其中智伯捞到的利益最多，所以势力也最为强盛。晋国的政事本来应该由国君执掌，由于卿大夫权倾公室，所以政事一变再变。先是六卿专权，范氏和中行氏被兼并之后，晋国的命运就由智、韩、赵、魏四家掌握了。四家之中，智氏最强，所以，晋国的政事都是他说了算。

智伯为了加强自己的势力，削弱其他三家的力量，就假托加强公室，要求赵、魏、韩三家各拿出100里的土地和户口来给晋室，其实是想据为己有。智伯先去威逼韩康子，韩康子本不愿意给，但他的谋臣劝他说："智伯贪得无厌，假借君命来剥夺我们的土地，如果不给，就违抗君命，他会借此来讨伐我们，不如先给他。他得到土地之后，一定又会向赵和魏索要。赵、魏若不顺从，必然会打起来，我们可以见机行事。"韩康子接受了谋臣的建议，把土地和户口如数地割给了智伯。智伯又用同样的办法向魏桓子索要，结果也如愿以偿。没想到的是，他在赵襄子那里碰了钉子，于是就联合韩、魏两家一起出兵攻打赵家，并允诺，灭赵之后，赵家的所有土地和户口由三家平分。

公元前455年，智伯瑶率韩、魏三家的兵马攻赵。赵襄子知道寡不敌众，于是就跑到了晋阳，以晋阳为根据地与三家对抗。智、魏、韩三家的兵马追踪而至，把晋阳团团围住。赵襄子的军队虽然被围，但士气很旺盛。他们固守城池，使敌方一时难以攻下。双方就这样相持了近两年的时间。智伯觉得长期下去不是个办法，于是在第三年即公元前453年，就设法引晋水淹晋阳城，企图以此逼迫赵襄子就范。几天之后，晋阳城的城墙差几尺就要全部被淹了。赵襄子既不愿意向智伯投降，又不愿意坐以待毙，正在无奈之际，他的家臣张孟给他出主意说："韩、魏割让土地也并非心甘情愿，跟智伯来攻打我们，实属貌合神离，不如去联络分化他们，以解困境。"赵襄子觉得他的计谋很高明，于是他就乘黑夜出城去分化魏、韩。魏、韩本来就对智伯不满，担心灭赵之后矛头对准自己。赵襄子派人来联络，不仅许诺归还他们割让出来的土地，而且答应灭智氏之后，三家平分其土地。魏、韩马上就同意了，遂订立了共同夹击智氏的同盟。

赵襄子决定以其人之道，还治其人之身。他先派人乘夜消灭了看护河堤的晋军，决堤放水淹了智伯的军队。接着，韩、魏两国军队从左右两翼夹击，赵国军队从正面攻击，打得智伯措手不及，最终被彻底消灭了。按照协议，先归还了魏、韩割让的土地，然后三家瓜分了智氏的全部土地。之后，赵、魏、韩各自建立了独立的政权。

公元前438年，晋哀公死，晋幽公即位。由于赵、魏、韩权势太大，晋国公室完全丧失了权利和地位，因畏惧权臣，不得不向韩、赵、魏三家行朝拜礼。于是韩、赵、魏干脆就瓜分了晋国的土地，只把绛城和曲沃两地留给晋幽公。公元前403年，周威烈王正式册封韩、赵、魏为诸侯。到公元前376年，韩哀侯、赵敬侯、魏武侯联合灭了晋国，瓜分了晋国的全部土地，把晋当时的国君静公废为百姓，晋完全为韩、赵、魏三家所取代。

晋国由六卿专权到三家分晋的整个历史过程，印证了孙子在《兵势篇》中所提出的用兵战略：善于调动敌人的人，无论向敌人展示出什么样的军形，敌人总是听从；给予敌人一点小利，敌人就必然会来夺取。用小利去诱动敌人，再用强兵劲卒去对付它。

TAKE AT THE RIGHT TIME
— The Houses of Zhao, Wei and Han Carved Up the State of Jin

According to *Sun Tzu's Art of War*, "Keep the enemy on the move by holding out the bait and then attack him with choice troops."

In 453 BC, the State of Jin was carved up by three houses — Zhao, Wei and Han, which were the original feudal clans of Jin, and they claimed to be "the Three Jin States".

The State of Jin was the vassal state of Tang Shuyu, the younger brother of King Cheng of the Zhou Dynasty. When Duke Wen came into power, he revived the State of Jin. Many times, he stabilized the Central Plains, and summoned meetings to form alliances between the dukes. He was appointed by the King of the Zhou Dynasty as "the Chief Duke" and was regarded as the most revered overlord without controversy in the Spring and Autumn Period. When Duke Xiang succeeded to the throne, he kept the powerful State of Qin out of the Central Plains, winning valuable time for the sustainable development of the culture on the Central Plains, and offering scope for development for the free contention of "*A Hundred Schools of Thought*". His successors, Duke Jing and Duke Dao maintained the dominance by following the strategy of preventing the State of Qin from expanding eastward. Therefore, among the Five Overlords of the Spring and Autumn Period, the State of Jin maintained the dominant position for the longest time.

However, in the late Spring and Autumn Period, the royal family of the State of Jin was on the wane, while some feudal clans, such as Viscount Zhi Boyao, Viscount Zhao Wuxu, Viscount Han Hu and Viscount Wei Ju, gained more power. Besides them, the State of Jin had two other feudal clans, Fan and Zhonghang, who had been annexed by these four powerful clans. The house of Zhi benefited the most from the annexation; therefore, it was the strongest in power. The Duke of the State of Jin should have been in charge of the political affairs, but as the feudal clans were powerful, the political power fell into their hands. At first, all the six feudal clans were in power, and then after the houses of Fan and Zhonghang were annexed, the other four clans were in control of Jin's destiny. The strongest among them was the house of Zhi, who had the final say.

In order to strengthen his own forces and weaken the power of the other three houses, on the pretext of the royal family, Viscount Zhi demanded that the other three houses present the State of Jin with a territory of 100 square *li* and its dwellers. But actually he wanted to appropriate them. Viscount Zhi coerced Viscount Han first, who was initially reluctant. But his advisor said to him, "Zhi is insatiably avaricious. Now he wants to deprive us of our land in the name of the King. If we disapprove, he will surely take the opportunity to invade us for our defiance. Let's take soundings by satisfying his demands first. After he gets our land, he will make the same demands on Zhao and Wei. If they disagree, they are sure to fight against him. In that case, we may use our discretion." Viscount Han accepted the advice and ceded the land and population to Viscount Zhi, who also got what he wanted from Viscount Wei in the same way. However, when he was unexpectedly rejected by Viscount Zhao, he formed alliance with the houses of Han and Wei to attack Zhao, and he promised that after the destruction of Zhao, they would evenly carve up and share Zhao's territory and population.

In 455 BC, Viscount Zhi led the three armies of Zhi, Han and Wei in an attack on Zhao. Realizing that his army was hopelessly out-numbered, Viscount Zhao escaped to Jinyang, where he confronted them. When the three armies of Zhi, Wei and Han reached Jinyang, they laid siege to the city. Despite the situation, the morale of the Zhao army was very high. They tenaciously defended the city so that the enemy could not win in a short time. The confrontation lasted for nearly two years. Viscount Zhi thought that a further stalemate would do nothing good, so in the third year (453 BC), he diverted the flow of the Jin River to inundate the city as a way to force Viscount Zhao into submission. Several days later, the city was only several feet above water level. Viscount Zhao neither wanted to submit, nor was he willing to wait passively for death. Seeing no way out of this dilemma, Zhang Meng, one of his vassals, suggested, "Han and Wei were far from willing to cede their land. They must have been forced to join Viscount Zhi in attacking us. They were seemingly in agreement but actually at odds. We may as well make contact with them and split them from Zhi. Only in this way can we turn the corner." Viscount Zhao thought that his idea was so brilliant that he asked Zhang Meng to go out of the city under the cover of darkness to contact the houses of Han and Wei. Zhang Meng promised not only to return the land that Wei and Han had ceded, but also to split Zhi's territories evenly with them after the destruction of the house of Zhi. Discontented with Zhi, both the Wei and Han were afraid of being targeted after the battle was won, so they immediately formed an alliance with Zhao to attack Zhi.

Viscount Zhao decided to pay Viscount Zhi back using his own tactics. Under the cover of darkness, the Zhao troops first killed the Jin soldiers who were standing guard over the dams and flooded the Zhi troops. Then, the Han and Wei troops attacked the Zhi troops from the sides while Viscount Zhao led his soldiers in the frontal attack. Completely unprepared, the Zhi troops were totally vanquished. According to the prior agreement, the houses of Han and Wei got back the land they had ceded and then they evenly distributed the territories of the house of Zhi. After that, the three houses established their independent respective regimes.

In 438 BC, after the death of Duke Ai of the State of Jin, Duke You succeeded to the throne. Because the three houses of Zhao, Wei and Han held much power, the royal family of the State of Jin completely lost authority and status and had to make obedience to the three houses. As a result, the three houses divided up all the Jin's lands, except for the two cities, Jiang and Quwo. In 403 BC, King Weilie of the Zhou Dynasty formally appointed the Viscounts of Han, Zhao and Wei as Marquis. In 376 BC, Marquis Ai of the State of Han, Marquis Jing of the State of Zhao and Marquis Wu of the State of Wei joined hands to destroy the State of Jin and partition the rest of its territory. They dismissed Duke Jing from his position and made him a civilian. The State of Jin was totally replaced by the three houses.

The whole historical process, in which the State of Jin underwent the dictatorship of the six feudal clans and was partitioned by the three houses, corroborated the military strategy stated in *Sun Tzu's Art of War*, "One who is skilled at making the enemy move does so by creating a situation, according to which the enemy will act. He entices the enemy with something he wants. He keeps the enemy on the move by holding out the bait and then attacks him with choice troops."

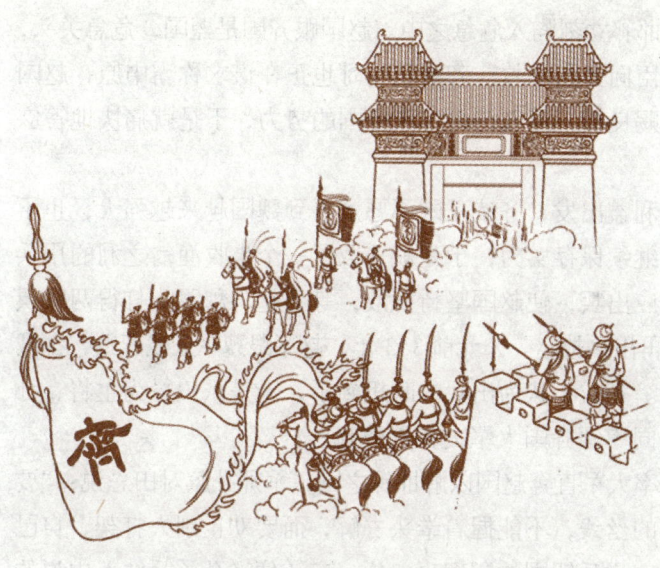

避实击虚——齐国围魏救赵

《孙子兵法·虚实篇》：用兵的规律像水的流动，水流动的规律是避开高处而流向低处；作战的规律是避开敌人雄厚的实力，攻击其虚弱的地方。

　　公元前 353 年，当时正处于战国时代的中期，各诸侯国为了扩张实力，不断相互吞并；为了争夺霸权，大国之间经常发生大规模的战争。齐国围魏救赵，就是在这种背景下发生的。

　　齐、魏、赵当时都是大国。齐国位于今山东地区，魏国位于今河南地区，赵国位于今河北地区，在它们之间还有一些小国或附属国。公元前 354 年，赵国向处于赵、魏之间的卫国发动进攻，企图吞并卫国领土，夺取战略上的有利地位，以便跟处于其南部的强国魏国抗衡。卫国是魏国的属国，现在赵国要吞并，魏国当然不能容忍，于是借口保护卫国，乘机出动大军直接包围了赵国的国都邯郸，赵国因出兵卫国而国内空虚，邯郸立刻陷入危急之中。赵国跟齐国是盟国，危急关头，赵王急忙派使臣向齐国求救。齐威王当时也正在谋求称霸中原，赵国求救，正是天赐良机，可以借机扩大齐国的势力，于是就痛快地答应了。

从齐国的利益出发，齐威王既不愿意看到魏国越来越强大，也不愿意邻国赵国继续保存实力，于是就采取了一个坐收渔翁之利的用兵战略，即先虚应出兵，使赵国坚持抗敌，等到赵、魏军队打得两败俱伤之时，齐国再出兵救赵。公元前353年，赵军跟魏军五战五败，都城邯郸危在旦夕。齐威王认为出兵的时机到了，于是派田忌为主将、孙膑为军师，一同率领齐国大军去伐魏救赵。

田忌打算率大军直奔赵国以解邯郸之围，军师孙膑对田忌说："要解开乱成一团的丝线，不能握着拳头去解，而要劝止别人打架，自己不能帮助去打。用兵解围的道理也一样，应该像《孙子兵法》中说的那样，'避实而击虚'，'击其所必救'。"孙膑提出直接进击魏国的都城大梁，一是魏军主力在外，国内空虚，乘虚而击，胜券在握；二是进击大梁，迫使魏军不得不回军自救，既解了邯郸之围，又使魏军兵力分散，疲于奔波，便于各个击破。田忌采纳了孙膑的计谋，率齐军主力直奔大梁。果然，魏军主帅庞涓接到大梁危急的消息，不得不分兵回救。这时，齐国军队已经在魏军的必经之地桂陵严阵以待。桂陵地势险要，又是魏军回救大梁的必经之地，齐军在此迎击魏军，以逸待劳，先占胜机。而魏军则是才离战场，又进征途，精疲力竭，士气不振，结果陷于被动挨打，惨败而归。这就是中国军事史上著名的齐魏桂陵之战。

在齐军伐魏救赵的过程中，孙膑灵活地运用了孙子"避实而击虚"、"攻其所必救"的战略思想，成功地制订了围魏救赵的战略方针，创造性地运用和发扬了孙子的兵法思想。"围魏救赵"成为家喻户晓的成语，"桂陵之战"则成为中国古代经典的战役之一。

AVOID THE ENEMY'S STRONG POINTS AND ATTACK ITS WEAK POINTS
— The State of Qi Besieged the State of Wei to Rescue the State of Zhao

According to *Sun Tzu's Art of War*, "An army may be likened to water, for as flowing water avoids the heights and hastens to the lowlands, so an army should avoid the enemy's strong points and attack its weak points."

In 353 BC, when China was in the middle of the Warring States Period, the vassal states still kept annexing each other in order to expand their respective strength. Big vassal states frequently initiated large-scale battles for power. It was under such circumstances that the State of Qi besieged the State of Wei to rescue the State of Zhao.

At that time, the states of Qi, Wei and Zhao were big vassal states. The State of Qi lies in Shandong Province today, Wei in Henan Province and Zhao in Heibei Province, with some small states and dependent states in between. In 354 BC, the State of Zhao launched an attack on the dependent state of Wei (one of Wei's dependent states) that lay between the State of Zhao and the State of Wei, attempting to annex its territory and to seize the strategically advantageous position so that it could rival the powerful State of Wei that lay to the south. The dependent state of Wei was attached to the State of Wei, so the latter could not tolerate Zhao's invasion. On the pretext of protecting its dependent state, the State of Wei sent troops to lay siege on Handan, the capital city of the State of Zhao. As the Zhao troops were sent to attack the dependent state of Wei, the capital was weakly defended and was immediately in danger. The King of Zhao quickly sent a messenger to appeal to the State of Qi, his ally, for help. Planning to dominate over the Central Plains, King Wei of the State of Qi thought that it was a heaven-sent opportunity to expand his strength, so he promised without any hesitation.

For the sake of the interests of the State of Qi, King Wei was unhappy with Wei's growing power and Zhao's existing strength, so he adopted the military strategy of "reaping the spoils of victory without lifting a finger". He first promised to send troops so that the State of Zhao could maintain their position, but then waited until both armies had been exhausted. In 353 BC, the Zhao troops suffered five successive defeats, and Handan was on the verge of destruction. King Wei thought that it was the time to come to Zhao's aid, so he appointed Tian Ji as the General and Sun Bin as the military advisor, who led the troops to attack Wei to rescue Zhao.

Tian Ji intended to march directly towards the State of Zhao to stop the siege of Handan, but Sun Bin said, "To sort the mixed string, you'd better use your fingers instead of your fist. To resolve a dispute, you mustn't get yourself entangled in it. The same is true of using forces to stop the siege. We should follow the advice in *Sun Tzu's Art of War* — 'avoid the enemy's strong points and attack its weak points' and 'attack a position where the enemy must move to defend'." Sun Bin suggested attacking Daliang directly, the capital city of the State of Wei. According to him, on the one hand, the major forces of Wei were on the battlefield and the capital was weakly defended, so the Qi troops were likely to win if they took advantage of this opportunity. On the other hand, the Wei troops had to rush back to Daliang's rescue and thus the siege of Handan could be stopped. Once led by the nose, the Wei forces were forced to disperse and could easily be destroyed one after another. Following Sun Bin's advice, Tian Ji led the troops directly to Daliang. As expected, when Pang Juan, the General of the Wei troops, got the news, he had no choice but to dispatch his troops to rescue Daliang. By this time, the Qi troops were prepared for the combat in Guiling, where the Wei troops must pass through. The terrain was strategically situated and difficult to access, so the Qi troops waited for the exhausted Wei troops and thus stood a chance of winning. As the Wei troops began their march immediately after they left the battlefield, they were extremely exhausted and demoralized. As a result, the Wei troops took the beating passively and were totally vanquished. This was the famous Battle of Guiling between the State of Qi and the State of Wei in Chinese military history.

In the process of Qi's besieging Wei to rescue Zhao, Sun Bin flexibly used Sun Tzu's strategic thinking — "an army should avoid the enemy's strong points and attack its weak points" and "an army should attack a position where the enemy must move to defend". Sun Bin successfully formulated the strategic principle of besieging Wei to rescue Zhao and creatively utilized and developed the military thinking of Sun Tzu. "Besieging Wei to Rescue Zhao" became a household idiom, whereas "the Battle of Guiling" became one of the classic battles in Chinese history.

因敌变化——管仲智破山戎伏兵之术

《孙子兵法·虚实篇》：用兵作战，既无一成不变的战场态势，也无一定的作战方式，能根据敌情变化而取胜的，才可叫做用兵如神。

公元前 664 年，山戎大举入侵燕国，燕王急忙向齐国求救，齐桓公带着管仲率领齐军前去救援。山戎是位于中国北部的游牧民族，勇猛善战，喜欢使用伏击之术战胜对手。春秋以来，中原诸侯争霸，战事不断，山戎趁机屡屡进犯中原，燕国深受其害。山戎听说齐桓公亲率齐军来救援，遂解围而去。齐军与燕军合力北出蓟门关追击，途中遭到山戎伏击，若不是后续部队及时赶到，齐军可能遭灭顶之灾。

春秋时代，中原诸侯军队的装备主要是战车，而山戎则是以骑兵为主。两者相比，山戎的骑兵不仅行动迅速，而且机动灵活，长于打突袭和伏击战。管仲是齐国文武兼备的思想家和军事家，他根据山戎和齐国军队的不同特点，及时重新调整了对付山戎的策略。一次，齐军追击山戎到达伏龙山区，为了防止山戎偷袭，管仲命令齐军把战车一辆接一辆地联结起来，围结如城，士卒居于"车城"之中，犹如"坚壁"。果然，山戎轮番进攻，都被"车城"阻隔，无法突破。山戎见攻坚不行，便又故伎重演，想引诱齐军出击，然后采取伏击。

山戎在屡攻不破之后，假装撤离，只留下小股兵力在"车城"附近活动。他们有时假装下马卧地休息，有时对齐军辱骂挑衅，企图把齐军诱出车城。管仲识破了山戎的阴谋，便将计就计，把齐兵分为三路：中间一路去迎击谩骂的戎兵，左、右两路相互接应，专门对付伏兵。一切准备就绪，齐军突然开门冲出"车城"，中间的一路直奔山戎的诱兵。山戎以为齐军中计，假意弃马而逃，齐军并不追赶，鸣金收兵而归。山戎没有料到齐军会返回去，本来埋伏在山谷里等待伏击的部队，只好杀出来追击齐军，正好与管仲派出的左、右两军相遇，两军合力夹击，把山戎打得落荒而逃。齐军放弃战车，骑马追击，直下500里，一直把山戎赶到沙漠深处。

俗话说："吃一堑，长一智"，管仲智破山戎伏兵之术，充分反映了军事斗争的一个重要规律：不可固守陈规，必须适时而变。管仲的这些军事斗争经验，在《孙子兵法》中都得到总结和发扬。孙子在《虚实篇》中说："故战胜不复，而应形于无穷。"又说："用兵作战，既无一成不变的战场态势，也无一定的作战方式，能根据敌情变化而取胜的，才可叫做用兵如神。"

MODIFY TACTICS IN ACCORDANCE WITH THE ENEMY SITUATION
— Guan Zhong Beat the Shanrong's Ambush

According to *Sun Tzu's Art of War*, "As water has no constant form, there are no constant conditions in warfare. Thus, one able to win the victory by modifying his tactics in accordance with the enemy situation may be said to be divine."

In 664 BC, the Shanrong people initiated a large-scale attack on the State of Yan. The King of Yan quickly appealed to the State of Qi for help, and Duke Huan of the State of Qi, accompanied by Guan Zhong, led the troops to their rescue. The Shanrong people, a courageous and skillful nomadic tribe in the north of China, were good at defeating their enemy by laying an ambush. Since the Spring and Autumn Period, as the dukes had been launching battles for power, the Shanrong troops took the chance to invade the Central Plains repeatedly, from which the State of Yan suffered. Hearing that Duke Huan of the State of Qi had come to Yan's rescue, the Shanrong troops stopped the siege and retreated immediately. Dashing out of the north gate of Jingmen, the troops of Qi and Yan pursued them, only to be ambushed on their way. Had it not been for the timely arrival of the follow-up units, the Qi troops would have been annihilated.

In the Spring and Autumn Period, chariots were the main military equipments of the vassal states on the Central Plains; whereas the cavalry was characteristic of the Shanrong troops. Compared with chariots, the cavalry with more mobility and flexibility was much faster. Besides, they were good at making a surprise attack and ambushing the enemy. Well versed in both polite letters and martial arts, Guan Zhong was a great thinker and military strategist in the State of Qi. According to different characteristics of the two troops, Guan Zhong modified the tactics of fighting against the Shanrong troops. Once, when the Qi troops pursued the Shanrong troops to Mount Fulong, in order to avoid sneak attacks, Guan Zhong ordered the soldiers to connect the chariots one after another. The troops remained in a "city of chariots", which looked like the "defensive walls". As expected, the Shanrong troops launched attacks but could not break through the "city of chariots". Realizing that it was useless to assault them, the Shanrong troops played the same old trick again — to lure the Qi troops into launching an attack and then ambush them.

The Shanrong troops pretended to retreat, leaving behind a contingent of forces hanging around the "city of chariots". In order to lure the Qi troops out of the "city of chariots", the remaining troops sometimes got off the horses, pretending to have a rest on the ground, or provoked the Qi troops by shouting insults. Seeing through their tricks, Guan Zhong decided to beat them at their own game. He divided the Qi troops into three groups: one group (the middle group) would launch a head-on attack on the decoys, while the other two groups (the left and right groups) would coordinate with each other to deal with the Shanrong troops in the ambush. When all was ready, the Qi troops suddenly opened the gate and dashed out of the "city of chariots", with the middle group charging directly at the decoys. The decoys thought that the Qi troops had fallen into the trap, so they deliberately abandoned the horses and fled. However, instead of pursuing them, the Qi troops beat the gongs and retreated. As this was unexpected, the Shanrong troops waiting in the ambush in the valley had to run after the Qi troops but encountered the other two groups. Under the attack from both sides, the Shanrong troops were defeated and fled in rout. Leaving the chariots behind, the Qi troops got on the horses and drove them 500 *li* down the road until deep into the desert.

One Chinese saying goes like this, "A fall into the pit, a gain in your wit." Guan Zhong's beating the Shanrong's ambush reflected a very important law in warfare — one should modify his tactics according to different circumstances instead of sticking to the old practices. Guan Zhong's experience in war was summed up and developed in *Sun Tzu's Art of War.* Sun Tzu said, "One should always respond to circumstances in an infinite variety of ways. As water has no constant form, there are no constant conditions in warfare. Thus, one able to win the victory by modifying his tactics in accordance with the enemy situation may be said to be divine."

以逸待劳——晋"三分四军"疲楚

《孙子兵法·虚实篇》：胜利是可以争取到的。敌人兵力虽多，也可以使其分散兵力无法与我战斗。

公元前564年，晋悼公采用中军元帅荀罃提出的分兵作战、轮番扰敌的办法对付强楚，实现以逸待劳的战略目的。这一计策，史称"三分四军"。

晋楚争霸，夹在中间的郑国成为争夺的战场。郑国既无力抗楚，也无力抗晋，只好采取"晋来归晋，楚来归楚"的滑头政策以自保。这一年，晋悼公听说郑国又叛晋归楚，非常恼火，意欲举诸侯之兵伐郑。中军元帅荀罃说："军队不能连续作战，如果连续打仗就会疲劳，就没有战斗力了。诸侯也不能连续劳烦他们，连续劳烦他们出兵打仗就会引起怨愤。如果在内疲而外怨的这种情况下去抗击楚国，是不会取胜的。"晋悼公说："这个道理我也知道，但是，对郑国的行为又不能坐视不管。"荀䓨说："郑国之所以反复无常，是因为楚国的力量大。如果楚国的力量足以与晋国争霸，那么郑国就会一直在晋楚两国之间摇摆不动。要想长期收郑，必须先削弱楚国的力量。不然，就难以长久收郑，更不要说御楚了。"晋悼公说："你的意见固然好，有没有什么弱楚的良策呢？"荀䓨说："三分四军，以逸待劳。"晋悼公见荀䓨分析得很有道理，于是就采纳了他的计策，并授权荀䓨实施这一战略。

晋国当时的军队编制有中军、上军、下军和新军四个部分，荀䓨所说的"三分四军"之策，就是把晋军的中、上、下、新四军各分为三支。军队分好之后，荀䓨命令其中的一支进入郑国牵制楚军，另外两支军队在本国养精蓄锐。进入郑国的晋军，采取敌进我退、敌退我进的战术与楚军周旋，弄得楚军求战不得、求息不成，而晋军则三支军队轮番使用，既有效地牵制和消耗了楚国的兵力，又使晋军免遭久曝于战场之苦，保存了军事实力，实现了"以逸待劳"的战略目标。成功的战略总是给后人以启发。五十多年之后，这一战略战术不仅被孙子和伍子胥成功地运用于吴楚之战中，而且有所发展。所以孙子在《虚实篇》说"胜利是可以争取到的。敌人兵力虽多，也可以使其分散兵力无法与我战斗。"

AWAIT THE EXHAUSTED ENEMY AT ONE'S EASE
— The State of Jin Exhausted the Chu Army by "Reorganizing the Four Armies into Three"

According to *Sun Tzu's Art of War*, "Victory can be achieved. Even if the enemy is numerically stronger, he can be prevented from engaging."

In 564 BC, following the advice of Xun Ying, the Commander-in-chief of the middle army, Duke Dao of the State of Jin dealt with the powerful State of Chu. Xun Ying suggested that the Jin army should be reorganized and then harass the Chu army in turn, with a view to realizing the strategic objective of "awaiting the exhausted enemy at one's own ease". This was historically known as the strategy of "reorganizing the four armies into three".

When the states of Jin and Chu struggled for power, the State of Zheng, located between the two states, became a battlefield that they scrambled for. Since it was powerless to resist either of them, the State of Zheng had no alternative but to adopt a flexible strategy of "submitting itself to whoever won the battle". One year, when Duke Dao was told that the State of Zheng had capitulated to the State of Chu again, he was so angry that he intended to raise troops from the vassal states to send a punitive expedition against it. Xun Ying said to him, "Troops cannot fight continuously; otherwise, they will lose combat effectiveness with fatigue. The vassal states cannot be constantly troubled either; otherwise, there will be discontent. If we attack the State of Chu in such a case, we will stand no chance of winning." Duke Dao said, "I know this well, but how can I sit by Zheng's betrayal?" Xun Ying said, "Zheng's fence-sitting is due to Chu's power. As long as Chu is our match, Zheng will swing like a pendulum. Therefore, the only way to bring Zheng under control for good is to weaken Chu's power. Otherwise, it will be difficult for us to keep Zheng for long, let alone resist Chu. " Duke Dao said, "Your suggestion sounds quite good, but how can we weaken Chu's power?" Xun Ying replied, "We may reorganize our four armies into three and await the exhausted enemy at our ease." Duke Dao felt that Xun Ying's analysis was so reasonable that he adopted it and authorized him to implement this strategy.

At that time, there were four armies in Jin's military establishment — the middle, the upper, the lower and the new army. According to Xun Ying, these four armies should be reorganized into three groups. After the division, Xun Ying ordered one group to enter the State of Zheng to occupy the Chu troops while the other two groups remained home to conserve strength and store up energy. The group entering the State of Zheng dealt with the Chu troops by retreating when the Zheng troops advanced, and advancing when they retreated. As a result, the Chu troops could seek neither battle nor rest. The three groups of Jin were sent there in turn to effectively occupy and "tire out" the Chu troops as well as to save themselves from too much exposure on the battlefield. Therefore, the Jin troops conserved strength and finally realized their military objective of "awaiting the exhausted enemy at one's own ease". Successful military strategies always inspire the posterities. More than fifty years later, this strategy was successfully used by Sun Tzu and Wu Zixu in the battle between the State of Wu and the State of Chu, and it was somewhat developed. Thus, in *Sun Tzu's Art of War*, Sun Tzu said, "Victory can be achieved. Even if the enemy is numerically stronger, he can be prevented from engaging."

兵诡必疑——晋军疑兵败齐军

《孙子兵法·虚实篇》：最大程度地把握敌军的内情，完全隐藏我军的真形，不露任何形迹，那么，纵使潜伏极深的间谍也窥探不到我方的底细，即使再有才智的人也无计可施。

公元前555年，晋平公会合了宋、鲁、卫、郑、莒、邾、滕、薛、杞、小邾等十二个诸侯国的兵马讨伐齐国，双方在齐国的平阴城下拉开了战幕。

齐本是东方的大国，春秋前期，齐桓公是第一位登上霸主地位的诸侯。桓公死后，齐国经历了内乱与外患，国力日渐衰落，不但失去了霸主地位，甚至沦为晋的附属国。公元前589年，在晋、齐鞍之战中，齐国惨败，不得不向晋国俯首称臣。这对齐国来说，不仅有失大国的尊严，而且利益上也是巨大的损失。所以，齐国并不甘于称臣，晋齐之间的摩擦时有发生，晋率十二国军队伐齐，就是一例。

齐灵公听说晋率十二国兵马来犯，命上卿高厚辅佐太子留守都城，自己亲率大军至平阴城阻击敌军。协助齐灵公作战的寺人夙沙卫曾建议道："晋率十二国军队来犯，其心未必齐，可趁其立足未稳之际出奇兵，先败其一军，其余的必然闻风丧胆。"齐灵公说："晋携诸侯来犯，齐、晋兵力对比悬殊，稳妥起见，还是守城为上。"夙沙卫说："要守，也得选个险要之地，凭险而守。区区平阴，仅靠几道沟壑怎么能挡住敌人的进攻呢？"齐灵公不听，遂命令士兵深掘壕堑，横广一里，选精兵把守，以御敌师。

中行偃为晋军主帅，他见齐军深沟高垒，掘堑而守，知道齐军不会轻易出城决战。于是他对部将们说："齐军害怕我们，采取深沟高垒，掘堑而守的战略，看来一时半会不可能出来与我们决战，我们必须用计谋来战胜敌人。"众将们回答说："愿听将军调遣。"于是，中行偃开始密授机宜，让各路大军分头行动。

根据中行偃的部署，鲁国和卫国两支军队从须句挺进，邾国和莒国的两支军队取道城阳向前进发，这两路兵马均由琅琊突入，晋国的主力军则从平阴正面突破。鲁、卫、邾、莒四国兵马出发之后，中行偃开始部署疑兵。他先命令部队扎了许多草人，准备许多旌旗和树枝，一切准备妥当之后，他对司马张君臣说："凡是山泽险要之处，都虚张旌旗；把草人蒙上衣甲立于空车之上，再把断木和树枝绑在车的后面，令士卒驱车往来于山谷之间。"司马张君臣依计而行。

布置好疑兵之后，中行偃又命令士兵把木石装上战车，命令步卒携带土袋，然后指挥三路兵马从左、中、右三个方向朝平阴城发起进攻，一边攻击敌人，一边用木、石、土袋填壕而进，一举突破了齐军的阵地。齐军大将析归父逃回平阴城，将联军填壕而进的危急情况报告齐灵公。齐灵公急忙跑到巫山上瞭望敌军态势，只见山泽险要之地，都有旗帜飘扬，车马奔驰，扬起的尘土遮天蔽日。齐灵公被眼前的场面吓懵了，以为诸侯的联军部队漫山遍野，平阴城岌岌可危，于是急急下令撤军，不战而逃。齐灵公虽然侥幸逃回临淄，但他手下的两员大将则被晋军俘获。

齐灵公一路逃进都城临淄，惊魂未定，收拾细软打算弃城继续逃亡。上卿高厚竭力劝谏道："诸侯联军远道而来，粮草用度大，必不能久战。平阴虽然失利，但齐国并非一败涂地。只要朝野协力，临淄必能守住。" 齐灵公勉强接受了高厚的建议，打消了弃城逃亡的念头，组织兵力守城。

楚国一直是晋国称霸的强劲对手，乘晋军率诸侯进击齐国之际，攻打晋国抗楚的桥头堡郑国。接到郑国求救的消息，晋军只好从齐国撤军。就这样，齐灵公躲过了一难。

孙子《虚实篇》中说："善于指挥作战的人，总是调动敌人而不为敌人所调动。能使敌人自动来到我预设地点的，是我用小利引诱它的结果；使敌人不来到我预设地点的，则是由于我使它感到有害的结果。所以，敌若休整良好，闲适安逸，我就设法烦而扰之，使之劳倦；敌若粮草丰足，我就设法使之饥困；敌若安守自固，我就挑而扰之使之不得安宁。"最大程度地把握敌军的内情，完全隐藏我军的真形，不露任何形迹，那么，纵使潜伏极深的间谍也窥探不到我方的底细，即使再有才智的人也无计可施。这正是晋胜而齐败的原因。

BE SUSPICIOUS OF DECEPTIVE FORCES
— Jin's Deceptive Forces Defeated the Qi Troops

According to *Sun Tzu's Art of War*, "Know the enemy situation to the greatest extent and conceal our troops without ascertainable shape, then the most penetrating spies cannot pry nor can the wise man conspire against you."

In 555 BC, Duke Ping of the State of Jin mustered troops from twelve vassal states (the states of Song, Lu, Wei, Zheng, Ju, Zhu, Teng, Xue, Qi and Xiaozhu, etc.) to attack the State of Qi. They started a battle outside Pingyin City of the

State of Qi.

The State of Qi was originally a big vassal state in the east. In the Spring and Autumn Period, Duke Huan of the State of Qi was the first overlord. After his death, the state power was dwindling because of internal disturbances and foreign invasions. Consequently, the state lost its dominant position and was reduced to becoming a dependency of the State of Jin. In 589 BC, in the Battle of An between the two states, the State of Qi suffered a severe defeat and had to submit itself to the rule of the State of Jin. The State of Qi was humiliated and suffered heavy economic losses as well. Since the State of Qi could not take it, conflicts frequently happened between them, one of which was Jin's invading Qi with troops from twelve states.

On hearing the news, Duke Ling of the State of Qi ordered Gao Hou, the superior official, to stay in the capital city to assist the crown prince while he personally led the troops to march towards Pingyin to block the enemy. Susha Wei, a eunuch accompanying Duke Ling, once suggested, "The twelve troops led by the State of Jin are not necessarily of one mind. We may launch a surprise attack before they gain a foothold. If we defeat one of them, the other troops will be panic-stricken." Duke Ling said, "Since the enemy's combined troops out-number ours, it's advisable that we defend our city instead of fighting." Susha Wei said, "If so, we had better choose a precipitous place rather than Pingyin. How can those several ditches in Pingyin work to prevent their attack?" But Duke Ling shut his ears to Susha's suggestion, and ordered deep ditches of one *li* in width and length to be dug. Then he chose choice soldiers to guard against the enemy.

Seeing that the Qi troops defended the city by high walls and deep ditches, Zhonghang Yan, the Commander-in-chief of the State of Jin, knew that the enemy would not easily come out for a decisive battle. So, he said to his officers, "The Qi troops are afraid of us so that they take such a strategy. It seems that they will not come out for a decisive battle with us soon. Therefore, we must defeat them by stratagem." His officers replied, "We are ready for your order." After that, Zhonghang Yan gave them confidential instructions and ordered all the troops to take actions respectively.

According to Zhonghang Yan's disposition, troops from the states of Lu and Wei would advance from Xuju while troops from the states of Zhu and Ju would march forward by way of Chengyang. Both troops would attack from Langya and the major forces of the State of Jin would break into Pingyin head-on. Zhonghang Yan started to deploy deceptive forces after the troops from the states of Lu, Wei, Zhu and Ju had set out. First he ordered the soldiers to make many straw men and prepare banners, flags and tree branches. After all was set, he said to Minister Zhang Junchen, "Put up banners and flags in all strategic mountain fields. Put up those armored straw men in empty chariots. Fasten broken wood and branches to the back of chariots. Then let soldiers drive the chariots to and fro in the valleys." Zhang Junchen did what he was told.

After the deceptive forces were deployed, Zhonghang Yan ordered his soldiers to load wood and stones into the chariots and ordered the infantry to take sacks of soil with them. Then he directed the three troops to launch an attack on Pingyin from the left, right and middle directions. While charging at the enemy, the three troops moved forward by filling the ditches with wood, stones and sacks of soil. They destroyed Qi's position at one stroke. Xi Guifu, the General of the Qi troops, escaped back to Pingyin and reported the emergency to Duke Ling. Duke Ling hurried to Mount Wu to have a bird's-eye view of the movement of the enemy, only to find banners and flags flying and chariots speeding in all strategic mountain fields. The dust blotted out the sky and the Sun Tzu. Extremely frightened by the scene, Duke Ling thought that the allied troops were everywhere and that Pingyin was in imminent danger, so he immediately ordered a retreat and fled without fighting. Though Duke Ling was lucky enough to escape back to Linzi, two of his generals were captured by the Jin troops.

After he escaped back to the capital city Linzi, Duke Ling was still in such a panicked state that he intended to abandon the city to flee with the valuables. Gao Hou, the superior official, did his utmost to admonish him, "The allied troops won't fight for long because of the long marching distance and their huge consumption of provisions. Although Pingyin is lost, our state does not fall utterly. As long as the imperial court and the ordinary people coordinate, Linzi is sure to be held." With reluctance, Duke Ling accepted his advice. He gave up the idea of fleeing and organized military strength to defend the city.

The State of Chu had always been a strong rival of the State of Jin who struggled for power, so it took the opportunity to attack the State of Zheng, the bridgehead of the State of Jin to defend against Chu. When asked for help by the State of Zheng, the Jin troops had to retreat from the State of Qi. As a result, Duke Ling survived the disaster.

In *Sun Tzu's Art of War*, Sun Tzu said, "Those skilled in war bring the enemy to the field of battle and are not brought there by him. One able to make the enemy come of his own accord does so by offering him some advantage. And one able to stop him from coming does so by preventing him with foreseeable consequences. Thus, when the enemy is at ease, try to tire him; when he is well fed, try to starve him; when he is at rest, try to make him move." Know the enemy situation to the greatest extent and conceal our troops without ascertainable shape, then the most penetrating spies cannot pry nor can the wise man conspire against you. This is how the Jin troops defeated the Qi army.

知有余与不足——魏舒"毁车为行"变战法

《孙子兵法·虚实篇》：通过筹划谋算，去了解敌人作战计划的得失；挑动敌军去掌握敌人的活动规律；通过展示军形，去察知敌人所处地形的有利与不利；通过与敌作试探性的接触，去摸清敌人兵力的虚实强弱。

　　公元前541年，晋军与无终、群狄的军队爆发了战事，因战场处于山地和丘陵地带，这对以车战为主的晋国军队来说，是个巨大的挑战。

　　在中国古代，把居于四方的少数民族分别称为蛮、夷、戎、狄，其中居于南方的叫蛮，东方的叫夷，北方的叫狄，西方的叫戎，故《春秋》上说"内诸夏而外夷狄"。与中原相比，这些少数民族地区的文化还不发达，当时称之为蛮、夷、戎、狄，是带有贬义的。

晋国的西边和北边与以游牧为生的戎、狄诸部落为邻。这些部落乘中原诸侯争强称霸战事不断之际，经常侵扰晋国边境地区，双方互有输赢。晋厉公在位时，荒淫无度，信任奸佞，随意诛杀忠良大臣，弄得民心不稳，内乱不断。后来晋大夫栾书、中行偃发动政变（公元前573年），杀死晋厉公，把住在国外的公子姬周接回国，拥立他为国君，称晋悼公。晋悼公是个有作为的国君，他举贤任能、革新朝政、节用民力，使晋国又逐渐恢复了强国的地位。公元前569年，无终部落的首领嘉父派使者孟乐带着贵重的礼品来找晋大夫魏绛，托他引见悼公，请求晋国与诸戎结盟讲和。魏绛引见了使者并说服晋悼公接受和解的建议，于是晋悼公派魏绛为使，到各戎狄部落缔结互不侵犯盟约。此后二十多年间，晋国解除了后顾之忧，集中力量与南方的劲敌楚国较量。但是到了公元前541年，晋与无终及群狄部落又爆发了战争，而战地对以战车为主要突击力量的晋军来说非常不利。

在汉代以前，中国古代军队最重要的装备就是战车。据说，最早使用战车的是夏王启，他指挥的甘之战中就使用了战车。春秋战国时期是中国战车鼎盛的时代。那时的战车，一般为独辀（辕）、两轮、方形车舆（车箱），四匹马或两匹马驾车。战车上配备三名甲士，中间一人为驭手，左右两人负责搏杀。依据功能，战车又分为轻车、冲车等多种类型。作战时，实施进攻的战斗队形以战车为核心，中间一乘战车，前左右三方各配属24名步兵，加上车上3名甲士，共75名，称为乘。这样一来，战车不仅是衡量军力强弱的标志，也是衡量国力强弱的主要标志。所以，在春秋时代，国家的大小或强弱，常以"千乘之国"、"万乘之国"来表达，军队投入战争数量，也以"百乘"、"千乘"来表示。战车适用于平原作战，跟以骑兵为主的戎狄在山地及丘陵地带作战，战车就不占优势了。这正是晋军遇到的问题。

战斗一开始，无终、群狄的骑兵机动灵活，而且运动速度快，晋军的战车虽然威武壮观，但是在崎岖的山地和凹凸的丘陵地带，不仅进军的速度缓慢，简直就像蜗牛在爬行，而且战阵也因受地形限制而无法排列，战车突击的威力完全无法施展，晋军因此受到不少损失。面对如此艰难的局面，晋将魏舒果断地提出"毁车以为行"。他说："若继续以战车应对敌人的骑兵，很难在这样险要的地形上取胜，我们不如放弃战车，专用步兵，在险要隘口之处阻击敌人，这样才有可能取胜。"将军荀吴坚决反对。他说："自古以来，战车包打胜仗，从来没有听说放弃战车只靠步兵能打胜仗的。我们怎么能丢掉祖先留下的传统而改用毫无先例的战法呢？这简直是胡闹。"魏舒说："根据地形变化，调整用兵之法。这是指挥者的责任。如果放弃战车改用步兵作战以前没有的话，那么从我们开始，以后不就有了吗？"荀吴还是抱着"战车包打胜仗"的观念不放，他断言，"毁车以为行"，必是送死。魏舒认为自己改革战法是"因势而制权"，毫不动摇。他果断地斩除了荀吴，巡行示众，表达了贯彻新的战略战术的决心。根据地势和敌情，魏舒对晋军作了"五阵(五种阵势)以相离"的配置，即前矩、前、后、左角、右角，引诱敌人进入险地，聚而歼之。最终，晋军夺取了这次作战的胜利，同时也打破了"车战"占统治地位的历史，为春秋末期由车战向骑兵战、方阵向线式阵形转换及变革开创了先河。

孙子在《虚实篇》中说："兵无常势，水无常形，能因敌变化而取胜者，谓之神。"然而在现实生活中，能够真正懂得这个道理并能付诸实践的人却很少。明代赵本学解《孙子兵法·始计篇》曾发出这样的感慨："古之良将全才者少，以小术而胜无术者多也。"所以，孙子非常强调将帅要善于通过实战来学习和总结。他在《虚实篇》中说："通过筹划谋算，去了解敌人作战计划的得失；挑动敌军去掌握敌人的活动规律；通过展示军形，去察知敌人所处地形的有利与不利；通过与敌作试探性的接触，去摸清敌人兵力的虚实强弱。"魏舒"毁车以为行"的改革，正是从实战中获得的经验和灵感。

LEARN WHERE THE ENEMY'S STRENGTH IS ABUNDANT AND WHERE DEFICIENT
— Wei Shu Changed the Law of War by "Abandoning Chariots and Switching Armored Soldiers to Infantrymen"

According to *Sun Tzu's Art of War*, "Analyze the enemy's plans so that you will know his shortcomings as well as strong points. Agitate him in order to ascertain the pattern of his movement. Lure him out to reveal his dispositions and ascertain his position. Launch a probing attack in order to learn where his strength is abundant and where deficient."

In 541 BC, a battle broke out between the State of Jin and the Wuzhong and Di tribes. Because the battlefield was located in mountainous areas and hilly lands, it was a great challenge for the Jin troops who were only good at chariot warfare.

In ancient China, the neighboring ethnic minority groups were called Southern Man, Eastern Yi, Northern Rong and Western Di respectively. Therefore, *The Spring and Autumn Annals* said, "Inside are the vassal states and outside are the Yi and Di ethnic minority groups." Compared with the Central Plains, cultures of these ethnic minority groups were backward, so the Chinese characters Man, Yi, Rong and Di were all derogatory at that time.

The nomadic Rong and Di tribes lived to the west and the north of the State of Jin respectively. At the time, dukes on the Central Plains continuously launched wars for power. The two tribes took the opportunity to frequently invade the borders of the State of Jin, and both sides had losses and gains. When Duke Li of the State of Jin was in power, he was excessively licentious, trusted treacherous officials, and killed faithful officials at will, which led to national panic and constant internal disturbances. Later, Minister Luan Shu of the State of Jin and Zhonghang Yan staged a coup (in 573 BC) and killed Duke Li. They welcomed Ji Zhou, the prince living abroad back to the state and crowned him ruler, who was known as Duke Dao. As a successful ruler, Duke Dao selected the worthy and promoted the capable, innovated court politics and economized on the financial resources of the people. As a result, the State of Jin gradually regained its status as a power. In 569 BC, Jia Fu, the leader of the Wuzhong tribe, sent Meng Le as a messenger to take valuable gifts to visit Minister Wei Jiang of the state. Meng Le pleaded with Wei Jiang for an audience with Duke Dao to request peace talks and creating an alliance with the ethnic minority groups. Wei Jiang introduced Meng Le and persuaded Duke Dao into accepting a compromise. Duke Dao sent Wei Jiang as a messenger to sign a non-aggression covenant with the Rong and Di tribes. In the following twenty years, without any fear of disturbance from the back, the State of Jin concentrated its strength to rival the powerful State of Chu in the south. However, in 541 BC, a battle broke out between the State of Jin and the Wuzhong and Di tribes, and the battlefield was extremely unfavorable for the Jin troops, who still depended on chariots in warfare.

Before the Han Dynasty (206 BC–220 AD), chariots were the most important piece of ancient Chinese military equipment. It was said that King Qi of the Xia Dynasty (2100 BC–1600 BC) first used chariots in the Battle of Gan. The use of chariots in China reached the peak in the Spring and Autumn Period. At that time, a chariot, drawn either by four or two horses, was composed of a single pole, two wheels and a square carriage. Each chariot was equipped with three armored soldiers. The man in the middle was the charioteer and the other two standing beside him were responsible for fighting. According to the military function, chariots were divided into many types, such as light ones, heavy ones and such. In warfare, the battle formation was centered on chariots. Each chariot also had 75 soldiers, 24 infantrymen in the front and on its left and right respectively, and 3 armored soldiers in the chariot. Chariots were not only a symbol of military strength, but also a sign of national strength. Therefore, in the Spring and Autumn Period, "a state of 1,000 chariots" or "a state of 10,000 chariots" were terms to indicate the strength or power of a state. Similarly, "100 chariots" or "1, 000 chariots" indicated the number of soldiers in warfare. Chariots were suitable in warfare on the plains, but they had no advantage over the cavalry of the Rong and Di tribes in the mountainous areas and hilly lands. This was the problem that the Jin troops encountered.

The cavalry of the Wuzhong and Di tribes were faster with more mobility and flexibility than the Jin chariots. Although the chariots looked mighty and spectacular, they were as slow as snails in the uneven mountainous areas and hilly lands. Besides, restricted by geographical features, the chariots could not be arrayed and fully put to use. As a result, as soon as the battle started, the Jin troops suffered great losses. Confronted with such a difficult situation, Wei Shu, the general, decisively put forward a strategy of "abandoning chariots and switching armored soldiers to infantrymen". He said, "If we continue to use chariots to deal with the enemy's cavalry, it will be difficult for us to win in such a strategic position. So we may as well abandon chariots and use infantrymen to check the enemy in strategic narrow mountainous passes. Only in this way can we win the battle." Xun Wu, another general, was absolutely opposed to him and said, "Since ancient times, chariots have guaranteed victories. No war was won by infantry rather than chariots. How can we give up the tradition of our ancestors and switch to an unprecedented law of war? This is simply nonsense." Wei Shu replied, "According to changes in terrain, a commander should adjust his tactics of using his forces. If there is no historical record of abandoning chariots and switching armored soldiers to infantrymen, we will be the first." Xun Wu still stuck to the idea that "chariots were a must in victory" and he asserted that Wei Shu's strategy was none other than suicide. Wei Shu was determined to carry out his reform in warfare because he "took the field situation into consideration and acted in accordance with what was advantageous". Without any hesitation, he beheaded Xun Wu publicly, expressing his resolution to carry out his new military strategy. According to the terrain and the enemy situation, Wei Shu deployed the Jin troops into "five formations at intervals", namely, the frontal square, the front, rear, left and right angles. The enemy could be lured into the strategic position, surrounded and then annihilated. Eventually, the Jin troops won the victory, and at the same time, they broke the dominance of chariots in warfare. This battle also set a precedent for the change in warfare in the late Spring and Autumn Period. Chariots were switched to cavalry and a phalanx formation to a linear one.

In *Sun Tzu's Art of War*, Sun Tzu said, "As water has no constant form, there are in warfare no constant conditions. Thus, one able to win the victory by modifying his tactics in accordance with the enemy situation may be said to be divine." However, in reality, few people can really understand this principle and apply it to practice. When Zhao Benxue of Ming Dynasty annotated *Sun Tzu's Art of War*, he sighed, "In ancient times, there were few able generals and all-round talents, while there were many people who use small tactics to defeat those who had no tactics at all." So Sun Tzu emphasized that generals should learn and summarize through actual combats. In *Sun Tzu's Art of War*, he said, "Analyze the enemy's plans so that you will know his shortcomings as well as strong points. Agitate him in order to ascertain the pattern of his movement. Lure him out to reveal his dispositions and ascertain his position. Launch a probing attack in order to learn where his strength is abundant and where deficient." The reform of "abandoning chariots and switching armored soldiers to infantrymen" was the very experience and inspiration Wei Shu obtained from the actual combat.

避锐击惰——齐鲁长勺之战

《孙子兵法·军争篇》：避开敌人的锐气，攻击敌人的惰气，这是掌握军队士气的方法。

公元前 684 年，齐国大举进击鲁国，起因是鲁国曾经插手齐国的政治，支持公子小白的政敌公子纠，后公子小白继位，即齐桓公。他先在乾时(今山东桓台县南)大败鲁军，威逼鲁国杀死了公子纠。接着又派大军进攻鲁国，以清算鲁庄公对自己的不敬。鲁国公被迫应战，君臣上下都很担心这场战争的结局。这时，有一个人求见鲁庄公，他的名字叫曹刿。

曹刿的一个同乡是鲁庄公的守门人，曹刿想通过他求见庄公。这位同乡对曹刿说："怎么打仗，是那些当官们的事儿，你是老百姓，何必去掺和呢？"曹刿说："那些当官的浅陋，不一定能深谋远虑。"同乡被说服了，答应去通报，于是鲁庄公召见了曹刿。

曹刿一见到鲁庄公就开门见山地问：现在齐国大军压境，您靠什么去和齐军作战呢？鲁庄公说："我在位以来，吃的、穿的、住的、用的，从不独占，总是分一些给别人；祭祀用的牛、羊、玉帛，从来都严格按照礼仪规定办理，一直是很虔诚的。"鲁庄公的意思是臣民们会为他去打仗；神灵会保佑鲁国打胜仗。曹刿说："单靠这两点还不足以应战。"鲁庄公又说："国内大小案件，我虽然不能全部亲自调查，但在处理的时候我是从不马虎的。"言外之意是说他执政清廉，力求避免冤假错案，注意维护民众的利益。曹刿说："您有这一条，抗击齐军就好办了。"曹刿的意思是，国家要打赢一场战争，光靠统治者身边少数常受恩惠的人是不行的，依靠神灵保佑也是不行的，只有政通人和、取信于民，这才是国家御敌取胜的根本。鲁庄公很欣赏曹刿的见识，于是就让他跟随自己一起去战场。

　　齐军和鲁军在长勺摆开战场。当时，战车是军队进攻和防守的主要装备，开战前，双方先把战车排列成一定的阵形，然后正面交战，战争的胜负往往由阵形保持得如何来判定。曹刿和鲁庄公坐在一辆战车上，齐军率先击鼓向鲁军发动了进攻，鲁庄公想马上下令反击，曹刿急忙对鲁庄公说："现在没到反击的时候。"鲁军严阵防守，齐军的第一次冲锋没能奏效，只好退回原地。不久，齐军又第二次击鼓冲锋，鲁庄公又想下令反击，曹刿马上阻止说："现在也还没到反击的良机。"鲁军继续巍然不动，严阵防守。鲁庄公不明白曹刿为什么一而再地不让反击。曹刿说："用兵打仗，靠的是士气，反复进攻，必然消耗士兵的体力，反复进攻又不能取胜，必然挫伤士兵的锐气，到敌军精疲力竭的时候再反攻，就能一举而胜。"曹刿的原话很精练，他说："夫战，勇气也。一鼓作气，再而衰，三而竭。彼竭我盈，故克之。"

　　过了一会儿，齐军第三次击鼓发起冲锋，曹刿对鲁庄公说："现在是时候了，您可以下令击鼓反击了！"中国古代打仗时，用金（金属）、鼓、旌旗指挥军队战斗，击鼓是进兵，鸣金是收兵，旌旗管节度。鲁庄公一声令下，鲁军鼓声大作，鲁国士兵早已经憋足劲儿要与齐军较量，听到鼓声大震，一起向齐军压了过去。已经疲劳不堪的齐军抵挡不住鲁军的猛烈冲击，军阵大乱，落败而逃。鲁庄公正要下令追击，曹刿说："且慢！"他跳下战车，仔细观察了一下齐军留下的车辙印，然后登上战车，又站在车前的横木上瞭望齐军的情况，有把握地对庄公说："可以追击。"原来，曹刿担心齐军诈退，他看到车辙痕迹很乱，齐军队伍不整，知道敌人是真败，可以追击。鲁军很快就追上溃逃的齐军，打了一个漂亮的胜仗。

长勺之战，鲁胜齐败，曹刿起了举足轻重的作用。他对战争胜败因素的认识，对士兵气、力与战场胜负关系的分析，对战机的把握以及战略战术等，都在《孙子兵法》中得到精彩的提炼和升华。比如，孙子在《始计篇》中说，战争是关乎百姓生死、国家存亡的大事，平时要从道、天、地、将、法等五个方面经营军事，战时才能取胜。孙子解释说："道者，令民与上同意也。"也就是曹刿说的那种关心百姓、取信于民的善政。孙子在《军争篇》中说，对于敌人的军队，可以使其士气低落，可以使其将帅的决心动摇。战场上军队的士气犹如天气早晚的变化，刚投入战斗时士气饱满；过一段时间，士气就会逐渐懈怠；到了最后，士气就会衰竭。所以，善于指挥作战的将帅，总是先避开敌人锐气，等到其懈怠和衰竭时再去打击他。再如《军争篇》中的"后人发，先人至"、"以逸待劳"等。孙子的这些思想和战略战术原则，既继承了曹刿论战的思想，又将以往的战争经验升华到理论的高度。

AVOID THE ENEMY WHEN HIS SPIRIT IS KEEN AND ATTACK HIM WHEN IT IS SLUGGISH
— The Battle of Changshao between the State of Qi and the State of Lu

According to *Sun Tzu's Art of War*, "Avoid the enemy when his spirit is keen and attack him when it is sluggish. This is the control of the morale factor".

In 684 BC, the State of Qi launched a large-scale attack on the State of Lu. The cause was that the State of Lu once interfered with the internal affairs of Qi and supported Prince Jiu, the political opponent of Prince Xiaobai who later succeeded to the throne and was known as Duke Huan. Duke Huan first routed the Lu troops in Qianshi (in the south of Huantai County of Shandong Province today) and intimidated the State of Lu into killing Prince Jiu. Then, he sent troops to attack the State of Lu in order to settle a score with Duke Zhuang, who was disrespectful to him. Duke Zhuang was compelled to meet the challenge. Both Duke Zhuang and his officials were worried about the outcome of the war. At that time, a man named Cao Gui requested an audience with Duke Zhuang.

One of Cao Gui's fellow villagers was a doorkeeper of Duke Zhuang, and Cao Gui turned to him for help to have an audience with Duke Zhuang. The man told Cao Gui, "It is the officials' responsibility to decide how to fight. You are nothing but a civilian. Why mess up?" Cao Gui replied, "The officials are shortsighted. They make no long-term plans." Having been persuaded, the man promised to report to Duke Zhuang, who then summoned Cao Gui.

When Cao Gui met the Duke, he straightly asked, "What encouragement do you have to fight since the Qi troops are crushing the border". The Duke said, "Since I came into power, I have never monopolized food, clothes, shelters or other necessities. I make a point of sharing them with others. Besides, I have been pious in offering sacrifices of cows, sheep and treasures according to the rites at worshipping ceremonies." What the Duke meant was that his officials would fight for him and the gods would bless him with a victory. Cao Gui said, "These are not sufficient to win the battle." The Duke said again, "I judge each case, big or small, fairly and reasonably, even though I couldn't make the investigation personally." The implication was that he was incorruptible so that he avoided miscarriages of justice and protected the interests of his people. Cao Gui said, "Well, you may venture the battle on that." What he meant was that a state could not win a victory simply by the minority around the ruler who often received his kindness or by blessings of the gods. A state would stand a chance of winning as long as its people lived harmoniously, the government functioned well and won the trust of its people. Appreciating Cao Gui's knowledge, Duke Zhuang challenged him to the battlefield.

The two armies confronted each other in Changshao. At that time, chariots were the primary equipment for both attack and defense and were arranged in certain formations before a battle. Then, the two sides would launch a frontal attack on each other and the outcome of a battle would be generally decided by how well the formations were maintained. Cao Gui and Duke Zhuang were in the same chariot. When the Qi troops took the lead to beat the drums to launch an attack, Duke Zhuang wanted to order an immediate counter-attack. But Cao Gui said hurriedly, "It is not the time to fight back." The Lu troops defended in full battle array. The first charge of the Qi troops was not effective, so they had to retreat to their original place. Soon they beat the drums to launch another attack. Duke Zhuang wanted to order a counter-attack but was stopped by Cao Gui again, who said, "The golden opportunity to fight back has not come yet." The Lu troops were still motionless. Duke Zhuang did not understand why Cao Gui did not allow a counter-attack. Cao Gui replied, "In fighting, all depends on the courageous spirit. When the drums beat for the first time, it excites the spirit. A second advance occasions a diminution of the spirit, and with a third, the spirit is exhausted. With our spirit at the highest pitch, we may fall on them easily when their spirit is exhausted and as a result, we can conquer them for sure."

After a while, when the Qi troops launched the third attack, Cao Gui said to Duke Zhuang, "Now comes the time. Your Lordship, please give orders to beat the drums and strike back." In ancient China, gongs, drums and flags were used to direct the operations of war. An army advanced at the beating of the drums and retreated when the gongs were struck. Flags were used to dispatch the forces. As soon as Duke Zhuang issued an order, the Lu troops sounded their drums. The soldiers could hardly wait to fight back against the Qi troops, so they bore down upon them at the beating of the drums. Unable to withstand them, the exhausted Qi troops were defeated and fled in a rout. When the Duke

Zhuang was about to dash after them, Cao Gui said, "Wait a minute!" He got down from the chariot and examined the tracks left by their chariot wheels. Then he remounted, got on the front-bar, and observed the fleeing enemy. After that, he said with confidence, "Pursue!" It turned out that Cao Gui was afraid that the Qi troops were feigning to retreat. But when he found the traces of their wheels were confused, he knew for sure that the enemy was actually defeated and could be pursued. Very soon the Lu troops caught up with the Qi troops and won a brilliant victory.

Cao Gui played a pivotal role in the outcome of the battle of Changshao between the State of Lu and the State of Qi. Greatly refined and sublimated in *Sun Tzu's Art of War* was Cao Gui's understanding of factors determining the outcome of a battle, his analysis of the impact of morale and strength of an army on the outcome of a battle, his ability to seize the opportunity to win a victory and his application of strategies. For instance, in *Sun Tzu's Art of War*, Sun Tzu said, "War is a matter of vital importance to the state, a matter of life or death, a road either to survival or to ruin. He who can manage an army through the following five factors — politics, weather, terrain, the commander and doctrine — will win a victory." Sun Tzu explained, "Politics means the thing which causes the people to be in harmony with their ruler." Politics here was actually what Cao Gui said to care about the common people and win their trust. In *Sun Tzu's Art of War*, Sun Tzu said, "An army may be robbed of its spirit and its commander deprived of his confidence. At the beginning of a campaign, the spirits of soldiers are keen; after a certain period of time, they flag, and in the later stage the soldiers are in no mood to fight." Therefore, those skilled in war avoid the enemy when his spirit is keen and attack him when it is sluggish and his soldiers homesick. There are other examples such as "setting out after the enemy and arriving at the battlefield before him" and "awaiting the exhausted enemy at your ease" in *Sun Tzu's Art of War*. All these thoughts, strategic and tactical principles not only reflect Cao Gui's thinking on war, but also are a theoretical distillation of the experience gained from the previous wars.

兵以利动——宋襄公违利致败

《孙子兵法·军争篇》：用兵作战以诈谋权术为其策略基础、以是否有利为行动原则，并以具体情况的变化灵活掌握兵力分散或集中为原则。

公元前 638 年(鲁僖公二十二年)3 月，宋襄公兴兵伐郑，招致郑国的友邦楚国的进攻，于是，宋、楚两军在泓水摆开战场。

自周平王东迁以后，诸侯乘王室衰落，纷纷夺城掠地，争当霸主。春秋初期，郑国首先站出来企图号令诸侯，但霸业未成就被齐国取而代之。在管仲的辅佐下，齐桓公北定诸戎，向南侵蔡伐楚，观兵召陵，成为中原第一霸主。齐桓公死后，宋襄公想取代齐桓公，按照周朝公、侯、伯、子、男五等公封等级，宋襄公的地位最高，但是宋国国力不行，诸侯在亳都会盟的时候，郑文公首先倡议尊国力雄厚的楚王为盟主，引起宋襄公的不满。后来，郑文公又带头去朝拜楚王，这让仍梦想当霸主的宋襄公无法忍受，于是兴兵伐郑。当然，楚王不会坐视不管，当宋、郑两军正在战场相持对抗的时候，楚王乘宋国国内空虚，发兵直接杀向宋国本土。宋襄公得到消息，急忙把宋军撤到泓水以抗击楚军。

楚军夜晚到达泓水，天亮后才开始渡河，对岸的宋军看得清清楚楚。宋将向宋襄公建议道："趁楚军过河之际，我们杀过去，一定大获全胜！"宋襄公说："宋乃仁义之师，楚军渡河未竟就攻打的话，不合乎仁义。"宋将对襄公说："宋军少，楚军多，等楚军渡完河再打的话，我们就很危险了。"宋襄公很自信地说："宋军仁义有余，一定能像当年周武王打败殷纣王那样，以少胜多。"

宋军已经渡河完毕，宋将又向襄公建议发起进攻。宋襄公还是不同意。按照当时作战的规矩，双方要鸣鼓列阵而战。所以宋襄公说："不鼓不成列！"在宋襄公看来，"半渡而击"是不仁义的，攻击未列好阵的对手也是不符合"仁义"标准的。所以，他坚持等待楚军渡完河、列好阵之后，再堂堂正正地开战。结果，兵力本来就弱的宋军一次又一次失去取胜的机会，最后被打得大败，宋襄公也受了重伤，差一点死在战场上。将士们埋怨他不该讲什么仁义，招致这样的惨败。宋襄公很生气地教训他们说："君子不重伤，不擒二毛。"意思是说：在战场上不打已经受伤的敌人，不抓已有白头发上了年纪的人，这样才称得上是君子。宋襄公至死都没有明白军事斗争的本质，不仅自己吃了苦果，死于箭伤，也害了宋军。

也许，宋襄公和宋军的血没有白流，泓水之战一百多年以后，《孙子兵法》对春秋时代的战争有许多精辟的总结。比如，孙子在《军争篇》说："用兵作战是以诈谋权术为其策略基础、以是否有利为行动原则，并以具体情况的变化灵活掌握兵力分散或集中为原则的。"在《行军篇》中说："如果敌军渡水来攻，有利的做法是不要在江河中迎战，而是要在他渡过一半、部分渡过时攻击他。"诸如此类的说法，必定包含了像宋襄公这样血的教训所换来的认识。

MOVE WHEN IT IS ADVANTAGEOUS
— Duke Xiang of the State of Song Was Defeated for Not Utilizing His Advantages

According to *Sun Tzu's Art of War*, "War is based on deception. Move when it is advantageous and create changes in the situation by dispersal and concentration of forces."

In March of 638 BC (In the twenty-second year of Duke Xi of the State of Lu), Duke Xiang of the State of Song sent a punitive expedition against the State of Zheng and thus incurred an attack from the State of Chu, a close ally of Zheng. The battlefield was at the bank of the Hong River.

Since King Ping of the Zhou Dynasty moved his capital eastwards, the royal court had declined. The neighboring states took the opportunity to plunder cities and lands continuously, struggling for power. In the early Spring and Autumn Period, the State of Zheng first attempted to issue orders to the other dukes, however, it was replaced by the State of Qi before it built up power. Under the assistance of Guan Zhong, Duke Huan of the State of Qi suppressed the Rong tribes in the north, sent punitive expeditions against the states of Cai and Chu in the south, demonstrated the military strength in Zhaoling, and finally became the first overlord on the Central Plains. After the death of Duke Huan, Duke Xiang of the State of Song wanted to take his place. In the Zhou Dynasty, the rankings of the five noble titles were Duke, Marquis, Count, Viscount and Baron. Duke Xiang of the State of Song was in the highest position but his national strength was weak. At the convention of all dukes in Haodu, Duke Wen of the State of Zheng first proposed honoring the King of the powerful State of Chu as the overlord, which irritated Duke Xiang. Later, Duke Wen took the lead in paying respects to the King of Chu and Duke Xiang could not tolerate it any longer. As a result, Duke Xiang sent a punitive expedition against the State of Zheng. Of course, the King of Chu would not sit by and tolerate this. When the Song troops confronted the Zheng troops in the battlefield, the King of Chu seized the opportunity to attack the State of Song. When Duke Xiang got the news, he hurriedly withdrew his troops to the bank of the Hong River to check the enemy's attack.

The Chu troops arrived at the river bank at night, and began crossing the river after daybreak. The Song troops saw everything clearly from the other side of the river. One general suggested to Duke Xiang, "If we attack them as they are halfway across the river, we are sure to win." Duke Xiang said, "Our troops are troops of benevolence. How can we attack them before they reach the opposite shore?" The general said, "The enemy is numerically stronger than us. If we wait for them to cross the river, we will be in danger." But Duke Xiang said confidently, "Just as King Wu of Zhou defeated King Zhou of Shang, a benevolent army like us will surely defeat the many with the few."

After the Chu troops crossed the river, the general proposed an attack but was refused again. According to the battle rules at that time, a war could only be started after the drums were beat and the battle formations were arranged. So Duke Xiang said, "Do not beat the drums! Do not line up the battle formation!" In his eyes, it was not benevolent to attack the enemy either when they were halfway across the river or before their battle formation was completed. As a result, he waited until the Chu troops landed on the bank and lined up the battle formation. The Song troops, which were numerically weaker, lost the chance of winning time and again and were finally routed. Duke Xiang had a narrow escape but was seriously wounded. The generals complained that it was his benevolence that caused such a severe defeat. However, Duke Xiang said angrily to them, "In fighting, the benevolent should not kill their enemies who are already wounded; neither should they capture the old and weak remnant troops." Duke Xiang did not understand the essence of military struggles even before his death. Eating the bitter fruit of war, he died from an arrow wound and brought a disaster to his troops.

Perhaps, both Duke Xiang and his troops did not shed their blood in vain, for more than one hundred years after the Battle of the Hong River, *Sun Tzu's Art of War* gave many penetrating summaries about the wars in the Spring and Autumn Period. For example, in *Sun Tzu's Art of War*, Sun Tzu said, "War is based on deception. Move when it is advantageous and create changes in the situation by dispersal and concentration of forces. When an advancing enemy crosses water, do not meet him in midstream. It is advantageous to allow half of his forces to cross and then strike." Such remarks must contain an understanding of Duke Xiang's lesson paid for in blood.

后发制人——晋楚城濮之战

《孙子兵法·军争篇》：要迂回绕道，用小利引诱敌人，做到比敌人后出动而先达到所要争夺的要地，这就是懂得了以迂为直的计谋了。

公元前632年，晋军与楚军在卫国境内的城濮打了一场有战略意义的战役，结果楚败晋胜，从此晋国取代楚国的霸主地位，这就是历史上著名的经典战役之一——晋楚城濮之战。

晋国位于黄河流域，楚国位于长江和汉水之间，一个在北方，一个在南方，两个并不搭界的诸侯国，却在他们之间的卫国打了一场恶仗，起因只源于两个字——争霸。

说起来，楚国还曾经有恩于晋国呢。当初晋国因争夺王位发生内乱，晋公子重耳流亡国外。途径楚国的时候，楚成王把他当作国宾一样隆重款待，他问当时身处逆境的重耳："如果公子将来回国执政，将如何报答楚国呢？"重耳回答说："倘若能借楚王您的威力回晋国执政的话，我愿意和楚国结为友好之邦。如果不得已和您楚王的军队在中原地区相遇的话，那么我将退避三舍。"中国古代军队行军，一般是三十里一停，称为一舍，三舍就是九十里。重耳的意思是说，如果有一天，晋楚两国军队发生战争，晋军退让九十里不战，作为对楚王您今日厚待之恩的报答。如果我退避三舍仍然不能使您停止进攻的话，那么我只好全副武装地与您周旋了。公元前636年，在外流亡了十九年的重耳在秦国的帮助下回到晋国执掌了国政，他就是历史上著名的一代霸主晋文公。

楚国是南方的大国，但是不满足于偏居东南一隅，早在楚文王时期，就开始向黄河流域扩张，先后攻占了申、息、邓等小国。楚文王死后，楚成王继位，此时齐桓公称霸中原，楚成王没有机会向北扩展。齐桓公死后，齐国发生内乱，国力衰落，楚成王借机向中原扩张。公元前633年，楚成王借口救援鲁国之名，发兵攻打齐国和宋国。宋国向晋国求援，晋文公正想遏制楚国向中原的扩张，于是就以救宋为名，出兵抗击楚军。

当时，晋国的兵力远不如楚国，晋文公听取大臣的建议，采取先攻楚的盟国曹、卫两国，迫使楚军分兵救援以解宋国之围，然后寻机与楚军作战。公元前632年初，晋文公以当年流亡时遭到曹国国君共公侮辱为由，向卫国借道伐曹，遭到卫国拒绝，于是晋文公命令晋军先攻破卫国，接着又拿下曹国，活捉了曹共公。但出乎意料的是，楚军并没有分兵来救曹、卫，而是继续围攻宋都商丘。这时晋文公有点左右为难了，去救宋吧，晋军的力量不如楚军，没有必胜的把握，而且直接进攻楚军，会背忘恩负义的名声；不去救吧，宋军最终必然投降楚军，晋国会失去盟友。正在为难之际，大臣先轸对晋文公说："可以利用矛盾智取。让宋国假装疏远晋国，然后备厚礼请齐国和秦国出面调停，请求楚军退兵。楚军若不接受，必然得罪了齐、秦两国，我们再联合齐、秦进攻楚军，必然大胜。"果然，楚成王不接受调节，触怒了齐、秦两国，结果晋、楚双方的力量发生了根本变化。

晋、楚两军的正面冲突终于爆发了，楚将子玉率楚军扑向晋军。晋文公见楚军来势凶猛，为了避其锋芒，遂命令晋军后撤。晋军将领不理解晋文公的用兵意图，说还没有打怎么就后撤呢？晋文公说："我当年曾许诺楚成王，晋楚万一发生战争，我一定退避三舍以报答他的恩德。现在我得恪守诺言。"晋军一连退了九十里，到达了卫国的城濮，这里地理条件等各方面对晋军都很有利。楚将子玉见晋军不战而退，以为是晋军不敢战，越发追得紧，最后在城濮相遇。楚将子玉依仗兵强，一扎好营寨就派使者去晋文公挑战。晋文公派使者回复子玉说："我因不敢忘记楚王的恩惠，才退避到这里。既然晋军退避仍得不到您的谅解的话，那也只好决战一场了。"

晋楚两军的决战开始了。子玉分楚军为左中右三路进攻，晋军以上、中、下三军应对。晋军根据楚将子玉骄傲轻敌和楚军左右翼相对薄弱的特点，先以下军攻楚右军。晋下军佐将胥臣命令士卒把驾战车的马用虎皮蒙上，出其不意地向楚右军冲杀过去。楚右军是由陈、蔡两国军队组成的，本来战斗力就弱，突然遭到晋军奇异的进攻，惊慌失措，纷纷奔逃。就在楚右军崩溃之际，晋上军主将狐毛故意在指挥车上高高竖起两面醒目的大旗，命令士兵一接触楚军就装作败阵，后撤时在战车后部绑上树枝，这样，树枝带起的尘土遮天蔽日，让楚军看不出晋军的真实情况。果然，站在高处指挥的子玉以为晋军溃败，立即下令左翼部队追杀，晋中军主帅先轸见楚军上钩，横空出击，晋上军回军夹击，楚左军基本上被歼灭了。子玉见左右两军均以失败，为了保住中军，急忙下令收兵，退出战场。城濮之战，最终以晋军胜利楚军失败而告终。

这一战，晋军先退而后战，做到了有理、有利、有节。晋军根据双方的实力和特点，抓住楚军的弱点，突然进击和诱敌深入，做到了知彼知己，战术灵活，最终创造了以少胜多的奇迹。城濮之战，不仅改变了晋楚两国的历史地位，楚国由此衰落，而晋文公则走上了霸主地位，而且，晋军出色的谋略和成功的战术，也为中国古代兵学增添了灿烂的一章，如孙子在《军争篇》中说的："后人发，先人至，此知迂直之计也。"又说："善用兵者，避其锐气，击其惰气，此治气者也。"还说："以近待远，以逸待劳，以饱待饥，此治力者也。"

GAIN MASTERY BY STRIKING ONLY AFTER THE ENEMY HAS STRUCK
— The Battle of Chengpu between the State of Jin and the State of Chu

According to *Sun Tzu's Art of War*, "March by an indirect route and divert the enemy by enticing him with a bait. So doing, you may set out after he does and arrive at the battlefield before him. One able to do this shows the knowledge of the artifice of diversion."

In 632 BC, a battle, which bore strategic significance, broke out in Chengpu of the State of Wei. It was between the State of Jin and the State of Chu, with the latter routed. Ever since, the State of Jin had replaced Chu's dominant position. This was one of the famous classical battles in history — the Battle of Chengpu between the State of Jin and the State of Chu.

The State of Jin was located in the Yellow River basin while the State of Chu between the Yangtze River and the Han River, with the former in the north and the latter in the south. Though these two states had no shared border, they had a difficult fight in the State of Wei, lying between them. The reason was simple indeed — struggling for power.

It was said that the State of Jin owed the State of Chu a favor. When internal fights for the throne broke out in the State of Jin, Prince Chong'er was forced to live in exile in a foreign land. When he got to the State of Chu, King Cheng treated him respectfully as if he were a state guest. He asked Chong'er, "How will you repay me when you return to your state and become ruler one day?" Chong'er replied, "If I'm honored to be the new king back to my state, I will form a friendly alliance with your state. If a war breaks out one day between us on the Central Plains, I will definitely order my troops to retreat three *she* (one *she* is equivalent to thirty *li* in ancient China, *li* is a Chinese unit of length equivalent to 1/2 kilometer)." What he meant was that if a war happened between the two states one day, the Jin troops would retreat ninety *li* in return for the King's favor, and if under that condition, the State of Chu did not stop attacking, he would have to fight back. In 636 BC, with the help of the State of Qin, Chong'er, after nineteen years of exile, finally went back to his state and succeeded to the throne. He was the famous overload in history — Duke Wen of the State of Jin.

The State of Chu was a big vassal state in the south, but it was not content with occupying a small southeast corner. When King Wen of the State of Chu was in power, he started to expand to the Yellow River basin, annexing several small states such as the states of Shen, Xi and Deng. After the death of King Wen, King Cheng succeeded to the throne and he had no chance to expand northwards because at that time Duke Huan of the State of Qi was dominating over the Central Plains. After the death of Duke Huan, internal disturbances broke out and the State of Qi was on the wane. King Cheng took the opportunity to expand to the Central Plains. In 633 BC, on the pretext of rescuing the State of Lu, King Cheng sent troops to attack the states of Qi and Song. The State of Song appealed to the State of Jin for help. Duke Wen was just about to constrain Chu's expansion to the Central Plains, so under the banner of helping the State of Song, he sent the troops to resist the Chu troops.

At that time, the Jin army was numerically weaker than that of the State of Chu. Following his minister's advice, Duke Wen decided to attack Chu's allies first — the states of Cao and Wei. This would force Chu to divide its troops to come to their rescue, and then the Jin troops might look for an opportunity to combat the Chu army. Early in 632 BC, on the pretext of having been insulted by Duke Gong of the State of Cao in his exile, Duke Wen wanted to attack the State of Cao by way of the State of Wei. But he was refused by the State of Wei. So Duke Wen ordered his army to take Wei first and then captured Cao. Duke Gong was caught alive. But against Duke Wen's expectation, the Chu army did not send its troops to rescue the two states, but instead, it continued to besiege

Shangqiu, the capital city of the State of Song. Thus, Duke Wen was in a dilemma. If he rescued the State of Song, he was not sure of success for his army was numerically weaker than that of Chu. Besides, if he directly attacked the Chu army, he would be devoid of gratitude. But if he did not come to its rescue, the Song army would finally surrender to the State of Chu, and the State of Jin would lose its ally. Just then, Xian Zhen, an official of the State of Jin, said to Duke Wen, "We can win a victory by producing conflicts. First we may ask the State of Song to pretend to chill its relationship with us, then present the states of Qi and Qin with substantial gifts and ask them to be the mediator, requesting the Chu army to retreat. If the Chu army does not accept the mediation, it will offend these two states. Then we may join hands with them to attack the Chu army and we will surely win a sweeping victory." As expected, King Cheng did not accept the mediation, which infuriated the states of Qi and Qin. As a result, a radical change took place in the military strength between the State of Jin and the State of Chu.

The head-on conflict finally broke out between the two armies. Ziyu, the General of the State of Chu, led the troops to storm the Jin army. Seeing that the Chu army was bearing down menacingly, Duke Wen ordered the Jin army to retreat so as to avoid a direct confrontation with it. His generals were confused and asked him why they retreated without any fighting. Duke Wen replied, "I made a promise to King Cheng that if there should be a war between us, I would order my army to retreat three *she* in return for his kindness. Now I must fulfill my promise." Duke Wen moved back his army ninety *li* till Chengpu, a city of the State of Wei, which was strategically favorable to him. Under the impression that the Jin army dared not to fight back, Ziyu pursued them relentlessly. Finally they confronted each other in Chengpu. As soon as the Chu army set camps, Ziyu sent an envoy to challenge Duke Wen. A messenger was sent by Duke Wen to Ziyu, saying, "We retreated here because my Duke dares not to forget your Duke's kindness. We have to fight back, since you are still not reconciled."

The decisive battle commenced. Zi Yu divided the Chu troops into the middle force, the left and right wings. The Jin troops confronted them with the middle, upper and lower armies. Ziyu was arrogant and always took his opponents lightly. His two wings were comparatively weak in strength, so the Jin lower army took advantage of their weaknesses to attack the Chu right wing first. Xu Chen, the Vice Commander of the Jin lower army, ordered his soldiers to cover the chariot horses with tiger hides and launched an urgent, vigorous assault on the Chu right wing. The Chu right wing, with weak strength, comprised completely of armies of the states of Chen and Cai. Attacked by the Jin army, they were panicked and fled in a rout. Meanwhile, Hu Mao, the Commander of the Jin upper army, deliberately put two huge eye-catching banners up high in his chariot. He ordered the soldiers to fake a retreat as soon as they met with the enemy. When they moved back, they fastened branches to the back of chariots, raising a dust fog to obscure their movements. As expected, Ziyu, who was directing his army on high, was deceived into believing that the Jin army had been defeated. He immediately ordered the left wing to pursue it. Seeing that the Chu army swallowed the bait, Xian Zhen, the Commander-in-chief of the middle army, attacked them and the Jin upper army joined the assault. As a result, the Chu left wing was almost annihilated. Seeing that both his wings were vanquished, Ziyu ordered a retreat in order to save the middle force. The battle of Chengpu ended in the victory of the Jin army.

In this battle, the Jin army first retreated and then fought back on just grounds, to their advantage and with restraint. According to the strengths and characteristics of both sides, the Jin army took advantage of Chu's weaknesses, made a sneak attack and then lured the enemy in deep. They knew themselves and the enemy well, adopted flexible stratagems, and created the miracle of defeating the many with the few. The Battle of Chengpu changed the historical positions of the State of Jin and the State of Chu. The State of Chu had been on the wane ever since, while Duke Wen stepped into the dominant position. Besides, Jin's outstanding strategy and tactics also added a bright chapter to the military science in Chinese history. As Sun Tzu said in *Sun Tzu's Art of War*, "By marching by an indirect route and diverting the enemy, you may set out after the enemy does and arrive at the battlefield before him. One able to do this shows the knowledge of the artifice of diversion. Those skilled in war avoid the enemy when his spirit is keen and attack him when it is sluggish and his soldiers homesick. This is control of the morale factor. Close to the battlefield, those skilled in war await an enemy coming from afar; at rest, they await an exhausted enemy; with well-fed troops, they await hungry ones. This is control of the physical factor."

将计就计——晋军反败为胜

《孙子兵法·军争篇》：兵以诈立。

　　在晋楚城濮之战前夕，即公元前632年初，晋文公为了救援友邦宋国，找借口讨伐楚的盟国曹、卫。在借道卫国伐曹遭拒绝后，先拿下卫国，接着兵逼曹国。曹国大夫于朗知道曹军不是晋军的对手，便使了一个诈降计，诱晋文公入城，趁机杀之。晋文公没有看破于朗的诈降阴谋，信以为真，准备带兵入城受降。晋军元帅先轸对晋文公说："您是一国之君，不可贸然进城，我们不如将计就计，先选一个人装扮成您带兵入城，看看虚实。"晋文公听从了先轸的建议。果然不出先轸所料，入城的晋军遭到伏击，死伤惨重，幸亏晋文公未去，否则后果不堪设想。

　　为了进一步打击晋军的士气，争取时间等待楚军的救援，曹军故意把晋军士兵的尸体堆在城上。晋军气恼于朗的欺诈，更痛恨曹军陈尸城上。为了报复，晋文公把军队移向城郊曹国的墓地，扬言如果曹军不把晋军尸体装在棺材里送出城来，就要掘曹人的祖坟。中国传统观念认为，人死了以后就会转到另一个世界——阴间生活，必须把死者体面地埋入坟墓，叫做"入土为安"，亲族要按时祭扫祖坟，一是敬祖，二是祈求祖先神灵的护佑。如果死者被陈尸示众，祖坟被掘开暴骨，都是莫大的侮辱，是无法忍受的。果然，曹军害怕祖坟被挖，答应把晋军的尸体用棺材装好送出城来，以换取晋国撤军。就在曹军打开城门往外送晋军尸体的时候，埋伏在外面的晋军趁机攻入城里，消灭了曹军，俘虏了国君曹共公。

晋军攻曹，本来拥有兵力上的优势，但是中诈降计后陷入被动。晋将先轸不愧是一个足智多谋的将帅，他先后两次将计就计，变被动为主动，最终反败为胜，保证晋军实现了预订的战略目标。

在军事谋略的技术层面，将计就计比通常的施计用谋难度更大。因为，首先要能识破对方的计谋，其次，对应的计谋必须不露任何破绽。这些都需要技高一筹才行。正因在军事斗争中谋略具有兵力无法替代的作用，兵学家孙子特别重视军事计谋。他说："兵者，诡道者也"、"兵以诈立"，它动作神速，有如飚风之疾；而舒缓行进，其行列齐肃则如林木之森然有序；其侵袭掠扰，有如烈火之猛，不可遏止；而其屯兵固守，则如山岳之固，不可动摇；其深密藏形，有如阴霾迷漫，莫辨辰象；而驱兵接仗，则如霆雷之威，触之者折。所有这些的确是真知灼见！

MAKE A COUNTERPLOT
— The Jin Army Converted Defeat into Victory

According to *Sun Tzu's Art of War,* "War is based on deception."

Before the Battle of Chengpu (in early 632 BC), on the pretext of rescuing the State of Song, Duke Wen of the State of Jin sent a punitive expedition against the states of Cao and Wei, the allies of the State of Chu. When Duke Wen borrowed a road from the State of Wei to invade the State of Cao, he was refused. After that, Duke Wen captured the State of Wei first and then attacked the State of Cao. Realizing that the Cao army was no match for the Jin army, Minister Yu Lang of the State of Cao feigned surrender. Actually he intended to lure Duke Wen to enter the city and then kill him. Duke Wen did not see through his conspiracy and was completely taken in. When he was ready to enter the city to accept the surrender, Xian Zhen, the Commander-in-chief of the Jin army, said to him, "As a ruler of a state, you should not enter the city rashly. We may as well counterplot. Ascertain the real situation in the city by selecting a man and dressing him up as you." Duke Wen followed his advice. As Xian Zhen expected, the Jin army was ambushed in the city and suffered heavy casualties. If Duke Wen had been there, the consequences would have been disastrous.

In order to further demoralize the Jin army and win time for the rescue of the Chu army, the Cao army deliberately piled up the Jin soldiers' bodies on the top of the city walls. The Jin army was infuriated by that as well as Yu Lang's fraud. In order to take revenge on them, Duke Wen mobilized his army to the suburban graveyards of the State of Cao, threatening to dig up the graves of their ancestors if they did not deliver those bodies in coffins out of the city. It was traditionally believed in China that after death people would go to another world — the nether world. The dead must be decently buried in graves. This was known as "Earth is the best shelter." Their clans would offer sacrifices at the graveyards on time, showing respect and praying for blessings of their spirits. If the dead were exposed publicly or their graves were dug up, it would be a great shame. As expected, the Cao army was afraid so that they acceded to their request. When the Cao army opened the gate, the Jin troops who had laid in ambush outside took the chance to break into the city. The Cao army was annihilated and Duke Gong was caught alive.

The Jin army outnumbered the Cao army at the beginning, but they were thrown into an unfavorable situation after they got tricked. Xian Zhen deserved to be called a wise and resourceful commander, who counterplotted twice, regained the initiative, and finally converted defeat into victory, realizing the planned strategic objective.

In terms of strategic techniques, the stratagem of counterplotting was generally more difficult to apply than any other stratagems, because, on the one hand, one should be able to see through the enemy's stratagem; on the other hand, he must cover his own stratagem. All these require more skills. It was because military strength was no match for stratagems in warfare that Sun Tzu, the military strategist, attached special significance to stratagems. He said, "All warfare is based on deception.", "War is based on stratagems." and "When campaigning, be swift as the wind; in leisurely marching, be majestic as the forest; in raiding and plundering, be fierce as fire; in standing, firm as the mountains. When hiding, be as unfathomable as things behind the clouds. When moving, fall like a thunderbolt." All these remarks were indeed a penetrating judgment.

攻心为上——烛之武退秦师

《孙子兵法·军争篇》：故军队的锐气可以使之衰懈，将帅的意志和决心也可以使之动摇。

晋文公在城濮之战大胜楚国之后，会合诸侯，连一向归附楚国的陈、蔡、郑三国的国君也都来了。郑国虽然跟晋国订了盟约，但因害怕楚国，暗地里又跟楚国结了盟。晋文公知道这件事，决定再一次会合诸侯去讨伐郑国。大臣们说："会合诸侯已经好几次了。晋国的兵马已足够对付郑国，不必再麻烦别国了。"晋文公说："不过秦国曾与我有约，有事一起出兵，不能不告诉秦国。"秦穆公正想向东扩张势力，接到晋文公的消息，亲自带着兵马跟晋国一起去攻打郑国。

公元前630年，秦晋联军兵临郑国都城，晋军驻扎在西边，秦军驻扎在东边。郑国的都城被晋、秦两军围得水泄不通，郑文公非常着急。大夫佚之狐对文公说："国家处于险境，如果派烛之武去见秦君，秦国军队一定会撤退。"郑文公听从了他的建议，请烛之武去游说秦君。烛之武推辞说："我在壮年的时候尚且不如别人，现在已经老了，做不了什么事了。"郑文公明白烛之武师是在抱怨平时没有用他，于是恳切地说："我没有及早重用您，现在危急时才来求您，这是我的过错。然而郑国灭亡了，对您也不利啊！"烛之武答应了文公的请求。

当天夜里，郑军守城士兵把烛之武用绳子从城墙上坠下去，借夜色的掩护，烛之武偷偷地进入秦军大营拜见秦穆公。烛之武开门见山地对秦穆公说："秦、晋两国围攻郑国，郑国已经知道就要灭亡了。如果郑国灭亡对穆公您有好处，那就值得烦劳您的军队。可是，秦国在晋国的西边，郑秦东西相距千里，秦国能越过其他国家而在远方设置边邑吗？如果不能，那么郑国的土地将被晋国得到，邻国强大了，您秦国就显得弱小了，难道亡郑以陪邻就是您兴师动众的目的吗？"秦穆公默然无对。烛之武继续说："如果秦军不灭郑国，使郑国成为您东方道路上的主人，贵国使臣来往经过，供应他们的食宿给养，这对您也没有坏处。"这就是"东道主"一词的来历，意思是东路负责招待的主人，后来演化为指请客的主人。

烛之武见秦穆公已经心动，语气更加恳切地说："再说，您也曾经有恩于晋君，他答应给您焦、瑕两地作为报答，可是他早晨刚刚渡河回国，晚上就在那里筑城防御，这些都是您所知道的。那个晋国，哪里有满足的时候？它既以郑国作为东边的疆界，又要扩张它西边的疆界，如果不损害秦国，它到哪里去夺取土地呢？损害秦国而有利于晋国，您还是好好儿考虑一下这件事吧。"秦穆公听了烛之武的一席话，幡然醒悟，于是就单方面跟郑国订立了盟约，然后委派杞子、逢孙、杨孙三人带领两千士卒留下戍守郑国北门，自己率领秦国大队人马回国了。

晋军见秦军不辞而别，很生气。大夫子犯建议袭击背约的秦军。晋文公说："不可，当年要不是秦君支持我回晋国继位，我到不了今天这个地步。如果依靠过别人的力量再去损害别人，是不仁义的，由此失去同盟国，不是聪明的选择，我们还是回去吧。"于是，晋国也以撤军为诱饵，使郑国与晋结为盟国。晋军遂撤离了郑国。就这样，郑国没动一刀一枪、没用一兵一卒便解了城下之围。一场剑拔弩张的战争，被烛之武以"攻心"的策略消解了。孙子在《始计篇》中说：对于敌军，可"若气势汹汹，乘怒而来，就设法使之屈挠；若词卑行敛，就设法使之骄惰"。在《军争篇》中说："故军队的锐气可以使之衰懒，将帅的意志和决心也可以使之动摇。"这些都属于军事斗争中的"攻心"战略。所以，中国古代兵学讲究"攻心为上"。

PSYCHOLOGICAL OFFENSIVE IS THE BEST POLICY
— Zhu Zhiwu Averted the Qin Army

According to *Sun Tzu's Art of War*, "An army may be robbed of its spirit and its commander deprived of his confidence."

Having defeated the State of Chu in the Battle of Chengpu, Duke Wen of the State of Jin held a summit conference of all dukes. Even the dukes of the states of Chen, Cai and Zheng, who had been attached to the State of Chu, attended the meeting. Out of fear of the State of Chu, the State of Zheng allied itself with Chu in secret though it formed an alliance with the State of Jin. When Duke Wen knew this, he decided to hold a summit conference to ask the other dukes to join him in the punitive expedition against the State of Zheng. However, his officials said, "We have already had the summit conference several times, besides, our forces are strong enough to deal with the State of Zheng and there is no need to bother them again." Duke Wen said, "But I have an agreement with the State of Qin that we will dispatch troops together in any emergency. So I have to let it know." Hearing the news, Duke Mu of the State of Qin, who was just about to extend his influence eastward, personally led the troops to attack the State of Zheng with Duke Wen.

In 630 BC, the allied forces of Jin and Qin arrived at the gates of the capital of the State of Zheng. The Jin army was stationed in the west while the Qin army in the east, densely surrounding the city. Duke Wen of the State of Zheng was extremely worried. Minister Yi Zhihu said to him, "Our state is in danger now. Your Lordship, if you ask Zhu Zhiwu to have an audience with the Duke of the State of Qin, the Qin army will surely retreat." Duke Wen followed his advice. But when asked to be the lobbyist, Zhu Zhiwu declined, saying, "When I was young, I was less capable than others. How could I do anything great at such an old age?" Knowing that Zhu Zhiwu was complaining that he had not been much valued, Duke Wen said earnestly, "I did not put you in an important position in the past but at this critical moment I am asking you for help. All is my fault. However, if our state is destroyed, it will do you no good." Zhu Zhiwu agreed with his request.

On that night, Zhu Zhiwu was lowered with a rope down the city wall by the guards. Under the cover of darkness, he sneaked into the Qin camp to have an audience with Duke Mu. Zhu Zhiwu said directly, "Our state has already known its destiny under the siege of the states of Qin and Jin. If our destruction does you good, it is worthwhile to mobilize your troops. However, your state lies to the west of the State of Jin. And our two states are a thousand *li* apart. Can you make us your remote dependency with several states between us? If not, then our territories will fall into the hands of the State of Jin, which will grow stronger than your state. Isn't it your purpose to mobilize so many troops, only to strengthen your neighbor at our expense?" Duke Mu said nothing. Zhu Zhiwu resumed, "If you do not destroy our state, but make it a host on your way to the east, it will be good to you, for we can accommodate your envoys who pass by." This was the origin of the word "host" in Chinese, which meant a person in the eastern road who was responsible for entertaining guests. Later, "host" was used to refer to a person who stood treat.

Seeing that Duke Mu was already swayed, Zhu Zhiwu said with more sincerity, "Besides, the Duke of the State of Jin owed you a favor. In return, he had promised to cede two cities Jiao and Xia to you. However, as you know, when he crossed the river and returned to his state in the morning, he fortified the area at night. At what time can the State of Jin be satisfied? It takes our state as its eastern border and also plans to expand its western border. Where can Jin plunder lands without damaging your interests? Your Lordship, please think it over." On hearing his words, Duke Mu came to realize his mistake. As a result, he signed a treaty of alliance with the State of Zheng. Then he led his major forces back to his state, with Qi Zi, Peng Sun and Yang Sun guarding the north gate of the State of Zheng with two thousand soldiers.

The Jin army was irritated that the Qin army left without saying goodbye. Minister Zifan suggested making a sneak attack on the Qin troops who betrayed the agreement. Duke Wen said, "No. But for the support of the Duke of the State of Qin in early years, I would not have succeeded to the throne; neither could I accomplish anything today. It is not benevolent to hurt those who once offered you help; neither is it wise to lose an ally because of this. So let's go home. " Therefore, using withdrawal of the army as bait, the State of Jin formed an alliance with the State of Zheng. Then the Jin army retreated too. Thus, the siege of the State of Zheng was stopped without any fighting. A bloody battle was eliminated by Zhu Zhiwu's stratagem of "psychological offensive". In *Sun Tzu's Art of War*, Sun Tzu said, "If your opponent is of choleric temper, try to irritate him. If he is arrogant, try to encourage his egotism. An army may be robbed of its spirit and its commander deprived of his confidence." All these belonged to stratagems of "psychological offensive" in military struggles. Therefore, "psychological offensive is the best policy" is always stressed in the history of the Chinese military science.

避锐击惰——晋襄公不应秦战

《孙子兵法·军争篇》：避其锐气，击其惰气。

公元前624年，秦将孟明视请求秦穆公发兵伐晋，以报崤山之仇，秦穆公很痛快地就答应了。

公元前627年，秦军企图偷袭郑国，因计谋败露未能实施，自郑返国途径崤山，遭到晋军伏击，全军覆没，秦将孟明视、西乞术、白乙丙被俘。晋文公的夫人文嬴是秦穆公的女儿，见秦军三将被俘，便向晋襄公请求道："他们三个的确损害了秦晋两国的亲近关系，秦穆公如果得到这三个人，恨不能吃了他们的肉。您不如把他们三个放回去，让他们到秦国去受刑，以满足穆公的心愿，何劳您亲自去惩罚他们呢？"晋襄公觉得文嬴的话有道理，就答应了她的请求，命令放了孟明视、西乞术和白乙丙。晋将先轸朝见襄公，问起秦国的囚徒押到哪里去了。襄公说："夫人为这事特地来请求我，我已经把他们放了。"先轸一听，顾不得君臣之礼，愤怒地对襄公说："士卒们花了那么大的力气才把他们从战场上俘虏来，妇人几句谎话您就把他们放走，毁了晋军的战果，而助长了敌人的气焰，亡国没有几天了！"晋襄公也感到后悔，急忙派阳处父去追孟明等人。阳处父追到河边，孟明视、西乞术和白乙丙已经登舟离岸了。阳处父解下驾车的马，对孟明等三人说："将军慢走，晋襄公特地派我来给你们送马，请三位将军上岸来带走。"孟明视知道有诈，肯定是晋襄公后悔了，派人来追。他在船上对阳处父叩谢道："贵国国君宽宏大量，没有用我们的血来涂抹战鼓，让我们回到秦国去受死刑，如果秦君杀死我们，那我们死了也不会忘记。如果遵从晋君的好意赦免了我们，三年后将要来拜谢晋军的恩赐！"意思是：三年之后，要来报仇。

果然，孟明视、西乞术、白乙丙回到秦国后，秦穆公不但没有责罚他们，而且一再检讨是他未能听蹇叔和百里奚的劝告，以致大败，害得三位将军受辱。此后三年间，孟明视刻苦训练士卒，不断积累作战经验，这次向秦穆公建言伐晋，就是要兑现三年报仇的诺言。他发毒誓说："若今番不能雪耻，誓不生还！"

出征前，孟明视优抚出征将士家属，该安置的安置，该送财帛的送财帛，上上下下，大有一去不返的气势。军队出征了，秦穆公亲自督战，指挥浩浩荡荡的大军向晋国扑来。军队刚一渡过黄河，孟明视即下令焚烧了所有渡船。秦穆公不解其意。孟明视说："兵以气胜。焚舟自绝归路，意思是告示三军，此次出征是有进路无退路，非胜即死，宁死勿归。以此激励他们的斗志。"秦穆公对此大加赞赏。

孟明视亲自做先锋，逢山开路，遇河架桥，长驱直入，一举拿下了王官城，兵锋直逼晋国都城绛州。晋襄公召集群臣商议抗敌之策。大将赵衰说："自崤山之战以来，秦军已经连续三次被晋军打败，上上下下已愤怒到了极点，这次倾一国之兵来战，必定奋死决战。我们不如暂避其锐气，让其稍稍得点便宜，免得两国争斗不休，兵祸连连，对谁都没有好处。"晋襄公很赞同赵衰的想法，于是命令晋军坚守四境，不与秦军正面接战。秦穆公见晋军只守不战，认为晋国已经胆怯和屈服了。乘着兵威，在当年晋军伏击秦军的崤山战场，隆重祭祀了崤山阵亡将士，为秦国和秦国军队挽回了面子。之后便奏着凯歌回国了。

这一次战争，秦晋并没有太大的正面接触，然而双方对结果似乎很满意。秦国达到了报仇雪恨、挽回国家和军队面子的目的，晋国也实现了最大限度地降低损失的战略目标。这样一个双方都满意的结果，应该归功于晋国所采取的正确战略和战术，即如孙子在《作战篇》中所说的那样："不尽知用兵之害者，则不能尽知用兵之利。""故善用兵者，避其锐气，击其惰气。"这确实是真知灼见啊。

AVOID THE ENEMY WHEN HIS SPIRIT IS KEEN AND ATTACK HIM WHEN IT IS SLUGGISH
— Duke Xiang of the State of Jin Did Not Meet Qin's Challenge

According to *Sun Tzu's Art of War*, "Avoid the enemy when his spirit is keen and attack him when it is sluggish."

In 624 BC, General Mengming Shi requested Duke Mu of the State of Qin to send a punitive expedition against the State of Jin in revenge for the battle of Mount Xiao. The Duke agreed without any hesitation.

In 627 BC, the Qin troops attempted to make a sneak attack on the State of Zheng but did not take actions because the plan had leaked out. When passing by Mount Xiao on their way home, the Qin army was ambushed by the Jin army and was wiped out, with the Qin generals Mengming Shi, Xiqi Shu and Baiyi Bing captured. Wenying, the wife of Duke Wen of the State of Jin, was the daughter of Duke Mu. When she got the news, she requested Duke Xiang of the State of Jin,

"They three really impaired the intimate relationship between our two states. If Duke Mu gets them, he will be only too ready to eat their flesh. To satisfy his wish, you may as well release them and let them be punished in their own state. So, why bother to punish them yourself?" Thinking what she said was reasonable, Duke Mu agreed and ordered their release. When Xian Zhen, the general of the State of Jin, had an audience with Duke Xiang, he asked where the captives were imprisoned. Duke Xiang said, "I have already set them free at the request of my queen mother." On hearing that, regardless of the ritual between the ruler and ministers, Xian Zhen said to him angrily, "It almost drained our soldiers to capture them on the battlefield. But you let them go because of a woman's slick talk. You not only spoil the fruit of our army, but also encourage the enemy's arrogance. Our state will perish in days!" Feeling regretful, Duke Xiang quickly sent Yang Chufu to pursue the three Qin generals. When Yang Chufu arrived at the riverbank, the three generals had already left the shore in a boat. Yang Chufu loosened horses which drove the chariots and said to them, "Wait a minute, generals. My Duke specially sent me to present you with horses. Please get ashore to take them home." Mengming Shi knew that Duke Xiang must have been regretful and sent Yang Chufu to pursue them, so he kowtowed in thanks in the boat, saying, "It is magnanimous of your Duke to spare our blood to smear your battle drums. Instead, he let us return home to get killed. If our Duke kills us, we will never forget your Duke's benevolence. If our Duke is so nice as to pardon us, we will be back to extend our gratitude to your army three years later." His implication was that he would take revenge in three years' time.

As expected, when Mengming Shi, Xiqi Shu and Baiyi Bing came back to the State of Qin, Duke Mu did not punish them; instead the Duke repeatedly made a self-criticism — if he had listened to Jian Shu and Bali Xi, his army wouldn't have been routed and the three generals wouldn't have been humiliated. In the following three years, Mengming Shi assiduously trained his soldiers and continuously accumulated experience in warfare. So, this time he intended to meet his promise that he would take revenge in three years. He cursed, "If I cannot wipe out the humiliation this time, I will not be back alive!"

Before the expedition, Mengming Shi gave special care to the family members of the whole army. He either made proper arrangements for them or gave them money and silk. It seemed as if the whole army would never return. Under the supervision of Duke Mu, the Qin army marched with great strength and vigor towards the State of Jin. As soon as the army crossed the river, Mengming Shi ordered his men to burn all the ferries. Duke Mu could not figure out his intention. Mengming Shi explained, "Victory is based on soldiers' high spirit. Burning the ferries to cut off the retreat actually warns the whole army that we have no choice but to advance; we either win or die on the battlefield; we would rather die than return alive. In this way our soldiers' fighting spirit will be aroused." Duke Mu spoke highly of his idea.

Mengming Shi acted as the Vanguard himself. The army overcame all difficulties on their way by cutting paths when they came across mountains and building bridges before rivers. Marching unchecked, they took the city of Wangguan at one stroke and then marched towards Jiangzhou, the capital city of the State of Jin. Duke Xiang of the State of Jin summoned his officials to discuss countermeasures. General Zhao Cui said, "Since the battle of Mount Xiao, the Qin army has been routed by us three successive times. They are so furious that they turn out in full strength this time and they are sure to fight desperately. We may as well avoid their keen spirit and let them gain some petty advantages lest there be turmoil caused by frequent wars, which will do no good to either of us." Approving of his idea, Duke Xiang ordered the army to defend the borders instead of having a head-on clash with the Qin army. At the sight of this, Duke Mu thought the enemy was already afraid and gave in. Therefore, at Mount Xiao where his army had been ambushed by the Jin army, Duke Mu grandly offered sacrifices to those who died in the battle, saving face for his state and his army. Then, they returned home amidst songs of triumph.

In this battle, although both sides did not have too much face-to-face confrontation, they seemed to be content with the outcome. For the State of Qin, it achieved the goal of taking revenge and saving its face; while for the State of Jin, it realized the strategic objective of reducing losses to the maximum possible extent. The outcome, satisfying to both of them, should be attributed to the proper strategy and tactics adopted by the State of Jin. Such was what Sun Tzu described in *Sun Tzu's Art of War*, "Those unable to understand the evils inherent in employing troops are equally unable to understand the advantageous ways of doing so. Those skilled in war avoid the enemy when his spirit is keen and attack him when it is sluggish." This was indeed a penetrating judgment.

虎卑狸缩——勾践复国灭吴

《孙子兵法·军争篇》：两军争利中最难的地方是把迂回曲折的弯路变为直路，化害为利。

公元前473年，越王勾践举兵伐吴，这是自二十年前惨败于吴国以来，越国首次发动复仇雪耻的战争。

公元前496年，吴王阖闾乘越王允常逝世、其子勾践新立之机，率精兵三万伐越。勾践以弱对强，以奇制胜，吴国军队惨败，吴王阖闾也受了伤和惊吓，死于撤军途中，其子夫差继位，发誓要为父报仇。两年之后，即公元前494年，夫差倾吴国之兵伐越。吴、越两军在夫椒（今太湖椒山）会战，吴军一举打败越军。越王勾践带领五千余残兵败将逃到会稽山上，紧接着又被夫差以重兵包围。勾践仰望苍天长叹道："我真的就这样完了吗？"大夫文仲是个很有智谋和远见的人，他劝勾践说："想当初，商汤曾被困在夏台，周文王曾被囚于羑里，但后来却一举成王；齐公子小白（齐桓公）曾避乱他乡，晋公子重耳（晋文公）曾逃往异国，后来却一举成霸。眼下可为韬晦之计，暂卑辞厚礼向吴王求和，日后再图翻身。"勾践别无良策，就接受了文仲的建议，主动向吴国求和。

吴王夫差身边有一位宠臣贪财好功，越王勾践先派文仲携带美女和贵宝贿赂他，然后求他劝吴王接受求和。果然，吴王夫差被说动。于是勾践带着家眷作为人质来到吴国。在吴国期间，勾践过着奴隶一样的屈辱生活，为死去的国君阖闾守墓，为现任的国君夫差当马夫。为了取得夫差的信任，勾践对夫差毕恭毕敬。每次夫差出门，勾践都在车前牵马缰绳，服务得细致入微。夫差病了，勾践不但端屎端尿，甚至亲口尝夫差的粪便，以确诊其病情的阴阳寒热。勾践的行为，一方面让夫差很感动，认为他忠心耿耿，值得信任；另一方面，勾践的行为也让夫差觉得他失去了大志，已经不是个威胁。于是在勾践服侍他三年之后，即在公元前491年将他释放回越国。

古人说，虎卑其势，将有击也；狸缩其身，将有取也。越王勾践正是以"虎卑""狸缩"的韬晦之计赢得了吴王夫差的信任。事实上，勾践一天都没有忘记复国报仇的计划。他一回到越国，立即着手实施强国富民计划。勾践一方面深入民间，激励百姓，发展生产，鼓励生育；另一方面广泛招贤纳士，整饬内政外交，征聚兵员，加强军事训练。为了麻痹吴王对越国的戒备，勾践不但每年按时向吴国进贡，还挑选绝色佳人送给吴王夫差，引诱他陷入犬马声色之中不能自拔。为了鞭策自己，勾践睡在柴草上，每天舔一下悬挂的苦胆，激励自己不要忘记在吴国的耻辱生活。就这样，卧薪尝胆，励精图治，十年生息，十年积聚，经过二十年的精心准备和艰苦奋斗，越国又复兴起来。到了公元前473年，勾践终于认为时机成熟，亲自率领精兵数万伐吴，攻破了吴国都城，吴王夫差被围困在阳山（今江苏吴县西北），他也重演了越王勾践当年屈尊求和的一幕，所不同的是，勾践比当年的夫差头脑清楚，他拒绝了夫差的请求。无奈，吴王夫差只得掩面自杀。打败了吴国，逼死了夫差，勾践终于报了仇，雪了耻。

越王勾践"虎卑狸缩"了二十多年，在这二十多年间，始终像孙子在《始计篇》中说的那样："能而示之不能，用而示之不用。"韬光养晦，最终才能一举成功。所以孙子专门讲了迂直之计，强调要采取表面迂远的进军路线去迷惑敌人，并用小利去引诱敌人。这样，即使在敌人之后出发，也能比敌人先期到达战地。

A HUMBLE TIGER AND A CROUCHED LEOPARD CAT
— Goujian Destroyed the State of Wu to Restore His Own State

According to *Sun Tzu's Art of War*, "What is the most difficult in the art of manoeuvring for advantageous positions is to make the devious route the direct route and to turn disadvantage to advantage."

In 473 BC, King Goujian of the State of Yue sent a punitive expedition against the State of Wu. It was the first battle that the State of Yue launched to take revenge after its army was defeated by the State of Wu twenty years before.

In 496 BC, King Yunchang of the State of Yue passed away and his son, Goujian, succeeded to the throne. King Helü of the State of Wu took the opportunity to lead 30,000 crack troops to invade the State of Yue. Although numerically weaker in strength, the Yue army won the battle by using the extraordinary means. The Wu army was defeated. Wounded and frightened, King Helü died in the retreat. When Fuchai, his son, succeeded to the throne, he swore that he would take revenge for his father. Two years later (In 494 BC), Fuchai led the whole army of the State of Wu to attack the State of Yue. When they met at Fujiao (Mount Jiao around the Tai Lake today), the Yue army was defeated at one swoop. King Goujian, followed by 5,000 remnants, fled to Mount Kuaiji. There they were densely surrounded by the Wu army. Looking up to the sky, Goujian sighed deeply, "Am I doomed here?" Minister Wen Zhong, resourceful and far-sighted, counseled him, "As recorded in history, King Tang of Shang Dynasty was once besieged at Xiatai and King Wen of Zhou was once imprisoned at Youli, but later both of them became great rulers. Prince Xiaobai (Duke Huan of the State of Qi) and Prince Chong'er (Duke Wen of the State of Jin) sought refuge in a foreign land, but they both became overlords afterwards. For the time being, we may lie low and bide our time by suing for peace with humble words and lavish gifts." Without any other good plan, Goujian had to follow his advice and sued for peace.

There was a favored courtier at King Fuchai's side, who was eager to earn wealth and merit. Wen Zhong was sent to bribe the courtier with beauties and valuables, asking him to persuade King Fuchai to accept their request for peace. As expected, King Fuchai was talked round. As a result, King Goujian, together with his family, went to the State of Wu as the hostage. During his stay in the State of Wu, Goujian lived a humiliating life like that of a slave. He kept the grave of King Helü, and acted as the groom for Fuchai. In order to win the trust of Fuchai, Goujian showed great respect to him. Each time Fuchai went out, Goujian led the horse by the bridle, with great care and meticulousness. When Fuchai was sick, Goujian cleared away his excrement and urine. He even tasted his excrement to make a diagnosis of his condition — chill or fever. Moved by Goujian's behavior, Fuchai thought he was extremely loyal and trustworthy. Besides, Fuchai was under the impression that Goujian had lost his ambition and was not a threat to him any longer. Therefore, Fuchai released him back to the State of Yue three years later (in 491 BC).

A saying goes like this in ancient China, "A humbly posed tiger will make an attack and a crouched leopard cat will get its prey." King Goujian won the trust of King Fuchai by using the tricks of "humble tigers" and "crouched leopard cats". In fact, Goujian did not forget to take revenge or restore his state at all. When he returned to the State of Yue, he went about implementing the plan to strengthen his state and enrich his people. On the one hand, Goujian went among the masses, encouraging them to boost agricultural production and give birth. On the other, he invited men of wisdom and virtue on a large scale, rectified domestic and foreign affairs, recruited soldiers and strengthened military training. In order to slacken Fuchai's vigilance, Goujian paid tribute to him annually. Besides, he presented stunning beauties to Fuchai, who was thus unable to extricate himself from sensual pleasures. In order to spur himself on, Goujian slept on the brushwood, tasting the hanging gall once each day. In this way he could be reminded of the humiliating life in the State of Wu. Sleeping on the brushwood and tasting the gall, Goujian exerted himself to make the state prosperous. After ten years of procreation and another ten years of accumulation (twenty years in total of meticulous preparation and hard work), the State of Yue was finally restored. In 473 BC, thinking that the time was ripe for action, Goujian led crack soldiers to attack the State of Wu. The capital city of the State of Wu was taken and King Fuchai was hemmed in at Mount Yang (in the northwest of Wu County in Jiangsu Province today). He sued for peace just as King Goujian did in the early years. But what was different was that Goujian was more sober-minded than the then King Fuchai, and refused his request. King Fuchai had no choice but to kill himself. Defeating the State of Wu and pushing Fuchai to death, Goujian finally wiped out the humiliation.

King Goujian acted as "a humble tiger and a crouched leopard cat" for more than twenty years, when he complied with the words in *Sun Tzu's Art of War*, "When capable of attacking, feign incapacity; when active in moving troops, feign inactivity." Only by hiding his capacities and biding his time could he succeed at one stroke. Therefore, Sun Tzu specified the artifice of diversion, emphasizing that one should march by an indirect route and divert the enemy by enticing him with bait; by doing so, one might reach the battlefield earlier than the enemy even if he sets out later.

知兵安国——周亚夫平七国之乱

《孙子兵法·九变篇》：凡用兵之法，……军有所不击，城有所不攻，地有所不争，君命有所不受。

公元前 154 年，汉王朝的吴、楚等七个诸侯王联兵发动叛乱，汉景帝派周亚夫率兵去平乱。

汉王朝建立之初，为了巩固统治地位，汉高祖刘邦采取分封刘氏子弟为王的政策，以加强家族统治、防止异姓篡权。当时分封的同姓王主要有齐、燕、赵、梁、代、吴、楚、淮阳等。这些同姓王的封地占有九郡，皇帝直辖十五郡。朝廷规定，诸王掌握封地内的经济支配权，而法令和军队则由朝廷统一掌控。但是，随着诸侯王的实力不断增强，分庭抗礼乃至武装割据的势头也越来越明显。到了汉景帝时期，已经达到了危及中央政权的地步。御史大夫晁错建议景帝实行削藩，即削减诸王封地，收归朝廷统辖。他在给景帝的《削藩策》中分析了削藩的利弊，他说，"今削之反，不削亦反。削之，其反得快，祸小。不削，其反得慢，祸大。"汉景帝接受晁错的建议，先后以各种罪名削去楚王戊的东海郡，赵王遂的常山郡和胶西王的6个县。削藩引起诸王的不满，当朝廷的削藩诏书送到吴国时，吴王刘濞下令诛杀了由朝廷派来的官员，并以"清君侧，诛晁错"为名号召诸侯国反叛，于是以吴、楚为首的"七国之乱"就这样爆发了。

汉景帝接到诸侯王叛乱的消息，派周亚夫率朝廷主力军去迎击吴楚叛军。周亚夫出征前与景帝分析战争局势。他说："吴军士气正盛，很难与他们正面争锋，我们可以暂时把梁国舍弃给吴国，然后断绝叛军的粮道，这样就能制服他们了。"汉景帝同意了这一作战计划，于是周亚夫率大军从长安向洛阳进军。从长安到洛阳，原定的行军路线要经过崤山、渑池至洛阳。部将赵涉提醒周亚夫说："将军出征，吴王一定知道您的动向，不如改变进军路线，由蓝田出武关至洛阳。这条路虽然比原来多一两天的路程，但可以隐蔽地到达洛阳，以控制那里的军械库。"周亚夫采纳了他的建议，军队顺利地抢先占领了战略要地荥阳，控制了洛阳的武器库。

这时，吴、楚联军开始向梁国发起进攻，梁王率军在棘壁与叛军交战，结果惨败。退守睢阳后，又被吴、楚联军包围，情况非常危急。梁王急忙向周亚夫求援，但周亚夫没有救援梁王，而是率领军队奔昌邑，在那里修筑坚固的防御阵地，准备坚守。梁王屡次派使求援，周亚夫坚持原定战略，没有发兵救梁，为此，梁王上书景帝。梁王是汉景帝的弟弟，又是太后最疼爱的小儿子，景帝遂派使者命令周亚夫率兵救梁。周亚夫奉行"将在外，君命有所不受"的古训，继续坚守营垒。为了缓解梁王的压力，也为了整个战局的胜利，周亚夫派轻骑兵迂回到吴、楚联军的背后，截断其粮道。吴、楚联军既久攻不下睢阳，粮草供给又被切断，进退无路，于是转而寻找周亚夫的主力部队决战。

周亚夫对于吴、楚联军的挑战不予理睬，继续深沟高垒固守。叛军只好采取声东击西之计，假装攻击汉军营垒的东南角。周亚夫识破了敌人的计谋，遂加强西北面营垒的军事防御力量，当吴楚联军佯攻东南、实攻西北的时候，狠狠地给敌人以打击。吴楚联军攻又攻不破，打又打不胜，粮草不继，只好引军撤退。周亚夫趁机派精锐部队追击。撤退的吴、楚联军本来就疲惫不堪，士气低落，根本经不住汉军精锐部队的冲击，被打得七零八落。楚王刘戊被迫自杀，吴王刘濞带领几千人逃到丹徒，周亚夫乘胜追至丹徒，将其将士全部俘获。吴王刘濞藏匿起来，周亚夫悬赏千金捉拿吴王。一个多月后，东越王在汉军的威胁和利诱下，诱杀了吴王刘濞，吴、楚联军作为七国叛乱的主力军，被彻底地消灭了。至此，周亚夫仅用了三个月的时间，就把一场席卷大汉帝国的七国之乱平息了。

七国之乱，是西汉中央与地方、皇帝与诸侯王之间一次决定性战争。影响战争胜负的因素很多，正如孙子在《始谋攻》中说的那样："知胜有五：知可以战与不可以战者，胜；识众寡之用者，胜；上下同欲者，胜；以虞待不虞者，胜；将能而君不御者，胜。"单从军事的角度来，周亚夫知兵且善于用兵，无疑是迅速平定七国治乱的决定因素。首先，他能准确地把握军事斗争的形势，制订出胜算在握的作战计划，并征得汉景帝的认可；其次，他善于接受建议，及时采纳了部将赵涉提出的改变进军路线的主张；第三，在梁王求援、汉景帝下令发兵的情况下，能够坚持正确的战略决策，真正做到了《孙子兵法》中所说的那样："军有所不击，城有所不攻，地有所不争，君命有所不受。"始终是一个清醒的指挥者。孙子在《作战篇》中说："知兵之将，安国之主也。"此言不虚。

UNDERSTAND HOW TO EMPLOY TROOPS AND KEEP THE STATE SECURE
— Zhou Yafu Suppressed the Rebellion of the Seven States

According to *Sun Tzu's Art of War*, "In general, the system of employing troops is ... There are some troops which must not be attacked, some cities which must not be assaulted, and some ground which should not be contested. There are also occasions when the commands of the sovereign need not be obeyed."

In 154 BC, seven dukes (of the states of Wu, Chu, etc.) of the Han Dynasty (206 BC – 220 AD) staged a rebellion. King Jing of the Han Dynasty sent Zhou Yafu to suppress the riot.

In the early years of the Han Dynasty, in order to consolidate his ruling position, strengthen the dominance of his clans and prevent usurpation of power by the people of different surnames, Liu Bang, the first emperor of the Han Dynasty adopted a policy of appointing dukes who had his surname. At that time, the major vassal states were the states of Qi, Yan, Zhao, Liang, Dai, Wu, Chu and Huaiyang. All the fiefdoms of these dukes occupied nine counties, while the King was directly in control of fifteen. According to the rules of the imperial court, the dukes were in charge of the economy within their fiefdoms, while laws and armies were under the unified control of the imperial court. However, as the dukes grew more powerful, they began to act independently and defiantly, and even to establish separate regimes through armed struggles. By the time of Emperor Jing, the dukes had already become a threat to the central government. Minister Chao Cuo recommended cutting down the sizes of the vassal states, namely, reducing the number of the dukes' fiefdoms and reclaiming them. In *A Policy of Cutting down the Sizes of the Vassal States* to Emperor Jing, Chao Cuo analyzed the advantages and disadvantages. He said, "They are going to rebel anyway whether we cut down their sizes or not. It will be better to let them rebel earlier than later, when they might be more prepared and thus bring us more trouble." Emperor Jing followed his advice. By inventing various charges, he reclaimed Donghai County from Duke Liu Wu of the State of Chu, Changshan County from Duke Liu Sui of the State of Zhao and six counties from Duke Liu Ang of the State of Jiaoxi, which aroused great dissatisfaction among the dukes. When the imperial edict was sent to the State of Wu, Duke Liu Bi ordered the officials from the imperial court executed. Under the pretext of "ridding the emperor of 'evil' ministers and executing Chao Cuo", Duke Liu Bi called on other dukes to rise in rebellion. Thus, "the Rebellion of the Seven States", headed by the states of Wu and Chu, broke out.

When Emperor Jing got the news, he sent Zhou Yafu to lead the major forces of the imperial court to combat the rebel armies. Before the expedition, Zhou Yafu analyzed the war situation with the emperor. He said, "The Wu army has high morale now, so it will be difficult to have a direct battle with them. For the time being, we may give up the State of Liang to them, and then cut off their supplies. In this way we can subdue them." Emperor Jing approved of the plan. Zhou Yafu led the troops and left Chang'an for Luoyang. Following the original march route, the troops would pass by Mount Xiao and Mianchi. Zhao She, his subordinate, reminded Zhou Yafu, "The Duke of the State of Wu must have known our movement. So, it will be better to change the route, that is, we may get to Luoyang via Lantian and Wuguan. Though it will take one or two more days, we may arrive at the destination in secret and occupy the arms depot there." Following his suggestion, Zhou Yafu led his army to smoothly seize Xingyang, the strategic post, and bring the arms depot in Luoyang under his control.

At the same time, the allied forces of the states of Wu and Chu began to attack the State of Liang. After having been defeated by the enemy at Jibi, the Liang army retreated to Suiyang. There they were densely surrounded by the enemy again. The situation was desperate. The Duke of the State of Liang quickly pleaded for help but was turned down by Zhou Yafu, who led the army to head for Changyi instead, where he constructed the solid defensive position, preparing to hold fast to it. Repeatedly, the Duke sent envoys to appeal for aid, but Zhou Yafu stuck to the original strategy and did not come to his rescue. As a result, the Duke submitted a written statement to Emperor Jing. Because the

Duke was his younger brother and also the youngest son most doted upon by Empress Dowager, Emperor Jing ordered Zhou Yafu to come to Liang's rescue. Following the old maxim that "A general in the field is not bound by orders from his sovereign", Zhou Yafu still held his ground. However, in order to ease the Duke's tension and win the final victory, Zhou Yafu sent the light cavalry to the rear of the allied forces to cut off their supply lines. Unable to capture Suiyang quickly, and with supplies cut off, the allied forces could neither advance nor retreat, so they had to seek a decisive battle with Zhou Yafu's major forces.

Ignoring the challenge of the enemy, Zhou Yafu kept defending the position by high walls and deep moats. Adopting the strategy of "making a feint to the east and attacking the west", the rebel army pretended to assault the southeast side of the Han camp. Seeing through the enemy's plan, Zhou Yafu strengthened the military defense capabilities in the northwest and gave them a good beating when they actually stormed the northwest side. Without supplies, the allied forces could neither break through nor have a chance of winning, so they had to retreat. Taking the opportunity, Zhou Yafu sent the crack troops to pursue them. Extremely exhausted and demoralized, the allied forces could not resist the charge of the opponent, only to be badly battered and thrown into confusion. Duke Liu Wu of the State of Chu was forced to commit suicide. Followed by thousands of his men, Duke Liu Bi of the State of Wu fled to Dantu. Following up the victory, Zhou Yafu pursued them there and captured Liu Bi's men. Liu Bi went into hiding and Zhou Yafu offered a reward of one thousand taels of gold to get him. More than one month later, threatened and lured by the Han army, the Duke of the State of Dongyue trapped Liu Bi and killed him. The allied forces of the states of Wu and Chu, the major forces of the seven rebellious states, were completely destroyed. Until then, Zhou Yafu spent only three months suppressing the rebellion which swept across the Han Empire.

The Rebellion of the Seven States was a decisive battle between the central and the local governments, the emperor and the dukes. There were many factors which influenced the outcome of the battle, just as Sun Tzu said in *Sun Tzu's Art of War*, "There are five points from which victory may be predicted: He who knows when he can fight and when he cannot will be victorious; he who understands how to fight in accordance with the strength of antagonistic forces will be victorious; he whose ranks are united in purpose will be victorious; he who is well prepared and lies in wait for an enemy who is not well prepared will be victorious; he whose generals are able and is not interfered with by the sovereign will be victorious." From the military perspective, Zhou Yafu's understanding of employing troops and his skills in war were undoubtedly the decisive factors in the battle. First, he was able to properly grasp the military situation, to formulate the war plans which guaranteed a victory and to get the approval of Emperor Jing. Besides, he was good at accepting other's advice and he promptly adopted Zhao She's suggestion of changing the march route. In addition, in spite of Duke Liang's pleading and the Emperor's order, he could stick to the right tactics and really acted on what was said in *Sun Tzu's Art of War*, "There are some troops which must not be attacked, some cities which must not be assaulted, and some ground which should not be contested. There are also occasions when the commands of the sovereign need not be obeyed." He was a soberminded commander at all time. In *Sun Tzu's Art of War*, Sun Tzu said, "The general who understands how to employ troops is the arbiter of the nation's destiny." What he said really sounded reasonable.

令文齐武——孙子吴宫教战

《孙子兵法·行军篇》：用怀柔的手段来颁布政令，用严格的手段去管束士兵，这样的军队打仗必胜。

　　吴王阖闾读了孙子的《兵法十三篇》，非常敬佩孙子的见解。但是不知道孙子的这些用兵办法真正实行起来怎么样，吴王想让孙子给他实际演练一下看看。孙子爽快地答应了吴王的要求。吴王又问孙子，可不可以用女子来演阵。孙子说可以，于是，吴王就命令从宫中调来180个宫女临时充当士兵供孙子演练阵法。

　　孙子让宫女们先穿上铠甲，拿好武器，然后到操场集合。孙子先把180个宫女分为两队，选派两个最受吴王宠爱的妃子担任队长。他又请求吴王派几个执掌兵法的人以壮军威，吴王都痛快地答应了。

　　孙子首先向宫女们宣令问："你们知道自己的前心、后背和左右手吗？"宫女们回答说："知道。"于是孙子宣布军令道："令向前，就是看前心所对的方向；令向左，则看左手方向；令向右，就是看右手方向，令向后，则是看背所对的方向。"宫女们回答说："明白了。"接着，孙子命令道："第一，队伍不许混乱；第二，不许喧哗吵闹；第三，不许违反军令。"又命令执军法的人把执法的刑具铡刀、大斧头排列出来，宣布军法，并三令五申。

演练正式开始了，孙子命令击鼓向右，宫女们听到鼓声后都大笑起来。孙子大声地对宫女们说："规定不明确，约令不熟悉，是将帅的过错。"于是，他又大声地把三道命令重复了一遍，再次命令击鼓向左。宫女们看到孙子认真的样子，听到鼓声，依然大笑不止。孙子严正地说："规定不明确，约令不熟悉，是将帅的过错。但是，现在命令已发布清楚，却不去执行，这就是队长的罪过了。按照军法，当斩两队之长。"说完，下令执法官将两个队长拉去斩首。

吴王在殿上观看孙子指挥演练阵法，见此情状，急忙派人前去对孙子说："我已经知道您的用兵能力了，我要是没有了这两个美姬，连吃饭都不香了，请务必不要斩她们。"孙子严肃地对来人说："请你回禀吴王，我已受君命为将，将领在军中，应该按军法行事，若不严肃军纪，军法岂不是成了儿戏？这样怎么能训练出可以调动的军队来？没有任随调动的军队，又怎么能打胜仗呢？吴王既然已经授命我统军演练，那么，将帅在军中，有权处置，君命若不合乎军情，可以不接受。"说完之后，果断地命令执法官："马上执行！"。

孙子回到队伍前，又指定两名宫女担任新的队长，然后开始击鼓进行操练。这时，全场除了脚步声以外，再也没有嬉闹欢笑的声音了，列队整齐，步调一致，俨然是训练有素的军队。这时，孙子派人向吴王报告："队伍已经训练完毕，请大王检阅吧！只要您需要，命她们赴汤蹈火都没有问题。"吴王阖闾还在为失去两个宠妃而生气，于是没好气地回答说："让他回去休息吧，我不愿再去看了。"孙子说："吴王您只是爱好兵法的词句，却不能真正按兵法实行。"

吴王生气归生气，但毕竟知道了孙子的军事才能。后来，在伍子胥的开导下，吴王终于化解了对孙子斩其两个美姬的不满，任命孙子担任吴国的上将军，让他跟伍子胥一起辅佐自己争强争霸。

吴宫教战的故事，反映了孙子"令之以文，齐之以武"，即用政治道义教育部队，用军纪军法来统一步伐的治军的思想。孙子认为：只要严明军规、军法，即便是宫廷里的女子，也能够把她们训练成一支能够赴汤蹈火的勇敢军队。平素能认真贯彻命令、教育士卒，士卒就会养成服从的习惯，将帅与士卒就能相互取得信任，否则就不可能做到令行禁止。"令之以文，齐之以武"是孙子文武兼施、德威并重的治军思想和治军原则的具体体现。

COMMAND AN ARMY WITH CIVILITY BUT KEEP THEM UNDER CONTROL BY IRON DISCIPLINE
— Sun Tzu's Training of an Army in the Palace of the State of Wu

According to *Sun Tzu's Art of War*, "Command an army with civility but keep them under control by iron discipline, and it may be said that victory is certain."

After reading *Sun Tzu's Art of War*, King Helü of the State of Wu admired Sun Tzu's views very much. However, he wondered how well these military tactics would work in practice, so he asked Sun Tzu to demonstrate them to him. Sun Tzu readily agreed. Then King Helü asked Sun Tzu if he could try those tactics out on women. The reply was "yes". Therefore, King Helü called in one hundred and eighty palace maids, who acted as temporary soldiers for Sun Tzu.

The maids were asked to assemble in the arena after they put on armor and took weapons. Sun Tzu organized the maids into two teams and appointed two of the King's favorite concubines as team leaders. Then he asked the King for several military law enforcers to strengthen the military might. The King approved without any hesitation.

First of all, Sun Tzu asked the palace maids, "Do you all know the positions of your heart, your back, your left and right hands?" The maids answered, "Yes." Then Sun Tzu ordered, "When I say forward, face in the direction of your heart. When I say left, face in the direction of your left hand, and when I say right, face toward your right hand. When I say rear, face in the direction of your back." The palace maids answered, "We've got it." Sun Tzu continued, "First, don't mess up; second, don't make any noise; and third, don't violate the orders." He ordered the military law enforcers to lay out choppers and big axes, the implements of punishment, and he repeated the orders again and again.

The training began. When Sun Tzu beat the drum and commanded the palace maids to look in the right direction, they laughed. Sun Tzu said to them loudly, "If the rules of movement are not well-explained or if the troops have not been made to remember the orders, this is the fault of the general." So, he repeated the three orders, and then beat the drum again, ordering them to look in the left direction. Seeing that Sun Tzu was so serious-looking, the palace maids still kept laughing. Sun Tzu said in seriousness, "If the rules of movement are not well-explained or if the troops have not been made to remember the orders, this is the fault of the general. But now the orders have been made clear, so that's the team leaders' fault not to obey them. According to the military law, the two leaders must be beheaded." After that, he ordered the enforcers to behead the two leaders.

Seeing that, King Helü, who was watching the training in the palace, immediately sent someone to Sun Tzu, saying, "I have learnt your ability of using troops. But if I lose my two beautiful concubines, I'll have no appetite for meals. So please spare their lives." Sun Tzu said to him seriously, "Please tell the King that I have received the orders to act as the General, and a general must act on the military law. If military discipline is not enforced, the military law will be a trifling matter. Then how can he train the troops ready to obey his orders? How can he win a victory without the well-trained troops? Since the King asked me to train them, I have the right to do anything and I may reject his orders if they do not tally with the military situation." After that, he firmly ordered the enforcers, "Execute them right now!"

When Sun Tzu came back to the troops, he appointed two palace maids to be the new team leaders and then went on with the training. This time only the sound of footsteps rather than the laughter could be heard in the arena. The palace maids lined up orderly and acted in unison, just like a well-trained army. Sun Tzu sent someone to report to the King, "The troops have completed training, please have an inspection on them. Now they may even cross through boiling water or walk on fire as long as you give them an order." The King was still not happy with the loss of his two favorite concubines, so he replied angrily, "Let him have a rest. I am not in the mood to watch." Sun Tzu said, "The King only likes military theories, but actually he cannot act according to military tactics."

Although King Helü was not happy about what had happened, he realized Sun Tzu was capable in military operations. Thereafter, talked around by Wu Zixu, King Helü finally removed the dissatisfaction and appointed Sun Tzu as the Senior General. With the help of Wu Zixu and Sun Tzu, King Helü struggled for dominance.

The story of Sun Tzu's training his army in the palace of the State of Wu reflected Sun Tzu's thoughts in the management of an army — command an army with civility but keep them under control by iron discipline. According to Sun Tzu, as long as strict discipline was observed, even the palace maids could be trained into a brave army who dared to cross through boiling water or walk on fire. If orders were consistently carried out to instruct the troops, they would be obedient, and thus the general and the soldiers would trust each other. Otherwise, strict enforcement of orders and prohibitions could not be guaranteed. The saying that "Command an army with civility but keep them under control by iron discipline." concretely embodied Sun Tzu's thoughts and principles in the management of an army — to combine civility with discipline and lay an equal stress on kindness and severity.

以弱对强——勾践奇招制胜

《孙子兵法·行军篇》：兵不是越多越好，只要不轻敌冒进，集中兵力，判明敌情虚实，取得部下信任也就够了。

公元前496年，吴王阖闾乘越王允常逝世、其子勾践新立之机，率精兵三万伐越，越王勾践率军抗击吴军。

吴越两国同处长江下游，自春秋诸侯纷争以来，两国因地缘关系交恶很深，《孙子兵法》中就透露出这样的信息。孙子在《九地篇》中论及使部队在作战时能相互策应、团结奋战的方法时，就曾举吴越人为例。他说，善于统帅军队的人，能使部队像蛇一样。打蛇的头，它的尾巴就会来救应；打它的尾巴，头就会来救应；打它的腰，头尾都会来救。吴国人和越国人本来相互仇恨，但当他们同坐一条船渡河，遇到风暴时，他们也会像一个人的左手和右手一样相互救援。成语"同舟共济"就是这么来的。 由此可知，吴越相恶由来已久。吴王阖闾，乘越国治丧和新君继位之机兴兵伐越，只不过是吴越争斗事件中的一例。

自从孙子和伍子胥帮助吴王打败楚国之后，阖闾便觉得自己不可一世，常常以霸主自居，威压邻国，稍有不顺，便以兵戎相见。此次兴兵伐越，伍子胥等老臣曾劝阻吴王，但阖闾根本不听，亲自率兵出征。吴、越两军相距十里安营扎寨，几经交锋，吴军都没有占到什么便宜。吴王很生气，列阵督战，期待能一举打败越军。越王勾践深知兵力不敌吴军，又见吴军阵营严整，知道硬拼肯定是打不赢的。他对诸将说："吴军势众，不可硬拼，必须用计谋才能战胜他们。"越军组织了一支五百人的敢死队，连续向吴军发起三次突击，希望把吴军阵脚冲垮，然后主力部队乘势掩杀。但是，三次突击都没有能够撼动吴军的阵营。正在无奈之际，越王勾践手下的一员大将出了一个"怪招"。越王听了，认为值得一试，于是就下令诸将分头去准备。

　　第二天，吴、越两军依然对阵，越王勾践密令把准备好的三百个死囚分为三队，列于阵前。每个死囚都袒胸露怀，手持大刀，把大刀架在自己的脖子上，一声令下，这些死囚一起向吴军阵营走去。快到阵前时，为首的一个死囚大声地对吴军将士说："越王不自量力，得罪于上国，使吴王震怒，兴兵讨伐。我们愿意以死代替越王赎罪，请吴王宽恕。"说罢，三百个死囚便一个接一个地在吴军阵前抹脖子自杀。吴军将士被眼前的情景惊呆了，他们从未见过这种场面，吴军不由得放松了警惕，纷纷议论越王是真赔罪还是假赔罪。就在这时，越军阵中鼓声大作，左司马畴无余、右司马胥犴各率领一支敢死队杀向吴军。吴军顿时阵脚大乱。勾践随即率领主力部队掩杀过来。大将诸稽郢、先锋灵姑浮奋勇当先，撕开吴军阵营左突右冲，所向披靡。混战中，吴王阖闾的脚被灵姑浮砍了一刀，吴国大将专毅也负了重伤，吴军只好败退。可怜三万精兵，经此一战，死伤过半。吴王阖闾本来年纪就大，又受了伤，连惊带吓，在败归的途中就因刀伤发作而死了。阖闾的儿子夫差继位，他发誓要为父亲报仇。此后，吴、越之间的征战杀伐愈演愈烈。

　　此次吴越之战，无论国力还是兵力，越都处于劣势。勾践明了双方的力量对比，果断地选择不硬拼而以奇策应对，打败了吴军。正如孙子在《兵势篇》中说："凡战者，以正合，以奇胜。"孙子论兵，非常注重智谋，他在《行军篇》中就明确地说："兵不是越多越好，只要不轻敌冒进，集中兵力，判明敌情虚实，取得部下信任也就够了。"吴王阖闾曾在孙子和伍子胥帮助下战胜强邻楚国，此次却因不听伍子胥的劝阻而又没能灵活地运用孙子兵法，惨败于弱邻越国，教训惨痛！

BEAT THE STRONG WITH THE WEAK
— Goujian Took the Enemy by Using Special Tactics

According to *Sun Tzu's Art of War*, "In war, numbers alone confer no advantage. It is sufficient if you do not advance relying on sheer military power. If you estimate the enemy situation correctly, gain the trust of your soldiers and then concentrate your strength to overcome the enemy, there is no more to it than this."

In 496 BC, King Yunchang of the State of Yue passed away and his son, Goujian, succeeded to the throne. King Helü of the State of Wu took the chance to lead 30,000 crack troops to invade the State of Yue. King Goujian led the troops to fight back against them.

Both the State of Wu and the State of Yue lay in the lower reaches of the Yangtze River. Since the struggle for power among dukes in the Spring and Autumn Period, the two states had been on bad terms with each other because of the borders, which was recorded in *Sun Tzu's Art of War*. In *Sun Tzu's Art of War*, Sun Tzu once took the people of Wu and Yue as an example to expound the method of letting troops coordinate and cooperate with each other in warfare. He said, "The troops of those adept in war are used like a snake. When struck on the head, its tail attacks; when struck on the tail, its head attacks; when struck in the waist, both head and tail attack. Although the people of Wu and Yue hate one another, if together in a boat tossed by the wind, they would cooperate like the right hand does with the left." This was the origin of the idiom of "crossing a river in the same boat". As shown in his words, the hatred was long-standing between the two states. A case in point was King Helü's attacking Yue at the time of Yue's arranging the funeral and the succession of the new king.

Since King Helü defeated the State of Chu with the help of Sun Tzu and Wu Zixu, he had been overwhelmingly arrogant. He often posed as an overlord, oppressing the neighboring states. If they were not obedient, he would resort to arms. When he intended to invade the State of Yue, he was dissuaded by Wu Zixu and other senior officials, but he shut his ears to their advice. He personally led his troops to go on the expedition. The two armies were encamped ten *li* away from each other. After several clashes, the Wu army did not gain any advantage. King Helü was extremely irritated so that he supervised the operations, expecting to rout the Yue army at one stroke. At the sight of the neat formation of the outnumbering Wu troops, King Goujian knew that fighting recklessly would not guarantee a victory. He said to his officers, "The enemy outnumbers us, so we cannot fight recklessly. We have to resort to stratagems." So the Yue army organized 500 soldiers of the dare-to-die corps and assaulted the enemy three times in succession, hoping to shatter its front line and then to make a surprise attack by using the major forces. However, they did not succeed. King Goujian felt helpless, when one of his generals came up with a "strange stratagem". On hearing that, King Goujian thought it was worth trying. So, he ordered his officers to make preparations separately.

The next day, the two armies were still poised for action. King Goujian secretly ordered to divide 300 condemned prisoners into three groups and then arranged them in front of the formation. Each of them bared his chest, holding a broadsword around his neck. At the word of command, all of them marched towards the Wu's camp. They nearly got to the enemy's position, when the head prisoner shouted to the Wu army, "Our King far overestimated his abilities. He offended your state and irritated your King. Now your King sent a punitive expedition against us. To gain his forgiveness, we would like to die to atone for our King's crime." After that, the 300 condemned prisoners cut their own throats one after another, which shocked the Wu army. They had never seen such a scene before, so they relaxed their vigilance, arguing the truth of King Goujian's atonement. At that very moment, the Yue army beat the drums. Chou Wuyu, the left minister of war, Xu An, the right minister, respectively led a dare-to-die corps to charge at the Wu army. The Wu front line was immediately shattered. King Goujian thereupon led the major forces to make a sneak attack. Fighting bravely in the van, General Zhuji Ying and Vanguard Linggu Fu shattered the Wu camp, charged at the enemy here and there, and carried all before them. In the confused fighting, King Helü was cut in the foot by Linggu Fu and General Zhuan Yi was seriously wounded. As a result, the Wu army had to retreat in defeat. It was a pity that more than half of the 30,000 crack troops were decimated in the battle. Being old, wounded and terrified, Helü died of the sword wound in the retreat. Fuchai, his son, succeeded to the throne and he swore that he would take revenge for his father. Thereafter, the rivalry between the two states became increasingly acute.

In this battle, the State of Yue was inferior both in national power and military strength. Realizing that, Goujian firmly chose special tactics to deal with the opponent rather than fighting with them recklessly and finally routed the Wu army. Such was what Sun Tzu said in *Sun Tzu's Art of War*, "During a war, the general should adopt the normal way of confronting the enemy, while using special tactics to take the enemy by surprise." When talking about troops, Sun Tzu laid great emphasis on stratagems. In *Sun Tzu's Art of War*, Sun Tzu said clearly, "In war, numbers alone confer no advantage. It is sufficient if you do not advance relying on sheer military power. If you estimate the enemy situation correctly, gain the trust of your soldiers and then concentrate your strength to overcome the enemy, there is no more to it than this." With the help of Sun Tzu and Wu Zixu, King Helü once routed the powerful neighboring State of Chu. But, this time he did not listen to Wu Zixu's advice, nor did he flexibly use Sun Tzu's military tactics, so he was defeated by the weak neighboring State of Yue. What a bitter lesson it was!

知彼知己——郑国"县门不发"退楚军

《孙子兵法·地形篇》：知彼知己，胜乃不殆。知地知天，胜乃可全。

公元前 666 年，处于长江流域的楚国出动六百乘兵车去攻打位于北方的郑国。

春秋时期，军队的编制以战车为基础，四匹马拉一辆战车叫做一"乘"，是战车的基本单位，每乘上有三名甲士，一人驾车，一人射箭，一人刺杀。实施进攻时，战斗队形以战车为核心，每乘战车的左、右和前方各配属 24 名步卒，加上战车上的 3 名甲士，每乘兵力是 75 人。这样算来，楚国出动的军队就是 45000 人。那时候，衡量诸侯国国力和兵力的强弱及多寡，都是以"乘"来计算的。楚国一下子出动 600 乘去攻打郑国，用兵规模在当时算相当大的了。这是楚国逐渐强大以后，企图称霸中原的开始。

楚国进兵迅速，军队很快就推进到郑国都城的近郊，郑国与齐国于前一年即公元前 667 年结有盟约，郑文公急忙派人去向其盟国齐国求援，同时召集文武官员商量破敌之策。楚国大军压城，如何破楚军保全郑国，大臣们的意见不一。有人主张向楚军请求和谈解决；有人提出坚守城中，等待盟国救援；有的大臣对楚国侵郑愤愤不已，主张背城一战；还有的人认为，目前楚军来势汹汹，力量对比悬殊，都城危在旦夕，主张郑文公最好先"奔桐丘"，避过此难，然后再作他图。看到大臣们莫衷一是，郑文公心里非常焦急。作为一国之君，他既不愿意屈尊求和，也不愿意夹着尾巴逃跑，可如何挽救郑国都城之危，大臣们提出的对策，没有一个让他觉得满意。就在郑文公左右为难之际，一直没有开口的大臣叔詹说话了，他对郑文公说："臣自有计退之!"听到这个话，所有的人一下子都安静下来了。郑文公问："你有什么妙计？" 叔詹不慌不忙地说："楚君早有野心想当霸主，这些年楚国不断用兵，兼并了不少小国，国力也逐渐增强了。这次侵郑，出动了 600 乘，用这样强大的兵力去打仗，对楚国来说还是第一次。楚君下如此大的力量，志在必胜。因此，楚军统帅子元在指挥作战时，一定会谨慎小心，稳扎稳打，不敢冒大的风险。我们就利用楚军怕败和不敢轻举妄动的弱点，制订退兵良策。"郑文公觉得叔詹的分析很有道理，于是就委派叔詹负责指挥郑军守城退敌。

　　古代都城的建造分为"城"和"廓"两部分，"城"在内，"廓"在外，是环"城"而建的外城，"城"和"廓"均有城墙和城门。就在叔詹依计调动军队的时候，士卒前来报告，楚军的战车已经突破外廓的城门，到达城外大路两旁的市场——逵市了。情况十分危急，君臣上下都有点沉不住气了。叔詹冷静地说："不要怕! 按我说的办，万无一失。"

　　叔詹的对策是：先把郑国的军队都埋伏在城内，使楚军在城外看不到一兵一卒，然后把城门开得大大的，让城内的百姓像平常一样，来来往往，轻轻松松，繁忙而井然有序，即城内的军队和老百姓都要做到内紧外松，给楚军以错觉。果然，楚军前锋推进到城门口，看到不

仅城门上的 "县门"没有使用，而且城门大开，百姓来来往往，根本没有要打仗的样子。"县门"即"悬门"，古代"县"与"悬"字音同义通。"悬门"是中国古代用于守城的防御设施，通常是用厚木板制成的门扇，平常悬于城门上方，遇到敌军临城，则关闭城门，启动机关放下悬门以坚壁拒敌。这次楚军压城，郑军不但不使用"悬门"，还把城门开得大大的，后人称之为"县门不发"。这一反常现象令楚军很困惑，认为其中必有诡计，贸然闯进，必然会陷入埋伏，于是就在城外停下来，等待主帅子元率大军来到再作定夺。

楚将子元率大军随后赶到，听到前锋的报告，急忙登上高处向城内眺望，只见城内旌旗整肃，甲士林立，秩序井然。他也猜不透郑国葫芦里装的是什么药，贸然攻城的话，万一失利，回去无法向楚王交代。于是，他命令部队先在城外驻扎下来，等进一步弄清情况后再进行攻城。第二天，子元还未弄清情况就接到楚军后队的报告，说齐国联合了鲁、宋两国派大军援救郑国，其前锋马上就要追上后队了。子元闻报，害怕腹背受敌。他想，反正楚军已经到达了逵市，这就算是取得胜利了，保险起见，还是马上撤军为好。他急忙率领楚军撤退，离开郑国国境之后，子元让部队高唱凯歌，做出打了大胜仗的样子，回去向国君报喜。

"县门不发"是郑国创造的一种战术，这段历史见载于《左传》之中，历史演绎小说《东周列国志》第二十回有详细的描写。有人说，"县门不发"是郑国的"空城计"，诸葛亮的"空城计"肯定是从郑国"县门不发"演化而来的。不论事实如何，但有一点是可以肯定的，那就是历史总是给后人以启发，后人总是从历史中汲取营养，可以把孙子的"知彼知己，胜乃不殆。知地知天，胜乃可全"看做是对"县门不发"的理论概括。

KNOW BOTH THE ENEMY AND YOUR-SELF
— The State of Zheng Averted the Chu Army by "Not Lowering the Hung Door"

According to *Sun Tzu's Art of War*, "Know the enemy, know yourself, your victory will never be endangered. Know the ground, know the weather, your victory will then be complete."

In 666 BC, the State of Chu, lying in the Yangtze River basin, sent 600 chariots to attack the State of Zheng, which lay in the north.

In the Spring and Autumn Period, military forces were mainly based on chariots. *Sheng* was the basic unit of chariots. A chariot drawn by four horses was known as one *sheng*. Each chariot was equipped with 3 armored soldiers, one of whom was the charioteer and the other two were the archer and the spearman respectively. In an attack, the battle formation was centered on chariots. Each chariot had 75 soldiers, to wit 24 infantrymen in the front and on its left and right respectively, in addition to 3 armored soldiers in the chariot. So the State of Chu sent 45,000 soldiers in total. In those days, "*sheng*" was used to measure national power and military strength of the vassal states. The State of Chu attacked the State of Zheng with 600 chariots, which was considered to be a large-scale use of troops. This battle was the first attempt made by the State of Chu to dominate over the Central Plains after it gradually grew stronger.

Marching at full speed, the Chu army soon arrived at the suburbs of Zheng's capital. A year ago (in 667 BC), the State of Zheng formed an alliance with the State of Qi, so Duke Wen quickly sent someone to appeal to the State of Qi for help. At the same time, he called in civil and military officials to discuss tactics. As the Chu army was bearing on the city, the officials differed from each other on how to defeat them and save the State of Zheng. Some advocated reconciliation, while others maintained defense, awaiting the aid of the allied states. Some were so irritated by the invasion that they advocated a last-ditch fight, while others recommended that Duke Wen "leave for Tongqiu" to avoid this calamity first and then make further plans because the Chu army was bearing down menacingly, overwhelming in number and the capital was in an imminent danger. Seeing that the officials could not reach consensus, Duke Wen was worried. As a ruler of a state, he was not willing to lower himself to sue for peace, neither was he willing to escape with his tail between his legs. But none of the suggestions of the officials sounded good to him. Duke Wen was at a loss about how to protect the capital city when Minister Shu Zhan who kept silent all the time said to him, "I have my own way of averting the enemy." On hearing that, everybody was quiet. Duke Wen asked, "What is your strategy?" Shu Zhan replied in a deliberate manner, "The Duke of the State of Chu has long dreamt of becoming the overlord. During these years, the State of Chu became stronger in national strength by using troops to annex many small vassal states. This time it sent 600 chariots to attack our state, which is the first time Chu has mobilized so many soldiers. The reason is that the Duke of Chu is determined to win the battle. Therefore, when Ziyuan, the Commander-in-chief of the Chu army, is commanding, he will be cautious enough to play safe, without taking any big risks. They fear defeat and dare not to act rashly. This is their weakness. We may as well make use of it in making our plan to avert them." Thinking that his analysis was quite reasonable, Duke Wen appointed Shu Zhan to command the Zheng army to defend the capital.

In ancient China, a capital was divided into two parts, "*cheng*" and "*kuo*". "*Kuo*" was an outside city built around "*cheng*". Both "*cheng*" and "*kuo*" had city walls and gates. When Shu Zhan was moving his troops as planned, a soldier came to report that the Chu chariots had already broken through the Chun Gate of "*kuo*" and arrived at the Kui market, which was near the main roads outside of "*cheng*". The situation was so desperate that both the Duke and his officials could not keep calm. Shu Zhan said calmly, "Do not panic! Do as what I say, and we are sure of success."

Shu Zhan's strategy was as follows: first lay the Zheng troops in ambush in "*cheng*" so that the Chu army could not see a single soldier from the outside; then open the gate wide with the civilians in "*cheng*" coming and going as usual with ease, busy but in good order. Both the army and the civilians were relaxed outwardly but vigilant inwardly, which gave the Chu army a false impression. As expected, when the Chu vanguard marched forward to the gate of "*cheng*", they noticed that the "hung door" was not lowered, and the gate was opened wide with the civilians coming and going. There was no sign that they were going to fight. In ancient China, a "hung door" was one of the defensive facilities to guard a city. A "hung door" was usually made of a thick board, ordinarily hung over the gate. When the enemy attacked, the gate would be closed, with the "hung door" lowered to enhance the defense and keep out the opponent. The Chu army was crushing the city by force, but the Zheng troops did not use the "hung door". Instead, they opened the gate wide, which was known as "not lowering the hung door" by the later generations. The unusual appearance bewildered the Chu army, who thought there must be some intrigue and if they rashly broke into the gate, they would definitely fall into the ambush. Therefore, they stopped outside of "*cheng*", waiting for the arrival of Ziyuan and the major forces.

Soon afterwards, Ziyuan, the Commander-in-chief, arrived there with the major forces. When he was told about the situation, he ascended to the height to have a bird's view of the city, only to find that the city was in good order, with orderly flags and clustered soldiers inside. He could not figure out what the State of Zheng had got up its sleeve. If he was defeated by rashly attacking the city, he could not account to his Duke. As a result, he ordered the troops to be stationed outside "*cheng*". He would not assault the city until he found out the real situation. The next day, before Ziyuan got a clear idea of the situation, he received a report that combined forces from Qi, Lu and Song were on their way to Zheng's rescue and their vanguard was catching up with his rearguard. In fear of being attacked front and rear, Ziyuan thought that he might as well order a retreat for the sake of security since the Chu army had arrived at the Kui market, which could be reckoned to be a victory. Therefore, he immediately led his army in retreat. After leaving the border of the State of Zheng, Ziyuan ordered the troops to sing songs of triumph as if he had won a sweeping victory, ready to report the good news to the Duke.

"Not lowering the hung door" was a military strategy invented by the State of Zheng. The event was recorded in *Zuo Commentary*, and described in great detail in Chapter Twenty of the hiotorical novel, *Annals of the States in the Eastern Zhou Dynasty*. It was said that "not lowering the hung door" was the "empty fort strategy" of the State of Zheng, which was the prototype of Zhuge Liang's "strategy of the empty fort". No matter what the fact is, one thing is certain — history always enlightens the posterities, who in turn receive nourishment from history. Sun Tzu summarized "not lowering the hung door" in theory, "Know the enemy, know yourself, your victory will never be endangered. Know the ground, know the weather, your victory will then be complete."

兵因地强——晋假"虎牢"抗楚

《孙子兵法·地形篇》：如果我先占据险形地区，必用重兵封锁关口等待敌军来攻。……地形是用兵的辅助条件。

公元前571年，晋悼公联合宋、齐、鲁、卫等国营建虎牢关，巧妙地利用地形营建军事堡垒，大大提高了晋军防御强敌楚军的能力，实现了兵因地强。

虎牢关，又名武牢关，位于今河南省荥阳县汜水西关。其南边与嵩山相连，北边与广武山及黄河相连，是东西交通的咽喉之地。因其地势险要，大有"一夫当关，万夫莫开"之势，故以关相称。传说周穆王时，有一天他率领臣子们到郑狩猎，突然遇到一只猛虎，那只虎皮毛发亮，斑斓多姿，威猛可爱。随行的一位勇士将虎擒下献给穆王，穆王大喜，命令把老虎豢养于东虞，"虎牢关"由此而得名。

春秋时代，"虎牢关"为郑国的属地。据说，早在公元前718年，郑国军队曾凭借虎牢关之险，打败了前来替卫国复仇的燕国军队，这大概是春秋时代最早利用虎牢关天险进行作战的战役。不过，那时郑军只是利用自然天险，还没有建造军事营垒。一百多年之后，晋国开始从军事战略重地的角度设兵把守，秦代正式设立为关口。

春秋时代中期，崛起于北方的晋国和崛起于南方的楚国是争霸的死敌，地处晋、楚之间的郑国成为两国争霸的战略要地。到了晋悼公时期，晋国与楚国的争霸战已经进入白热化。晋悼公是继晋文公、晋襄公之后又一个比较有作为的君主。他继位之后，一方面采取"和戎狄"之策，与西部的戎狄和睦相处，保证中原地区的发展；另一方面，积极会盟各国，使诸侯听命于晋，保持晋国自文公以来所占据的霸主地位。为了控制晋楚之间的战略要地郑国，也为了有效地防御楚国向北扩张，晋悼公召集了宋、齐、鲁、卫、曹、莒、邾、滕、薛等盟国的大夫，共同商量"谋郑""御楚"之计。大夫孟献子说："何不请城虎牢以逼郑？"鲁国大夫仲孙鼠也建议说："虎牢关地势险要，扼楚军北上的大门，要是能在那儿建城立兵以把守，不仅能够防止郑国叛晋归楚，还可以阻止楚军向北扩张，一举两得。"晋悼公采纳了两个人的建议，遂决定由盟国共同建造虎牢关。根据协议，大国出千人，小国出五百或三百人，组成联军在虎牢关筑垒设防，共御其地。从此，虎牢关便成为晋国御楚的战略要地。

晋军得虎牢关天险，又派精锐部队驻军把守，楚军由此北上，久攻不下，只好放弃这条北上的捷径，改走别的路线。自晋楚争霸之后，虎牢关成为历代封建王朝兼并战争的古战场之一。比如：楚汉争霸时期，刘邦、项羽在此争城夺关；东汉末年，吕布在此大战刘（备）、关（羽）、张（飞）；唐代李世民在此大战窦建德；宋代岳飞大破金兵于竹芦渡。一直到元、明、清时期，虎牢关仍是鏖战纷繁，时闻杀声。宋代著名的史学家、诗人司马光曾为虎牢关题诗："天险限西东，难名造化功，路邀三晋会，势压两河雄。除雪沽枯草，警飚卷断蓬，徒观战争处，今古索然空。"由此可见，像虎牢关这样的山关隘口，在军事斗争中起重要作用。孙子在《地形篇》中说："地形者，兵之助也。料敌制胜，计险厄远近，上将之道也。知此而用战者，胜；不知此而用战者，必败。"所谓兵因地而强，就是这个道理。

TROOPS BECOME POWERFUL BY VIR-TUE OF THE TERRAIN
— The State of Jin Intercepted the Chu Army by Virtue of "Hulao Pass"

According to *Sun Tzu's Art of War*, "If I first occupy narrow passes, I must block the passes and await the enemy…Conformation of the ground is of the greatest assistance in battle."

In 571 BC, Duke Dao of the State of Jin assembled allied forces from the states of Song, Qi, Lu and Wei to construct Hulao Pass (Tiger Cage Pass), which was a military fortress established by clever use of the terrain. The fortress largely enhanced Jin's defense capability against the powerful Chu army, strengthening Jin's military power with the help of the terrain.

Hulao Pass, alias Wulao Pass, lies at the West Pass of the Si River in Xingyang County of Henan Province today. As a vital passage connecting the west and the east, Hulao Pass linked Mount Song in the south, and Mount Guangwu and the Yellow River in the north. It was known as a pass, because it was strategically important, with the momentum that "if one man guards the pass, ten thousand cannot get through". It was said that one day when King Mu of the Zhou Dynasty, followed by his officials, was hunting in the State of Zheng, he ran across a fierce tiger, which was powerful and lovely with shining hair, bright color and varied postures. One warrior caught the tiger and presented it to the King, who was very delighted and ordered it kept at Dongyu. Thus came the name Hulao Pass (Tiger Cage Pass).

In the Spring and Autumn Period, "Hulao Pass" was a dependency of the State of Zheng. It was said that as far back as in 718 BC, by virtue of the natural barrier at Hulao Pass, the Zheng troops defeated the Yan troops which took revenge for the State of Wei. This was, perhaps, the earliest battle conducted by using the natural barrier at Hulao Pass in the Spring and Autumn Period. However, at that time, the Zheng army only utilized the natural barrier but they did not establish a military camp there. Over one hundred years later, considering it a military strategic position, the State of Jin began to send troops to Hulao Pass for defense. In the Qin Dynasty, Hulao Pass was formally established as a strategic pass.

In the middle Spring and Autumn Period, the State of Jin springing up in the north was a sworn foe of the State of Chu emerging in the south. The State of Zheng lying between the two states became a strategically important place which they contested. By the time of Duke Dao of the State of Jin, the struggle for power between the two states turned white-hot. Following Duke Wen and Duke Xiang, Duke Dao was another successful ruler. After Duke Dao succeeded to the throne, he lived in harmony with the Rong and Di ethnic minority groups in the west by adopting a strategy of "making peace with them", thus guaranteeing the development of the Central Plains. On the other hand, he actively met with the dukes of other states, making them at his beck and call, thus maintaining the dominant position that the State of Jin had achieved since the reign of Duke Wen. In order to control the State of Zheng, the strategically important post between the states of Jin and Chu, and effectively prevent the State of Chu from expanding northwards, Duke Dao assembled officials from his allied states (the states of Song, Qi, Lu, Wei, Cao, Ju, Zhu, Teng and Xue) for a strategy of "striving to gain the State of Zheng" and "guarding against the State of Chu". Minister Meng Xianzi said, "Why not build Hulao Pass to press the State of Zheng?" Minister Zhongsun Shu of the State of Lu, also advised, "Strategically situated, Hulao Pass is the gate to stop the State of Chu from moving northwards. If we establish a fort and send troops there, we may 'kill two birds with one stone' — on the one hand, we may prevent Zheng from crossing over to Chu and on the other, we may hinder the Chu army from expanding northwards." Following the two men's suggestions, Duke Dao decided to construct Hulao

Pass with his allied states. According to an agreement, each big state would send 1,000 soldiers there while a small state would provide 500 or 300. They formed allied forces to put up ramparts, defending Hulao Pass together. Since then, Hulao Pass had become a place of strategic importance to the State of Jin in resisting the State of Chu.

As the Jin army occupied the natural barrier at Hulao Pass, and stationed crack troops there for defense, the Chu army attacked it for a long time, but without success. As a result, the Chu army had to give up this short cut to the north and changed its route. Since the struggle for power between the State of Jin and the State of Chu, Hulao Pass had been one of the ancient battlefields for the annexation of the feudal dynasties of the past ages. For example, in the battle between Chu and Han, Liu Bang competed with Xiang Yu for the Pass; in the late Eastern Han Dynasty, Lü Bu fought with Liu Bei, Guan Yu and Zhang Fei here; in the Tang Dynasty (618 – 907), Li Shimin had a fierce battle with Dou Jiande; in the Song Dynasty (960 – 1279), Yue Fei defeated the Jin troops at Zhulu Ferry Crossing. Even during the Yuan, Ming and Qing dynasties, battles still frequently broke out and battle cries could be often heard at Hulao Pass. Sima Guang, a historian and poet of the Song Dynasty, wrote a poem for Hulao Pass:

The west and east of the Central Plains is seperated by the natural barrier, Hulao Pass,

A stroke of good fortune, which is too wonderful for words.

The states of Han, Zhao and Wei are linked by the winding roads,

While on the banks of the two Rivers, graciously stand the tall cliffs.

Withered grass and thawing snow clinging to the stairs,

The heavy gale rolls up the broken fleabanes beside the roads.

Though in history Hulao Pass experienced many wars,

Everything is as transient as fleeting clouds.

It can be said that passes like Hulao Pass played a vital role in military struggles.

In *Sun's Art of War*, Sun Tzu said, "Conformation of the ground is of the greatest assistance in battle. Therefore, virtues of a superior general are to estimate the enemy situation, and calculate distances and the degree of difficulty of the terrain so as to achieve victory. He who fights with full knowledge of these factors is certain to win; he who does not will surely be defeated." This is the so-called "troops becoming powerful by virtue of the terrain".

兵学传薪——吴起强兵与用兵

《孙子兵法·地形篇》：视卒如婴儿，故可与之赴深溪；视卒如爱子，故可与之俱死。

孙子治军，非常注重军心与民意。比如他在《始计篇》中论述审视敌我双方的情况时，第一条就是"道"。他说："道者，令民与上同意也，故可以与之死，可以与之生，而不畏危。"在论述如何治军时，他在《地形篇》中说：对待士卒就像对待婴儿一样，那么士卒就可以与之赴汤蹈火；对待士卒就像对待爱子一样，那么士卒就会与之同生共死。吴起是孙子之后的又一了不起的兵学家，作为先秦兵学的传薪之人，吴起在强兵、用兵方面，继承和发展了孙子的兵学思想。

吴起是战国时期卫国人，生年不详，死于公元前381年。传说吴起小时候家境不错，后来他想当官，四处游说，弄得家徒四壁，遭到乡邻的耻笑。吴起杀了诽谤他的人，然后逃离卫国。他喜好兵法，为此到各国游学，后在鲁国为臣。公元前412年，齐国进攻鲁国，鲁君想用吴起为将，但吴起的妻子是齐国人，所以有些犹豫。吴起知道后，就把妻子杀了，向鲁君表明心迹。于是鲁君就任他为将，率领鲁军抗击齐军，结果大胜。吴起得势后遭到妒忌，一些权臣在鲁君面前说他的坏话，批评他杀妻求将的行为。鲁君心生疑虑，于是就把吴起辞退了。吴起听说魏文侯是个贤明之君，于是就投奔了魏国。

魏文侯知道吴起善于用兵，就任命他守卫河西（在今陕西）以抗拒秦国和韩国。吴起镇守河西期间，强调兵不在多而在"治"，他认为不是每个人都可以成为士卒的，必须加以考查和挑选，并且制定了考查和挑选标准：凡能身穿全副甲胄，执 12 石之弩（12 石指弩的拉力，一石约今 30 公斤），背负矢 50 个，荷戈带剑，并携带三天的口粮，在半日内跑完百里者，方可入选为"武卒"，并对其进行严格训练，使之成为魏国的精劲之师。作为"武卒"，可以免除其全家的徭赋和田宅租税。吴起首创的考选士卒之法，为魏国建立强大的军事力量奠定了基础。

在治军方面，吴起继承了孙子"令之以文，齐之以武"的思想，主张严刑明赏、教戒为先。吴起认为，若法令不明，赏罚不信，虽有百万之军也没有战斗力。所以，他身体力行，和最下层的士卒同衣同食。睡觉时不铺席子，行军时不骑马坐车，自背干粮，和士卒共担劳苦。传说他曾亲自用嘴为生疮的士卒吸脓。这个士卒的母亲知道后大哭起来。别人觉得很奇怪，对她说："你儿子是个士卒，将军亲自为他吸脓治疮，你为什么还要哭呢？"这个母亲说："以前，吴将军曾经为他的父亲吸过疮上的脓，他父亲感激将军爱护之恩，作战时就一往无前地拼命，所以就战死了。现在吴将军又为我儿子吸疮上的脓，我不知他又将死到哪里了，所以我哭。"正因为吴起既懂得用兵治军，又懂得爱惜士卒，所以他总是打胜仗。公元前 409，他率兵攻取秦河西地区的临晋、元里。次年，攻秦至郑，筑造洛阴、合阳两城，把秦国的河西之地全部占领，置河西郡，任河西郡守。公元前 389 年，在阴晋之战中，吴起以五万魏军击败了十倍于己的秦军，成为中国战争史上以少胜多的著名战役，也使魏国成为战国初期的强大的诸侯国。

作为将军，吴起并不主张穷兵黩武，而是像孙子一样，主张国君要有治国之道。传说魏文侯死后，吴起继续为魏文侯的儿子魏武侯效力。有一次，魏武侯与吴起一起乘船顺河而下，船到中流，武侯说："美哉乎山河之固，此魏国之宝也！"吴起对他说："国家最宝贵的是君主的德行，而不在于地形的险要。从前三苗氏左边有洞庭湖（今湖南洞庭湖），右边有彭蠡湖（今江西鄱阳湖），但不讲求德义，夏禹把它消灭了。夏桀所处的地方，左边有黄河和济水，右边有泰华山，伊阙在南，羊肠在北，施政不讲仁爱，商朝汤王将他流放了。殷纣王的国家东面有孟门，西面有太行山，常山在北面，黄河在南面流过，地势也无比险要，但施政不讲道德，周武王把他杀了。由此看来，治理国家在于君主的德行，而不在于地形的险要。如果君主不讲德行，就是一条船中的人也都会成为敌国的人。"魏武侯很赞赏他的见解。

后来，魏武侯听信谗言，不再信任吴起。于是，吴起就投奔了楚国。楚悼王早就知道吴起的威名。吴起一到楚国，就被任命为宛地（今河南南阳）守；一年后便当上了令尹（相当于相国），执掌楚国军政大权。吴起认真地分析了楚国的情况。他向楚悼王建议说："楚国的地方很大，军队人数也很多，理应比其他诸侯国强大，可是现在却不能，主要原因是大臣的权势太重，受封食禄的贵族太多。他们对上威逼君主，对下虐待士民，这种现状不改是不行的。"当时尽管有许多人反对吴起的改革主张，但楚悼王很支持吴起在全国实行变法。于是吴起就按自己的想法来管理楚国。首先，他规定：凡分封后三代无功的，一律收回封爵和俸禄，从而限制了贵族，打破了分封制和世袭制；其次，"罢无能、废无用，损不急之官"，精简了国家政治机构，裁除了冗员，把省下来的财富用来供养士卒，奖励军功；最后，建立一支"魏武卒"那样的军队，由国君统一指挥，同时加强国都的防卫，以"厉甲兵以时争于天下"。这些措施，仅实行一年，就使楚国面貌一新。吴起的变法引起楚国贵族的不满，楚悼王一死，他们就把吴起杀死了。这一年是公元前381年。

吴起曾著有兵学著作《吴子》，在谋略思想、战略战术、治军料敌等许多方面都继承和发扬了孙子的兵学思想。特别是他亲为士卒吸脓治疮的故事，一直传为"爱兵如子"的佳话。

AN INHERITOR OF MILITARY SCIENCE
— Wu Qi Strengthened and Employed His Troops

According to *Sun Tzu's Art of War*, "A general regards his men as infants and they will march with him into the deepest valleys. He treats them as his own beloved sons and they will stand by him unto death."

In the management of an army, Sun Tzu attached great importance to morale and popular will of his soldiers. For instance, in *Sun Tzu's Art of War*, Sun Tzu put "politics" on the top of the list when he elaborated comparisons of the various conditions of the antagonistic sides. He said, "Politics means the thing which causes the people to be in harmony with their ruler so that they will follow him in disregard of their lives and without fear of any danger." On how to manage an army, he said, "A general regards his men as infants and they will march with him into the deepest valleys. He treats them as his own beloved sons and they will stand by him unto death." Wu Qi was an outstanding military strategist after Sun Tzu. As an inheritor of the pre-Qin military science, Wu Qi inherited and developed Sun Tzu's military thoughts in strengthening and employing troops.

Born in the State of Wei in the Warring States Period, Wu Qi died in 381 BC, yet his date of birth remained unknown. It was said that Wu Qi was born into a well-to-do family. When he grew up, he wanted to be a government official. So, he canvassed everywhere, only to leave his family completely destitute, which invited ridicule from his neighbors. Wu Qi fled to the State of Wei after he killed people who had slandered him. Because he liked military tactics, he studied them in other states. Later, he served in the State of Lu. In 412 BC, the State of Qi attacked the State of Lu. The Duke of the State of Lu wanted to appoint Wu Qi as General, but he hesitated because Wu Qi's wife was a native of the State of Qi. When Wu Qi knew that, he killed his wife to lay bare his sincerity to the Duke.

As a result, the Duke appointed him as General, who led the Lu army to resist the Qi army and won a sweeping victory. Wu Qi became the object of envy after he held sway. Some domineering ministers spoke ill of him before the Duke for his seeking the position at the expense of his wife's life. With some misgivings in his mind, the Duke dismissed Wu Qi. Hearing that Marquis Wen of the State of Wei was wise and able, Wu Qi sought refuge in the State of Wei.

Knowing Wu Qi's ability of using troops, Duke Wen of the State of Wei appointed him to defend Hexi (in Shanxi Province today) against the states of Qin and Han. When in office at Hexi, Wu Qi stressed that the management of an army outweighed its figure. He thought that not everyone was able to become a soldier. One could become a soldier only after an overall examination and careful selection. Wu Qi formulated the standards: whoever was eligible for the "armed soldier" must fulfill the following tasks — fully armored, he was able to carry a bow of 12 *dan* (12 *dan* refers to the pulling force of the bow, *dan* is a unit of dry measure for grain in China, roughly equivalent to 30 kilograms); he could cover 100 *li* in half a day, with 50 arrows, a dagger-axe, a sword and 3-day rations. After the careful selection, the armed soldiers would be strictly trained to become the crack troops of the State of Wei. The families of the "armed soldiers" were exempted from labor service, taxes and levies of their lands and residences. The method of selecting soldiers, pioneered by Wu Qi, laid a foundation for the State of Wei to build a great military force.

In the management of an army, Wu Qi inherited Sun Tzu's thoughts — command an army with civility but keep them under control by iron discipline. Wu Qi advocated the strict enforcement of discipline, fairness in meting out rewards and commanding an army with civility as well. Wu Qi thought that even an army with 1,000,000 soldiers would have no combat effectiveness if military laws were not made clear or rewards and punishments were not meted out fairly. Therefore, he practiced what he preached. He wore the same clothes and had the same meals as the lowest soldiers did. When he slept, he did not use a mat. In the march, he neither rode a horse nor sat in the chariot. He carried rations himself, sharing hardships with his soldiers. It was said that he once sucked pus from a sore of a soldier. When the soldier's mother knew that, she burst into tears. People were surprised and asked her, "Your son is only a soldier but the general could suck pus for him. What are you crying for?" The mother replied, "General Wu used to suck pus for my son's father. Deeply indebted to the general, my husband did not hesitate to fight desperately in the battle and was killed. Now the general sucked pus for my son, and I don't know where he will be killed. That's the reason why I am crying." It was because of his understanding of the management of an army and his love for soldiers that Wu Qi always won the battles. In 409 BC, he led the troops and captured Linjin and Yuanli in the Hexi area of the State of Qin. The next year, he attacked the Qin army to Zheng City and built Luoyin City and Heyang City, thus completely occupying the whole Hexi area. There, the State of Wei established Xihe County and Wu Qi was appointed as Mayor. In 389 BC, in the Battle of Yinjin, Wu Qi led 50,000 soldiers to rout the Qin army which was ten times the number of his troops. In the Chinese war history, this became a famous battle, where a numerically smaller army defeated a much larger force. The battle also turned the State of Wei into a powerful vassal state in the early Warring States Period.

As a general, Wu Qi did not advocate wantonly engaging in military ventures. Instead, like Sun Tzu, he maintained that a ruler should have his own politics of administering a state. It was said that after the death of Marquis Wen, Wu Qi continued to serve Marquis Wu, Marquis Wen's son. On one occasion, Marquis Wu, accompanied by Wu Qi, moved down the river in a boat. When the boat was in midstream, Marquis Wu said, "What a magnificent land! This is our national treasure!" Wu Qi said, "What is most valued for a state is the ruler's virtue rather than the strategically important position. In the past, the Miao ethnic minority group possessed Dongting Lake (Dongting Lake in Hunan Province today) on the left and Pengli Lake (Poyang Lake in Jiangxi Province today) on the right, but it did not lay stress on virtue or faith, only to be destroyed by Yü of Xia afterwards. The place where Xiajie lived had the Yellow River and Ji River on the left, Mount Taihua on the right, Mount Yique in the south and Yangchang in the north. However, Xiajie was not benevolent in his administration, only to be exiled by King Tang of the Shang Dynasty. King Zhou of the Yin Dynasty had Mengmen in the east, Mount Taihang in the west, Mount Chang in the north and Yellow River in the south. His state was strategically important, but King Zhou was not moral in his administration, only to be killed by King Wu of the Zhou Dynasty. It can be said that the management of a state lies in the ruler's virtue instead of the strategically important position. If the ruler does not pay attention to his virtue, even people in the same boat with him will become his foes." Marquis Wu thought highly of his opinion.

Later, Marquis Wu did not have trust in Wu Qi because he believed slanders. As a result, Wu Qi went to the State of Chu. Duke Dao of the State of Chu had long heard of the renowned name of Wu Qi. As soon as Wu Qi got there, he was appointed as Mayor of Wandi (Nanyang in Henan Province today) and was appointed as Prime Minister a year later, in charge of the military affairs of the State of Chu. After carefully analyzing the situation of the State of Chu, Wu Qi suggested to Duke Dao, "In theory, your state should be stronger than any other states, for it has a big territory with a large population of army. But it failed to be the strongest because there are too many powerful ministers and salaried nobles. They coerce Your Lordship and ill-treat the civilians. The present situation must be changed." Though at that time, Wu Qi's reforms were opposed by many people, Duke Dao supported him. As a result, Wu Qi administered the State of Chu according to his own idea. First, he made a regulation: officials' conferred titles as well as their pay would be reclaimed if they did not make any contribution three generations after their titles were granted. In this way, the system of enfeoffment and heredity were broken, thus putting restrictions on nobles. He then "dismissed officials who were useless, lazy or simply had no meaningful task to do", thus streamlining the administrative structures and cutting down the redundant personnel. He used the saved money to support soldiers and reward military merit as well. Finally, he established an army just like the "armed soldiers of the State of Wei", which was under the unified control of the Duke. At the same time, he reinforced the defense of the capital city, "awaiting an opportunity to struggle for dominance with armored soldiers ready". Only one year after the implementation of his reforms, the State of Chu took on a new look. Wu Qi's reforms enraged the nobles of the State of Chu, so he was killed by them after the death of Duke Dao. That year was 381 BC.

Wu Qi once wrote *Wuzi*, a book on military tactics, which inherited and developed Sun Tzu's military thoughts in many respects such as strategic thinking, strategies and tactics, the management of an army and estimation of the enemy. The story of his sucking pus for his soldier became an oft-told tale of "treating soldiers as one's beloved sons".

攻其不戒——秦晋崤山之战

《孙子兵法·九地篇》：从意料之外的途径，进攻其没有戒备的地方。

公元前 627 年，秦军偷袭郑国的阴谋，被郑国商人弦高破解了。秦军远道而来，无功而返，很不甘心，遂在撤军途中顺手捞一把，灭了小国滑。这些情况，被秦国的东邻晋国看得一清二楚。3 年前，晋秦曾相约联合攻郑，结果秦军中途撤兵，导致计划落空，那件事就引起晋国的不满。现在晋文公刚去世，晋襄公新继位，秦国又趁晋国正在发丧之机，举兵攻打晋的东邻郑国。晋国君臣上下对秦国的行为都觉得不可容忍，何况，秦国也是晋国称霸的一个重要障碍。晋襄公接受了中军元帅先轸的建议，决定在秦军返国的必经之路崤山设伏击敌。

崤山是秦晋两国的接合地带，位于今河南省西部和山西灵宝县、陕县南部，向东延伸的余脉称为邙山。崤山是秦岭山脉东段的支脉，隔黄河与山西省的中条山相望，共同构成一段岩石峡谷。那里高山绝谷，峻坂迂回，形势险要，自古以险峻闻名，是陕西关中至河南中原的天然屏障。晋军遂选择秦军必经的险要之地东、西崤山附近设伏。先轸估算了一下秦军达到东、西崤山的时间，根据地形，先派他的儿子先且居带领五千埋伏崤山的左侧，让胥婴率兵五千埋伏于崤山的右侧，令狐射姑引兵五千埋伏于西崤山。先轸还让士兵们预先砍伐树林，阻塞秦军的归路。最后又命梁弘和莱驹引兵五千伏于东崤山，先轸则带着一班宿将跟晋襄公一起率大军在离崤山二十里的地方安营扎寨。一切都布置就绪之后，就等着秦兵钻入"口袋"了。果然，正像先轸预计的那样，秦军按时进入晋军设伏的峡谷。

崤山是秦晋两国之间兵家的险地，秦军不是不知道。早在秦军预谋偷袭郑国的时候，老臣蹇叔和百里奚都曾提出过警告。百里奚告诫儿子白乙丙说："此次偷袭，郑国不足虑，值得担心的是晋国。崤山是兵家险地，你们要谨慎行事。"蹇叔在未能劝阻住秦穆公偷袭郑国之后，曾在送别秦军出师的时候，预言秦军会在崤山遭到伏击，哭着告诉他的两个儿子说："我将在那里为你们收尸。"秦军归来的时候，白乙丙想起父亲的告诫，提醒主帅孟明视要小心崤山之险。孟明视接受了白乙丙的提醒，把秦军分为四队，每队间隔一二里，逶迤而进。秦军的先锋部队与晋军莱驹投石问路的小股兵力相遇，晋军假装败退。孟明视接到报告，觉得危险已经过去，便命令部队四队合为一队，径直进入晋军的伏击口袋。晋军各路伏兵相互协同战斗，采取卡头、断尾、斩腰的战术，将秦军截为几段，围困在地形狭窄、险峻的峡谷之内。秦军欲进不能，欲退无路，虽有战车三百乘，却如笼中之兽，无法发威。结果晋军像包饺子一样，把秦军将士一网打尽。秦军三员将帅孟明视、西乞术、白乙丙都成了晋军的俘虏。

从根本上说，孟明视并不是不懂崤山是兵家险地，对伏击也不是没有一点心理准备。但是他觉得军队奔袭千里并无险阻，现在已到了国门口，不会有什么太大的危险，所以，他没有采取足够的预防措施，注定了全军覆灭的下场。《孙子兵法》中说："真正懂得用兵的将帅，行动起来绝不迷惑，没有失误，采取对敌措施必须变化无穷，所以说："了解敌方虚实，又了解自己的强弱，争取胜利不会有危险，了解天时，懂得地利，才能有十分的胜算。"秦军将帅不是不知地险，而是"动而迷，举而穷"，才招致惨败。而晋军则做到了像孙子在《虚实篇》中所总结的那样："知战之地，知战之日"，"从意料之外的途径，进攻其没有戒备的地方"，所以能"胜乃不殆"。

秦晋崤之战是春秋时代著名的战役之一，晋军的谋略和战术，秦军的惨痛教训必定给后世的孙子以启发，《孙子兵法》中诸多精彩的妙论，似乎可以看到秦晋崤之战的影子。

ATTACK THE ENEMY WHERE HE HAS TAKEN NO PRECAUTIONS
— The Battle of Mount Xiao between the State of Qin and the State of Jin

According to *Sun Tzu's Art of War*, "Make your way by unexpected routes, and attack the enemy where he has taken no precautions."

In 627 BC, the Qin army intended to launch a sneak attack on the State of Zheng, but the conspiracy fell through because of Xian Gao, a merchant of Zheng. But the Qin army did not want to go back empty-handed after such a long march, so in the retreat they conquered the State of Hua en route. The State of Jin, the eastern neighbor of the State of Qin saw everything clearly. Three years ago, the State of Jin and the State of Qin made an appointment to launch a concerted attack on the State of Zheng, but the Qin army retreated on the way. So the plan fell through, which irritated the State of Jin. Now Duke Wen of the State of Jin just passed away and Duke Xiang succeeded to the throne. The

State of Qin took this opportunity to attack the State of Zheng, the eastern neighbor of the State of Jin, which was intolerable to both Duke Xiang and his officials. Besides, the State of Qin was also an obstacle to Jin's seeking dominance. Following the advice of Xian Zhen, the Commander-in-chief of the middle army, Duke Xiang decided to lay an ambush at Mount Xiao, where the Qin army must pass through on their way back.

A contiguous zone of the states of Qin and Jin, Mount Xiao lies in the west of Henan Province and south of Lingbao County and Shan County of Shanxi Province today. The branch range extending eastwards is known as Mount Mang. As the eastern branch range of Ridge Qin, Mount Xiao faces Mount Zhongtiao of Shanxi Province across the Yellow River, thus creating a stretch of rocky gorges here. The area is the natural barrier from Shanxi Province to Henan Province. With high mountains, precipitous canyons and circuitous towering slopes, Mount Xiao is a strategically important terrain. Since ancient times, it has been well-known for its treacherousness. The Jin army chose to lay in ambush at Mount East Xiao and Mount West Xiao respectively, the strategically important positions, where the Qin army were bound to pass through. After estimating the Qin army's arrival time at Mount Xiao, Xian Zhen made arrangements according to the terrain: Xian Qieju, his son, to lay in ambush with 5,000 soldiers on the left of Mount Xiao, Xu Ying with 5,000 men to lay in ambush on the right of Mount Xiao, and Hu Shegu with 5,000 soldiers at Mount West Xiao. Xian Zhen ordered soldiers to cut down trees in advance to block the retreat route of the Qin army. Finally he ordered Liang Hong and Lai Ju, with another 5,000 soldiers, to lay in ambush at Mount East Xiao. While Xian Zhen, together with Duke Xiang and veteran generals, led the major forces to set camp twenty *li* away from Mount Xiao. When all was ready, the only thing to do was wait for the Qin army to fall into the ambush. As expected, the Qin army entered the gorges on time, where the Jin army lay in ambush.

Located between the State of Qin and the State of Jin, Mount Xiao was an important position for all strategists, as was known to the Qin army. When the Qin troops planned to launch a sneak attack on the State of Zheng, both Jian Shu and Baili Xi, senior officials, gave them a warning. Baili Xi warned Baiyi Bing, his son, "The State of Jin rather than the State of Zheng is a big concern this time. Mount Xiao is an important position for all strategists, so you cannot be too careful." Jian Shu's advice against the expedition fell on the deaf ears of Duke Mu. When seeing off the Qin troops, Jian Shu predicted that the army would be ambushed at Mount Xiao. He cried and said to his two sons, "I will pick up your bodies there." On the way back from the State of Zheng, Baiyi Bing remembered his father's warning and reminded Mengming Shi, the Commander-in-chief, of the treacherousness of Mount Xiao. Following his warning, Mengming Shi divided the army into four groups, each of them at regular intervals of one to two *li*, meandering their way forward. The Qin vanguard encountered with the contingent led by Lai Ju who "threw a stone to clear the road". The Jin army feigned retreat. When Mengming Shi received the report, he thought that the danger was passed. As a result, he ordered the four groups to be combined into one team, marching straight ahead into the ambush. Following the tactic of "blocking head, cutting off tail and striking waist", the Jin troops in ambush cooperated with each other to cut the Qin troops into several sections, besieging them in the narrow and precipitous canyon. The Qin troops could neither advance nor retreat. Their 300 chariots, just like caged animals, could not be put into full use. As a consequence, just like making dumplings, the Jin army annihilated the Qin army and captured the Qin's three generals: Mengming Shi, Xiqi Shu and Baiyi Bing.

Fundamentally speaking, Mengming Shi was clear about the strategic position of Mount Xiao and mentally prepared for ambush. However, he thought that they were not at risk since they arrived at the gate of their state after a long march without any difficulty. Therefore, he did not take enough precautions. It was due to his relaxed vigilance that the Qin army was doomed to be wiped out. As was recorded in *Sun Tzu's of War*, "When those experienced in war move, they are never bewildered; when they act, their resources are limitless. And therefore, I say: Know the enemy, know yourself, your victory will never be endangered; know the ground, know the weather, your victory will then be complete." The Qin generals did know the terrain was perilous, but "they were bewildered when they moved and their resources were limited when they acted", only to be routed. On the contrary, the Jin army followed what Sun Tzu summarized in *Sun Tzu's Art of War*, "If one knows where and when a battle will be fought, his troops can march a thousand *li* and meet on the field. Make your way by unexpected routes, and attack the enemy where he has taken no precautions." Therefore the Jin army's victory would not be endangered.

The Battle of Mount Xiao was one of the famous battles in the Warring States Period. The strategies and tactics of the Jin army as well as the bitter lesson of the Qin army must have enlightened Sun Tzu of a later generation. It seemed that the Battle of Mount Xiao was reflected by many ingenious remarks in *Sun Tzu's Art of War*.

不知不交——郑襄公"坐山观虎斗"

《孙子兵法·九地篇》：不了解诸侯各国的战略动向，就不能与他们结交。

公元前597年6月，楚庄王兴兵讨伐郑国，郑国求救于晋国，结果楚国伐郑变成了晋楚大战。

春秋时代，周王室日衰，诸侯纷纷争霸。最先出来企图称霸的是郑庄公，但霸业未成就被齐桓公取代了，所以，他是春秋时代第一个霸主。齐桓公死后，宋襄公企图取而代之，但宋国势单力薄，根本没有称霸的基础。继齐而起的是晋国，公元前632年晋楚城濮之战后，晋文公正式登上霸主的地位。楚国虽然在城濮之战中被晋军打败，但是楚王称霸的野心并没有被打掉，依然不断地向北方扩展势力，谋求取代晋国而称霸诸侯。郑国位于晋、楚之间，是两国称霸的必争之地，所以郑国屡次受兵祸之害。郑国力弱，无法与晋楚抗衡，只好采取楚来就楚、晋来就晋的随风倒策略。楚庄王兴兵讨伐郑国，就是怒郑襄公叛楚而就晋。

楚国的军队包围了郑国的都城，郑国急忙向晋国求救。可是与楚军相持了3个月，仍不见晋国的援军到来，郑军逐渐支持不住了，郑襄公只好屈尊亲自到楚军中赔罪，并请求与楚国结盟。楚庄王觉得目的已经达到了，于是接受了郑襄公的赔罪，并与郑国结盟，然后准备撤军回国了。就在此时，郑国得到报告，说晋景公派遣荀林父为大将，率领六百乘大军前来救援，部队很快就要赶到郑国了。郑襄公想，楚军走晋军来，郑与楚结盟的事必然会惹麻烦，遂召集群臣商讨对策。大夫皇戍说："晋、楚两个大国争霸，郑国夹在中间屡屡受害，不如利用这次机会让晋、楚进行决战，楚胜从楚，晋胜从晋，郑国亦可免遭晋军问罪。" 郑襄公觉得这个坐山观虎斗的计策不错，便采纳了。遂派皇戍前往晋军营中游说主帅荀林父与楚军决战，另派一名使者去游说楚军，说楚军一走，郑必遭晋军践踏，劝说楚军与晋军交战。

晋军主帅荀林父率援军到达黄河岸边，得知郑国已经降楚，楚已开始撤军，觉得进军已无意义，遂决定撤军。荀林父的副将叫先谷，他认为这是建立军功的好机会，于是仗着其先辈有军功、自己本事过人，私自带着部下渡过黄河去追赶楚军较量。面对副将违令贸然行动，荀林父不但不能果断加以惩治，反因顾忌先谷的身份背景而糊里糊涂也率军跟着渡过了黄河。

楚庄王见晋军追来，考虑到楚军已鏖战三个月，士气不如晋军旺盛，决定不与晋军接战，主动派使者去与荀林父讲和。荀林父本来就不想战，很快就答应了对方讲和的请求。可是，副将先谷却坚决反对，他手下一帮主战的将领还把楚国的使者辱骂了一顿。更糟糕的是，荀林父用人不当，派了一个跟先谷意见相同的魏奇到楚军营中议和，他不但未执行议和的使命，而且言语冒犯，当面向楚军挑战，惹恼了楚庄王，属将伍参也竭力怂恿楚庄王跟晋军决战。庄王遂收回了班师回国的命令，率军对晋军发动突然袭击。晋军毫无思想准备，仓促在郑（今河南开封）迎战楚军。经过激烈的战斗，原本占优势的晋军被打得溃败而逃，楚军一直追击到黄河渡口。晋军死伤无数，战斗以楚军大胜而告终。事后，坐山观虎斗的郑襄公自然是与楚国结好。

《孙子兵法》说："不知诸侯之谋者，不能预交。"又说："故不知用兵之害者，则不能尽知用兵之利。"郑襄公深知夹在晋、楚两国之间的利害，故怂恿晋楚决战，自己则坐山观虎斗，避免遭受楚、晋两军的连续打击，可谓知谋知兵。晋军驰援，占天时地利，但主帅荀林父优柔寡断，既不能有效地节制部将，又不能很好地应对事变，结果惨败。孙子在《作战篇》中说："知兵之将，安国之主也。"此言不妄。

ONE IGNORANT OF THE PLANS OF NEIGHBORING STATES CANNOT MAKE ALLIANCES WITH THEM
— Duke Xiang of the State of Zheng "Sat on the Top of the Mountain to Watch the Tigers Fight"

According to *Sun Tzu's Art of War*, "One ignorant of the plans of neighboring states cannot make alliances with them."

In June of 597 BC, King Zhuang of the State of Chu sent a punitive expedition against the State of Zheng, which appealed to the State of Jin for help. As a result, Chu's attacking Zheng turned out to be a battle between the State of Chu and the State of Jin.

In the Spring and Autumn Period, the royal court of the Zhou Dynasty was on the wane. The dukes took the opportunity to struggle for power. Duke Zhuang of the State of Zheng first attempted to seek dominance; however, he was replaced by Duke Huan of the State of Qi before he built up his power. Therefore, Duke Huan became the first overlord in the Spring and Autumn

Period. After the death of Duke Huan, Duke Xiang of the State of Song intended to become the next overload, but his state was too small to seek dominance. Following the State of Qi, the State of Jin developed quickly. After the Battle of Chengpu between the State of Jin and the State of Chu in 632 BC, Duke Wen of the State of Jin formally took the dominant position. Though defeated by the Jin army in the Battle of Chengpu, the King of the State of Chu still harbored the ambition of becoming the overlord. He kept extending his influence northwards, intending to substitute the State of Jin. The State of Zheng, located between the two states, became a battlefield they scrambled for. As a result, the State of Zheng frequently suffered from the turmoil. Since it was powerless to resist either one of them, the State of Zheng had no alternative but to adopt a flexible strategy of "submitting itself to whoever won the battle". Irritated by Duke Xiang's betrayal again, King Zhuang sent troops to attack the State of Zheng.

The Chu troops besieged the capital city of the State of Zheng, which quickly appealed to the Duke of the State of Jin for help. However, the Jin army did not turn up after the Zheng army confronted the Chu army for three months. Gradually, the Zheng army could not hold out, so Duke Xiang had to lower himself to apologize to the Chu army in person and requested an alliance with the State of Chu. Thinking that the objective was achieved, King Zhuang accepted his apology, made an alliance with his state and then prepared to withdraw his troops back home. Just then, the State of Zheng got the report that Duke Jing of the State of Jin sent 600 chariots led by General Xun Linfu to his rescue and the army was arriving soon. Duke Xiang thought that his alliance with the State of Chu would definitely get him into trouble. So he summoned his officials for countermeasures. Minister Huang Xu said, "We fall a victim to their seeking for dominance. We may as well take this opportunity to let the two states have a decisive fight. Then we may capitulate to whoever wins the battle. In this way we will be free from being denounced by the Jin army." The strategy of "sitting on the top of the mountain to watch the tigers fight" sounded good to Duke Xiang, so he followed. He sent Huang Xu to the Jin campsite, lobbying Xun Linfu, the Commander-in-chief, to have a decisive battle with the Chu army. Another envoy was sent to persuade the Chu troops to fight with the Jin army, saying that after they left, the State of Zheng would be trampled by the Jin army.

When Xun Linfu, the Commander-in-chief of the State of Jin, led the relief troops to the bank of the Yellow River, he was told that the State of Zheng had submitted itself to the State of Chu and that the Chu army began to retreat. Xun Linfu thought that it was pointless advancing, so he decided to retreat. Xian Gu, the assistant general of Xun Linfu, thought that it was a good opportunity to render meritorious service. So, relying on his forefathers' military merits and his extraordinary abilities, he, without permission, led his subordinates to cross the Yellow River to pursue the Chu army. Although Xian Gu disobeyed his orders and acted rashly, Xun Linfu did not punish him resolutely. Out of fear of Xian Gu's status and background, Xun Linfu led the army to follow him foolishly.

At the sight of the coming Jin troops, King Zhuang decided not to fight with them. According to him, the morale of his army was lower than that of the enemy as his army had fiercely been engaged for three months. As a result, King Zhuang voluntarily sent a messenger to have a peace talk with Xun Linfu. Xun Linfu immediately agreed with his request because he had not intended to fight at all. However, Xian Gu, the assistant general, strongly disapproved. His subordinates who advocated war even insulted the messenger. To make things worse, Xun Linfu sent a wrong person named Wei Qi to the Chu campsite to negotiate peace. Wei Qi was on Xian Gu's side. He did not perform his mission at all. Instead, he uttered offensive remarks and threw down the gauntlet to the Chu army, which enraged King Zhuang. Wu Shen, a subordinate general, tried to incite King Zhuang to fight. As a result, King Zhuang withdrew his order of going back home and led the troops to launch a sneak attack on the Jin army. Mentally unprepared, the Jin army hastily met the enemy head-on at Hao (Kaifeng in Henan Province today). After the furious battle, the Jin army, which was originally superior, were routed and fled in a rout. The Chu army pursued them till the ferry crossing of the Yellow River. With heavy casualties of the Jin army, the battle ended up in the victory of the Chu army. After the event, it naturally followed that Duke Xiang "who sat on the top of the mountain to watch the tigers fight" formed a friendly alliance with the State of Chu.

Sun Tzu's Art of War says, "One ignorant of the plans of neighboring states cannot make alliances with them. Those unable to understand the evils inherent in employing troops are equally unable to understand the advantages of the ways of doing so." Sandwiched between the two states, Duke Xiang was fully aware of the advantages and disadvantages. Therefore, he incited the battle, while he himself sat on the top of the mountain to watch the tigers fight, thus freed from successive attacks by both of them. In a sense, Duke Xiang knew the plans of his neighboring states and how to employ the troops. When the Jin troops rushed to the rescue, they had Heaven's favorable weather and Earth's advantageous terrain. However, Xun Linfu, the Commander-in-chief, was indecisive, unable to effectively restrain his officers or flexibly deal with emergencies, only to be severely defeated. In *Sun Tzu's Art of War*, Sun Tzu said, "The general who understands how to employ troops is the arbiter of the nation's destiny." What he said was quite reasonable.

置之死地而后生——项羽破釜沉舟战巨鹿

《孙子兵法·九地篇》：在死地，我将昭示士卒要有死战的决心。因此，军事上的情形是，士兵被包围就会协力抵抗；迫不得已就会拼死战斗，陷入危险的境地就会听从指挥。

公元前 209 年 7 月，陈胜、吴广在大泽乡首先揭竿而起，举起反秦的大旗，各地纷纷起兵响应。同年 9 月，项梁、项羽杀死会稽郡郡守殷通，聚众起义，队伍迅速由八千上升到十余万众。陈胜、吴广死后，实力最强的起义军是项梁率领的楚军，于是他便召集各部反秦将领共商灭秦大计。范增建议项梁复楚国，拥立楚王的后裔以得人心。项梁遂把楚怀王的孙子找来当楚王，仍称楚怀王。项梁自称武信君，率领项羽、刘邦等多次击败秦朝大将章邯的军队。公元前 208 年 9 月，项梁与章邯在定陶西北遭遇，项梁战死，起义军遭到重创。章邯得胜之后，率领秦军渡过黄河进攻赵地，围剿另一支反秦武装赵军。当时赵新立国不久，赵王歇和相国张耳、将军陈余深知不是章邯军的对手，退守巨鹿，接着又遭到秦将王离、涉间的重兵围困，情况十分危急。赵王歇只好向楚怀王求救。楚怀王遂任命宋义为上将军，项羽为次将，领兵北上救赵。

宋义以前是项梁的谋士，知道秦军的实力非常强大，率领大军到达安阳后，就驻扎下来，以期坐山观虎斗，坐收渔翁之利。他的如意算盘是：若秦胜赵败，秦军已疲，则乘秦军疲惫之时进攻，费力少而收获大；若赵军胜而秦军败，则乘势西入关中，夺取秦都咸阳。没想到，宋义这一观望就是一个多月。项羽心急如焚，建议宋义跟赵军来个配合，里外合击秦军。宋义斥责项羽太鲁莽。他说："论冲锋陷阵，斩将马前，我不如你。论运筹帷幄，决胜千里，你可就没有说话的份儿了。还是乖乖地服从命令吧。"为了防止项羽盲动，宋义特地下了一道军令："敢违反命令者，一律斩首！"

眼见着秦军对赵军屠戮围困而宋义却坐视不救，项羽终于忍不住了。第二天，他全身披挂来见宋义，再次请求出兵救赵。宋义一听就火了。他对项羽呵斥道："军令已下，难道你想以头试令吗？"项羽顿时被激怒了，他大声喝道："我现在就要借你的人头发令！"手起剑落，斩下宋义的头，一手拿着宝剑，一手提着宋义的人头走出中军帐外，向惊愕的将士们宣布道："宋义背楚王之命，按兵不动，坐失战机，我已奉怀王之命把他处死了。现在，大家都听我的号令。"项羽一边安排军务，一边派人去报告楚王。楚怀王无奈，只好接受这个事实，正式任命项羽为上将军，负责指挥救赵。

秦军统帅章邯是个智勇双全的人，他派大将王离、涉间、苏角率兵围攻巨鹿，自己则率军驻扎在巨鹿南边的棘原，负责拦截救赵的援兵。他还命令部队在棘原和巨鹿之间修一条两边建有土墙的甬道，作为给围攻巨鹿的秦军运送粮草的通道。布阵严密，无懈可击。项羽探知了秦军的部署，一个大胆的计谋在他的脑子里诞生了。恰好赵王派人来催问何时发兵救赵，项羽爽快地对赵国的使者说："你回去报告赵王，项羽不会辜负贵国的厚望，你们就等候佳音吧！"

项羽先派英布和蒲将军带领两万人马渡过黄河，作为解救巨鹿的先头部队，自己则率领主力部队来到漳河南岸，准备渡河。这时，赵国使者又来告急道："齐、燕等国援兵畏惧秦军凶悍势众，只是远远扎营观望，不敢出战。赵国的安危存亡，全系在将军身上了!"项羽送走使者，随即命令部队每人带足三天的口粮，次日一早渡河。第二天渡河前，项羽命令把行军做饭用的锅全部砸碎。渡河之后，项羽又命令士兵把用过的渡船全部砸沉，烧掉所有的行军帐篷，以破釜沉舟、自绝退路的行动，向将士们表示了不胜则死的决心。

项羽率领大军直插章邯和王离这两军之间的空隙，一面阻拦章邯去增援巨鹿，一面切断甬道，断绝巨鹿城下秦军的粮草供应。王离见失去了后援和粮草供应，急忙指挥兵马拦截项羽的军队。楚军将士知道已无退路，个个拼死作战，锐不可当，杀得秦军死伤无数。王离三进三退，才算逃回了本营。

章邯曾在东阿之战中与项羽交过手，领教过项羽的勇猛，这次前锋败北，粮道被断，王离交战失利，他不得不立即重新排兵布阵。章邯想诱项羽深入，然后聚而歼灭。章邯引楚兵深入阵中，以为项羽中计，却不料楚军因断了后路而作战格外勇猛。士卒三五成群，各自为战，以一当十，两天之内，秦军就连吃了9次败仗。项羽趁势派英布、蒲将军夺取了秦军甬道，杀了秦将苏角，活捉了大将王离，秦将涉间葬身火海。秦军统帅章邯见大势已去，被迫率领20万秦军投降项羽。这就是著名的巨鹿之战。这一战，基本上消灭了秦军主力，项羽因而赢得了威名。"破釜沉舟"也被传为千古佳话。

在巨鹿之战中，项羽的军队大大少于秦军，但他却以破釜沉舟的壮举，表达了必胜的决心和勇气，极大地激发了士卒奋勇死战的气概，创造了以少胜多的奇迹。孙子在《九地篇》中说："在死地，我将昭示士卒要有死战的决心。因此，军事上的情形是，士兵被包围就会协力抵抗；迫不得已就会拼死战斗，陷入危险的境地就会听从指挥。"这就是中国传统兵学中的"治气"、"治心"学说，现代军事学称之为军事心理学。巨鹿之战中，项羽把传统兵法运用得出神入化。

CONFRONT A PERSON WITH THE DANGER OF DEATH AND HE WILL FIGHT TO LIVE

— Xiang Yu Fought at Julu by Breaking the Cauldrons and Sinking the Boats

According to *Sun Tzu's Art of War*, "When you are in desperate ground, you must show your soldiers that there is no choice but a last-ditch fight. So a general must know the psychology of soldiers that they will resist when surrounded, fight desperately while being forced to and follow the general while they fall into dangerous situations."

In July of 209 BC, Chen Sheng and Wu Guang raised the standard of revolt at Daze Town, raising a great flag to rebel against the State of Qin. Peasants in other places rose in rebellion one after another. In September of that year, Xiang Liang and Xiang Yu staged an uprising after killing Yin Tong, Mayor of Kuaiji County. The number of their troops rose quickly from 8,000 to more than 100,000. After the death of Chen Sheng and Wu Guang, the strongest insurrectionary army was the Chu army led by Xiang Liang, who thus summoned generals from other armies for a strategy of destroying the State of Qin. Fan Zeng recommended that Xiang Liang restore the State of Chu and support a descendant of the kings of Chu, thus winning the popular will. As a result, Xiang Liang supported the grandson of King Huai to be the King of the State of Chu, who was still known as King Huai. Claiming to be Wuxin Monarch, Xiang Liang, followed by Xiang Yu and Liu Bang, defeated the Qin army led by General Zhang Han many times. In September of 208 BC, Xiang Liang was killed in the northwest of Dingtao, where his army encountered with Zhang Han's troops. Heavy casualties were inflicted on the insurrectionary army. After the victory, Zhang Han crossed the Yellow River to attack the State of Zhao, encircling and suppressing the Zhao rebel army. At that time, the State of Zhao was just established. King Xie, as well as Prime Minister Zhang Er and General Chen Yu, was fully aware that the Zhao army was no match for Zhang's army, so he decided to retreat to Julu and stand on the defensive. There, they were densely surrounded by Wang Li and She Jian, the Qin generals. The situation was desperate, so King Xie had to appeal to King Huai for help. King Huai appointed Song Yi as Senior General and Xiang Yu as his assistant to head north to rescue the State of Zhao.

As an advisor of Xiang Liang in the past, Song Yi was quite clear about the strength of the Qin army. When he arrived at An'yang, he stationed his troops, expecting to "sit on the top of the mountain to watch the tigers fight and then reap the spoils of victory without lifting a finger". His smug calculation was as follows: if the Zhao army was defeated, he would attack the Qin army which had been already exhausted. Thus he could get more advantages without much effort. If the Qin army was routed, he would take the opportunity to intrude into Guanzhong and capture Xianyang, the capital city of the State of Qin. Unexpectedly, Song Yi had been looking on for more than one month, so Xiang Yu was extremely anxious. He suggested that Song Yi cooperate with the Zhao army to attack the Qin army front and rear. Song Yi excoriated Xiang Yu for his recklessness. He said, "I cannot match you when it comes to charging the enemy lines and killing the generals. But as for mapping out campaign strategies and assuring victory a thousand *li* away, you'd better shut your mouth and obey my orders." In order to prevent Xiang Yu from acting harshly, Song Yi gave a special order, which said, "Anyone violating the order will be beheaded!"

At the sight of Song Yi's ignorance of the slaughtering and besieging of the Zhao army, Xiang Yu could not stand it any longer. The next morning, he put on his armor and went to request Song Yi again to relieve the Zhao army. However, Song Yi was furious, bawling, "The order has been issued. Don't you want to try it out with your head?" Xiang Yu was enraged at once. He shouted, "Now I will borrow your head to issue orders!" He raised his sword and chopped off

Song Yi's head. Then, he came out of the tent, the sword in one hand and the head in another, announcing to the surprised army, "Song Yi disobeys King Huai's orders and loses a golden opportunity by taking no action. At the command of King Huai, I killed him. Now you must obey my orders." Xiang Yu began to arrange the military affairs and at the same time he sent someone to report to King Huai. King Huai could do nothing but accept the fact and formally appointed Xiang Yu as Senior General to command the rescue.

Brave and sagacious, Zhang Han, the Commander-in-chief of the Qin army, ordered the generals Wang Li, She Jian and Su Jiao to surround Julu with troops, while he himself led the army stationed at Jiyuan to the south of Julu, intercepting the Zhao army's reinforcements. He also ordered a corridor built between Jiyuan and Julu with walls alongside to supply the forces surrounding the city. Tightly deployed, the Qin army was unassailable. When Xiang Yu was told about the disposition of the enemy, a bold strategy burst into his mind. By coincidence, King Xie sent someone to ask Xiang Yu when he would come to Zhao's rescue. Without any hesitation, Xiang Yu told the envoy, "Please tell your King that I will not let him down. Wait for the good news!"

Xiang Yu first sent generals Ying Bu and Pu with 20,000 men as the vanguard to cross the Yellow River to relieve Julu. Then he led the major forces to the south bank of the Zhang River. They were ready to cross the river, when the messenger of the State of Zhao came to report an emergency and asked for help again, saying, "For fear of ferociousness and numerical strength of the Qin army, the reinforcements from the states of Qi and Yan dare not to go into battle, instead they set camp in the far distance and are just looking on. The destiny of our state is in your hands!" After seeing off the messenger, Xiang Yu ordered the army to cross the river the next morning, with everyone carrying three days of rations. Before crossing the river the next morning, Xiang Yu ordered to break all the field cauldrons. After the army crossed the river, he ordered to sink all the boats and burn all the camp tents. Breaking the cauldrons and sinking the boats to make retreat impossible, Xiang Yu showed his soldiers that there was no choice but a last-ditch fight.

Xiang Yu led the troops to thrust directly into the space between the two armies of Zhang Han and Wang Li. He prevented Zhang Han from reinforcing Julu and disconnected the corridor, cutting off Wang Li's supply lines. Without reinforcements and supplies, Wang Li immediately commanded his soldiers to intercept Xiang Yu's army. The Chu troops knew that there was no way out, so they risked their lives and fought with irresistible force. Heavy casualties were inflicted on the Qin army. Advancing and retreating three times, Wang Li finally fled to his campsite.

Zhang Han had fought with Xiang Yu in the Battle of Dong'e, and he got to know his bravery. So, this time when the vanguard was routed with the supply lines cut off, Zhang Han had to immediately deploy his troops again. He intended to lure Xiang Yu's troops in deep and then assembled and annihilated them. When the Chu troops were lured into the disposition, Zhang Han thought that Xiang Yu had fallen into the trap. Out of his expectation, the Chu troops were incredibly fierce because their retreat was cut off. The Chu army, in threes and fours, fought independently, pitting one against ten. As a result, the Qin army was defeated nine successive times within two days. Xiang Yu took the opportunity to send generals Ying Bu and Pu to seize the corridor of the Qin army, killed Su Jiao and captured Wang Li alive. She Jian lost his life in fire. Realizing the situation was beyond salvation, Zhang Han, the Commander-in-chief of the Qin army, was forced to surrender himself and his 200,000 men to Xiang Yu. This was the famous Battle of Julu. The Qin major forces were almost destroyed in the battle, for which Xiang Yu rose to fame. "Breaking the cauldrons and sinking the boats" also became an oft-told tale throughout history.

In the Battle of Julu, the Qin army greatly outnumbered Xiang Yu's army, but Xiang Yu expressed his determination and courage to win by his brave feat of "breaking the cauldrons and sinking the boats", which greatly aroused the soldiers' spirit to fight till death. He created the wonder that a numerically smaller army defeated a much larger force. In *Sun Tzu's Art of War*, Sun Tzu said, "When you are in desperate ground, you must show your soldiers that there is no choice but a last-ditch fight. So a general must know the psychology of soldiers that they will resist when surrounded, fight desperately while being forced to and follow the general while they fall into dangerous situations." This was the theory of "control of morale" and "control of mind" in the traditional Chinese military science, which is called military psychology in modern society. In the Battle of Julu, Xiang Yu's application of traditional military tactics reached the acme of perfection.

先知者胜——晋、楚鄢陵之战

《孙子兵法·用间篇》：英明的君主、贤良的将帅，之所以能够一出兵就赢，成功高于众人，是因为事先掌握了敌情。

　　公元前 575 年，晋、楚两国在鄢陵（今河南鄢陵西北）展开了一场大战。这是两国长期争霸的继续。

　　春秋诸侯称霸，发端于郑庄公，成于齐桓公。桓公死后，齐国因内乱而衰落，宋襄公本欲继起，无奈宋国小力微，不足以称霸。晋楚城濮之战后，晋文公登上霸主地位，此后几代晋君维持着称霸的局面。处于长江上游的楚国日益强大起来，楚要想向北发展争霸中原，晋楚之间的郑国、宋国、卫国等是必争之地，而晋国要想遏制楚国保住霸主地位，必须把郑、卫、宋等国紧紧地掌握在晋国手中。所以，在晋楚长期争霸中，争夺郑、宋等国成为两国军事斗争的焦点。

　　公元前 579 年，在宋国大夫华元的调停下，晋、楚两国弭兵议和，实际上是想蓄积力量，等待时机，以利新的争霸决战。公元前576年，楚国背弃弭兵之盟，发兵进击郑国和卫国，迫使郑国叛晋附楚。第二年的春天，郑军进攻宋国，在勺陵（今河南宁陵南）把奋起抵抗的宋军全部消灭。于是，晋楚之间便爆发了鄢陵之战。

公元前575年4月，晋国君臣经过商议，决定发兵救宋。为了防止郑军阻遏晋军渡过黄河去救宋国，晋厉公首先让与晋结盟的卫国派兵占据鸣雁（今河南杞县北），威胁郑军侧背，使其不敢北进，然后开始调度盟军和晋军。晋厉公先分别遣新军主将郤犨、大夫栾黡去联络齐、鲁、卫等盟国，相约出兵会集郑地鄢陵，接着命令下军副将荀罃留守国内，自己亲自统领大军南下。

大约自西周开始，作战排列阵势时一般将参战部队分为左、中、右三个集群，号为"三军"，并按照集群的战术重要性又称为上军、中军、下军，总指挥居中军，所以中军地位最高。春秋战国时代，诸侯国之间战争频繁，各个诸侯国有所不同，有的有三军，有的有四军。晋国就是在上、中、下三军之外增加一个"新军"，所以晋有四军。晋厉公命令栾书统领中军，指挥全军，士燮为副将。郤锜统领上军，荀偃为副将。韩厥统领下军，郤至统领新军。晋厉公则率领公族亲兵居中军督战。楚共王知道晋军动向后，一点儿也不含糊。他随即命令司马子反为中军主帅，统领三军，令尹子重为左军主将，右尹子辛为右军主将，楚王自率亲兵戎车居中军迎战晋军。

当年5月，晋军渡过黄河，6月到达鄢陵。这时，齐、鲁、卫三国的军队尚在途中，而楚军已与郑军会合，并联合了夷兵，企图在晋国的盟军没有到达鄢陵之前先与晋军开战，以优势兵力制胜。6月29日，楚军利用大雾的掩护，将军阵摆到晋军的营门口，使晋军无法出营布阵。面对如此不利的局面，将如何应对，晋军将帅出现了分歧。主帅栾书自知兵力单薄，又被楚军逼营不能布阵，主张先避其锋，固营坚守，待诸侯援军到达，再转守为攻，乘楚军后退之际发动突击，一举打败敌人。新军主将郤至则认为，楚军将帅不和，郑军阵势不整，夷兵不能成阵，且部伍混杂，纪律松懈，彼此观望后顾，没有战斗意志，应该趁机速战而取胜。

晋厉公是个颇有见地的国君。听取了将帅们不同的意见之后，他认为，固守待援还需要时间，而战场情势千变万化，难以预料。晋军虽兵力不及楚军，若能利用楚军的弱点迅速展开决战，是可以创造胜利的奇迹的。遂采纳了郤至的意见，决定与楚军决一死战。有一位部属向厉公献策道："我们可以在营内填井平灶，扩大空间，就地列阵。这样既可摆脱不能出营布阵的困境，又能隐蔽自己的部署调整，给楚军意想不到的打击。"晋厉公欣然采纳了他的计策。

楚共王身边有一个谋士，叫伯州犁，是晋国的旧臣。当楚共王登巢车（瞭望车）观察晋军情况时，陪伴在身边的伯州犁只告诉他晋军的动向，但是不给提任何建议。晋厉公身边也有一个楚国的旧臣，叫苗贲皇。他陪伴晋厉公观察楚军阵势时，不仅说明楚军的动向，还针对楚军精锐集于中军的情况，建议分晋中军的精锐以加强两翼，先击破楚左、右军，然后合力围歼其中军。晋厉公和统帅栾书采纳了他的建议，决定用上军及部分中军攻击楚军实力较强的左军，用下军、新军及部分中军攻楚实力较弱的右军及郑兵，用护卫厉公的亲兵引诱楚军。一切布置妥当之后，晋军先发制人，打开营门发动攻击。晋军绕开营前泥沼，沿两侧而进。楚共王见晋厉公所在中军兵力薄弱，且晋厉公乘车陷于泥沼，乃率王族亲兵戎车攻厉公。统帅栾书想分兵救厉公，被其子栾鍼制止，以保持全军指挥不乱。危急中，晋大夫魏锜用箭射中楚王左目，迫使其后退，晋军恢复攻势。楚军得知共王负伤，军心动摇，锐气大减。楚右军及郑兵在晋重兵攻击下，兵力不支，很快就溃退下来。楚中军及左军失去右军和郑兵的协作，也只好向后退却。楚军在败退中阵势大乱，晋军乘胜全线追击，最终赢得了鄢陵之战的胜利。

孙子在《用间篇》中说："不知敌之情者，不仁之至也，非人之将也，非主之佐也，非胜之主也。故明君、贤将所以动而胜人，成功出于众人者，先知也。"事先掌握敌情，不可取自于鬼神，不可用相似的事情作类推，也不可天文地理来推算，而必须从了解敌情的人那里摸清虚实。分析晋楚在鄢陵之战中成败的因素，不难发现，在知彼知己方面，晋厉公始终高楚共王一筹，他不仅能够及时听取各方意见，采纳好的计谋，而且能够做到正确决策，及时调整战略，灵活应对不利局面，化被动为主动。楚军本来占有天时和地利的有利因素，但是楚王在"先知"方面输给了晋厉公，再加上不能灵活应对不利局面，致使大败。孙子在《兵势篇》中说，故善战者，追求的是势，而不责于人，能择人去造成有利于破敌的态势。善于造成有利于破敌态势的将帅指挥作战，就像转动木头与石尖。木石的特性是放在平地就比较稳定，放在陡险的地方就会滚动，形状方的不动，形状圆的容易移动。善战者追求的势如同圆石从千尺高山之上往下翻滚，不可阻挡。想必，鄢陵之战，也给予了孙子以思想的养分。

HE WHO CAN FORESEE THE DEVELOPMENT OF WAR WILL WIN
— The Battle of Yanling between the State of Jin and the State of Chu

According to *Sun Tzu's Art of War*, "An enlightened sovereign and an able general can defeat the enemy whenever they take action and achieve extraordinary accomplishments because they can foresee the development of war."

In 575 BC, a large-scale war broke out between the State of Jin and the State of Chu in Yanling (in the northwest of Yanling of Henan Province today), which was the continuation of the long-term fight for power between the two states.

In the Spring and Autumn Period, dukes fought for supremacy with each other. Duke Zhuang of the State of Zheng waged the first battle, with Duke Huan of the State of Qi becoming the final winner. After the death of Duke Huan, the internal power struggles resulted in the decline of the State of Qi. Duke

Xiang of the State of Song wanted to become the next overlord but his state was too small to realize it. After the Battle of Chengpu between the State of Jin and the State of Chu, Duke Wen of the State of Jin became the overlord. Since then, the rulers of the State of Jin had maintained the status of dominance for several generations. The State of Chu in the upper reaches of the Yangtze River increasingly got stronger and planned to expand to the north of the Central Plains. Lying between the two states were the states of Zheng, Song and Wei. In pursuit of power, either the State of Chu or the State of Jin had to contend for these three states. If the State of Jin wanted to stop the State of Chu and maintain the dominant position, it had to keep the neighboring states under control. As a result, the scramble for these neighboring states became the focus in the long-term struggle for dominance between the two states.

In 579 BC, under the mediation of Minister Hua Yuan of the State of Song, the two states called a truce and negotiated a peace treaty. In fact, both states wanted some time to build up strength and wait for an opportunity to launch a decisive battle for power. In 576 BC, the State of Chu broke the treaty, sent troops to attack the states of Zheng and Wei and forced the former to capitulate. The next spring, the Zheng troops attacked the State of Song, and in Shaoling (in the south of Ningling of Henan Province today) annihilated the Song troops who tenaciously resisted. Consequently, the battle of Yanling broke out between the State of Jin and the State of Chu.

In April 575 BC, after the discussion with his officials, Duke Li of the State of Jin chose to send troops to rescue the State of Song. In case the Zheng troops prevented the Jin troops from saving the State of Song across the Yellow River, Duke Li of the State of Jin first asked his ally, the State of Wei, to occupy Mingyan (in the north of Qi County of Henan Province today). By doing so, Duke Li intended to threaten the Zheng army from its side and hinder its march northward. He began to deploy the Jin troops and his allied forces. He sent Xi Chou, the General of the new army, and Minister Luan Yan to contact his allies (the State of Qi, the State of Lu and the State of Wei, etc.), with whom he reached an agreement that their troops would assemble in Yanling of the State of Zheng. After that, he ordered Xun Ying, the assistant general of the lower army, to remain in the State of Jin, while he personally led the major forces to the south.

Approximately from the Western Zhou Dynasty, in war the army was generally divided into the left, the middle and the right groups, which were called "*san jun*" (the three armies). According to the importance of military tactics, the three armies were also known as the upper, middle and lower armies, the middle army being in the highest position among them because the Commander-in-chief was in it. In the Spring and Autumn Period and the Warring States Period, and because of the frequency of wars, the number of armies varied from state to state, some states owned three armies and some states had four. "A new army" was added to the State of Jin, so it had four armies. Duke Li ordered Luan Shu to lead the middle army and direct operations, with Shixie as the assistant general. Xi Qi led the upper army with Xun Yan as his assistant. Han Jue led the lower army and Xi Zhi led the new army. Followed by his kinsmen and bodyguards, Duke Li supervised military operations with the middle army. King Gong of the State of Chu showed no sign of fear when he was informed of the situation. He immediately appointed Sima Zifan as Commander-in-chief of the middle army to command the troops, Prime Minister Zizhong as the General of the left army and Yin Ziyin as the General of the right army. Accompanied by his bodyguards, King Gong met the enemy head-on in his chariot.

In May of that year, the Jin troops crossed the Yellow River and arrived at Yanling in June. At that time, the troops of Qi, Lu and Wei were still on route, while the Chu troops had already met with the Zheng army and also teamed up with the Yi troops. The Chu troops attempted to wage a battle against the Jin army before the arrival of its allied forces. They wanted to win the victory by virtue of their superior forces. On June 29, under the cover of the thick fog, the Chu troops deployed the troops near the gate of the barracks of the Jin military administration, which made it impossible for them to go out to deploy their troops. Confronted with such an unfavorable situation, the generals of the Jin troops argued as to how to deal with it. Realizing that his forces were in an inferior situation and unable to deploy the troops, Luan Shu, the Commander-in-chief, maintained that they should avoid confrontation with the Chu troops, strengthen the barracks, and hold their ground until the arrival of the relief troops. Till then, they would easily turn defense into offense. They could launch an attack on the Chu troops at their retreat and finally defeat them in one move. While Xi Zhi, the General of the new army, suggested they should launch a quick war to win the victory. His reasons were as follows: firstly, there was discord between the generals and the commander-in-chief in the Chu troops; secondly, the Zheng troops were in disorder; thirdly, the Yi troops were loosely-disciplined and could not form arrays. Above all, the Chu troops were mixed up, in low spirits and lacked the determination needed to focus and succeed.

Duke Li was a ruler with sound judgment. Hearing the different opinions of the generals, he thought that waiting for the relief troops while holding on would take too much time and it was impossible to foresee the variables in battles. Although the Jin's military forces were no match for the Chu troops, they could miraculously win if they took advantage of the weaknesses of the enemy and launched a quick war. So, he adopted Xi Zhi's advice and decided to wage a life-or-death battle with the Chu troops. One official said, "We may fill up the wells and remove the cooking ranges to expand space for the deployment of the troops. In this way we may not only get the problem solved, but also disguise our plan and give the Chu troops an unexpected beating." Duke Li happily adopted his strategy.

King Gong of the State of Chu had an adviser, Bo Zhouli, a former official of the State of Jin. When King Gong mounted the lookout chariot to overlook the Jin troops, Bo Zhouli, who was standing by, told him only of the movements of the enemy but offered no suggestion. Coincidentally, Duke Li had a former official of the State of Chu, Miao Benhuang. When he accompanied Duke Li to observe the dispositions of the Chu troops, he not only specified their movements but also offered a suggestion. According to the observation that the superior forces of the Chu troops were in the middle army, Miao Benhuang advised that some superior forces of the Jin middle army be dispatched to reinforce the other two armies, which could first defeat the left and right armies of the Chu troops and then together with the middle army, they would surround and annihilate the Chu middle army. Duke Li and Luan Shu, the Commander-in-chief, adopted his advice. They decided to use the upper army and some forces of the middle army to storm the Chu's left army which was of high combat effectiveness. The lower army, the new army and some forces of the middle army would attack the Chu's right army and the Zheng troops who were of lower combat effectiveness. The bodyguards of Duke Li would lure the enemy. After everything was ready, the Jin troops took the initiative, opened the gate of the barracks and launched an attack. The Jin troops bypassed the mire before their barracks and marched along its two sides. Seeing that there were not enough forces in the Jin's middle army and that the chariot of Duke Li had sunk into the mire, King Gong led his imperial kinsmen and bodyguards to attack Duke Li. Luan Shu intended to dispatch some forces to rescue him, but was stopped by Luan Zhen, his son, because Luan Shu should keep the forces in perfect order. At the critical moment, Minister Wei Qi of the State of Jin, shot King Gong in the left eye with an arrow, which made him move back, and the Jin troops were on the offensive again. Hearing that King Gong was hurt, the Chu troops were greatly humbled with shaken morale. Under the attack of the massive forces of the Jin troops, the Chu's right army and the Zheng troops were unable to hold their own and were very soon defeated and dispersed. Losing the cooperation of the right army and the Zheng troops, the Chu's middle army had no choice but to retreat. The dispositions of the Chu troops were in great disorder during their retreat, and the Jin troops followed up the victory in hot pursuit on all fronts and finally won the Battle of Yanling.

In *Sun Tzu's Art of War*, Sun Tzu said, "If ignorant of the enemy's situations, he is, of course, completely devoid of humanity. Such a man is not a good general, not a good assistant to his sovereign, and no master of victory. Therefore, an enlightened sovereign and an able general can defeat the enemy whenever they take action and achieve extraordinary accomplishments because they can foresee the development of war." Such fore-knowledge cannot be obtained from ghosts and spirits, cannot be gained from analogous experiences, and cannot be achieved by calculating the positions of the Sun Tzu, the moon and stars. It must be obtained from those who are quite clear about the enemy's situations. Analyzing the decisive factors of the Battle of Yanling, we may easily find that Duke Li of the State of Jin knew the enemy and himself better than King Gong of the State of Chu. He not only listened to opinions from different parties in time and adopted good strategies, but also was able to make sound decisions, adjust strategies, flexibly confront the unfavorable situations and regain the initiative. At the very beginning, the Chu troops had favorable timing and geographical convenience, but King Gong was no match for Duke Li in terms of the ability to "foresee". In addition, King Gong was inflexible in the face of unfavorable situations. As a result, he was totally defeated. In *Sun Tzu's Art of War*, Sun Tzu said, "Therefore, a commander seeks victory from the situation and does not demand it of his subordinates. He selects suitable men and exploits the situation. He who utilizes the situation uses his men in fighting as one rolls logs or stones. The nature of logs and stones is that on stable ground they are static; on a slope, they move. If square, they stop; if round, they roll. Thus, the energy of troops skillfully commanded in battle may be compared to the momentum of round boulders which roll down from a mountain thousands of feet in height." Undoubtedly, Sun Tzu must have been inspired by the Battle of Yanling.